MANAGEMENT, ORGANIZATIONS, AND BUSINESS SERIES

Series Editor: John Storey

This wide-ranging series of texts, surveys and readers sets out to define the study of the management of people and organizations. Designed for both postgraduate and undergraduate students of business and management, it draws on the leading authors from the various contributing disciplines, including organizational psychology, sociology and industrial economics. A distinctive characteristic of the series is that these subject specialists make their work available to the general business and management student in a highly accessible way.

Published

Human Resource Management: A Strategic Introduction, Second Edition
Christopher Mabey, Graeme Salaman and John Storey

Changing Patterns of Management Development
Andrew Thomson, Christopher Mabey, John Storey, Colin Gray and Paul Iles

Strategy and Capability: Sustaining Organizational Change
Graeme Salaman and David Asch

Learning by Design: Building Sustainable Organizations
A. B. (Rami) Shani and Peter Docherty

Forthcoming

Motivation and Performance
David Guest

Learning by Design

Building Sustainable Organizations

A. B. (Rami) Shani and Peter Docherty

Blackwell
Publishing

350 Main Street, Malden, MA 02148-5018, USA
108 Cowley Road, Oxford OX4 1JF, UK
550 Swanston Street, Carlton South, Melbourne, Victoria 3053, Australia
Kurfürstendamm 57, 10707 Berlin, Germany

First published 2003 by Blackwell Publishing Ltd

Library of Congress Cataloging-in-Publication Data

Shani, Abraham B.
Learning by design : building sustainable organizations / Abraham B. Shani and Peter
Docherty.
　　p.　cm. — (Management, organizations, and business series)
　Includes bibliographical references and index.
　ISBN 0-631-23276-1 (hbk : alk. paper) — ISBN 0-631-23277-X (pbk : alk. paper)
　1. Organizational learning.　2. Organizational effectiveness.　3. Organizational change.
I. Docherty, Peter.　I. Title.　III. Series.
HD58.82 .S5453 2003
658.3'124—dc21

2002010437

A catalogue record for this title is available from the British Library.

Set in 10/12pt Book Antiqua
by Graphicraft Limited, Hong Kong
Printed and bound in the United Kingdom
by MPG Books Ltd., Bodmin, Cornwall

For further information on
Blackwell Publishing, visit our website:
http://www.blackwellpublishing.com

Contents

Figures

Tables

About the Authors

A. B. (Rami) Shani is Professor of Organizational Behavior and Change at California Polytechnic State University, San Luis Obispo, and visiting Research Professor in the FENIX programme at the Stockholm School of Economics, Sweden.

Peter Docherty is Professor of Services Operations Management at the Royal Institute of Technology, Stockholm, and a Senior Researcher at the National Institute for Working Life, Stockholm.

Foreword

I've often wondered why people in some organizations don't simply give up. It would seem to me that starting over would be easier than fixing the problems they report to me. Poor performance in the marketplace, competitive pressures, incompetent leaders, excess regulation, unreasonable customers, wasted effort, political gamesmanship, worn-out products, run amuck, poorly positioned assets, outdated talent, labor–management strife, product liability, a lack of vision for the future. These and many more issues detract from the success of some of our most important enterprises.

Why do people keep trying? Weighing against the seemingly hopeless list of maladies organizations suffer is the tremendous investment that people have made in creating what exists. Founding a company isn't easy. Enduring the lean early years, inventing and refining products and services, forging lasting relationships with loyal customers, beating off the creditors, managing growth wisely, deciding which markets to serve, diversifying talent, developing leadership. Then, as the organization becomes larger, there are more investments for people to make. Working one's way up the organization, developing an understanding of the market, gaining a feel for the competition, bringing out successful innovations, expanding into new geographies, defending patents, working out labor contracts, creating more stable arrangements with suppliers, acquiring firms that provide related opportunities for growth, transitioning leadership, drawing new organizational charts, improving quality and work processes, installing information systems. There's a lot to do just to keep the doors open and the lights burning.

Starting over in the face of problems would mean giving up these investments. Moreover, one is never certain that the next organization would be any different. While some organizations are better than others, at least for a short time, none are ever perfect or forever perfect. No, it makes just as much sense to continue on. But not *just* to continue on. To try to make things better.

That's where this book comes in. What Shani and Docherty have done, in *Learning by Design*, is to provide a window through which the reader can catch a glimpse of organizations in the act of learning, in the process of improving. We see people who haven't given up searching for ways to continue on, but not *just* to continue on. We see people and organizations trying to make things better.

What's more, we see different people, in different companies, in different countries, on different continents, finding different ways to make things better. That's what makes this book exciting and worth reading. The sheer breadth of experience captured here is astonishing and unparalleled. Reading this book makes it clear that learning is a *human* drive, not just the invention of modern scholars looking for a new path through an over-trodden field. The six cases from Europe, Israel, and North America documented here provide proof that when humans congregate in organizations, their inherent drive to learn is intensified.

As the authors take us through the cases, we learn that learning is not uni-dimensional, replicable, or even readily translatable from one organization or one country to the next. Learning isn't a formula or a program and it certainly doesn't have a convenient beginning or end. The cases here are riveting in their uniqueness, in the ways in which the context of each case has affected notions of what should be learned and how learning should take place in that particular setting. Once we bring people together to make an organization, we leave any hope of finding similarities in how people choose to learn at the door. What will strike you as you read this book is that learning is occurring in organizations all the time. Things that you might not have thought of as instances of learning suddenly come into sharp focus as learning events. Everything from improving work methods to developing a new IT infrastructure becomes an opportunity for learning.

And how do people in these organizations learn? The ways are as diverse as the topics. You will encounter familiar modes of gaining and exchanging knowledge in these cases such as classes, e-learning, tutors, and on-the-job experience. But you will also encounter novel approaches, like experience exchange workshops, project group dialogues, and parallel learning structures.

What Shani and Docherty do here is to go beyond inventorying the cases and methods. They attempt (and succeed) at exposing the underlying organizational design elements that give rise to learning and support its sustainability. As you read this book, you will discover that the act of learning in organizations both requires and creates structure. Like any other organizational activity, learning must compete with other priorities for attention. Once received, attention brings with it responsibilities to be fulfilled. People need forums in which to gather. They need to simplify the task of collecting and disseminating information. Their efforts must be recognized and sanctioned by the formal system, if the formal system is to benefit and change.

Investments in learning need to be justified and results measured. Things need to get done.

As individuals, we can choose to learn or not to learn. We can learn things that are valuable to our future, or things that are completely useless to know. It's our choice. In organizations, learning is a collaborative act. People decide together what to learn and how to learn. While the possibility for wasting time learning things that are totally irrelevant still exists in organizations, the possibility is greatly reduced by the imposition of structure, shared goals, reporting arrangements, measures of progress, and other organization design features that shape and direct collaborative learning behavior. Shani and Docherty expose the interface between organizational context, organizational learning needs, organizational learning methods, and organizational learning structures. They propose that alignment among these variables matters. I would suggest, after reading the cases, that alignment is ultimately inevitable.

Learning processes and learning structures seem to co-evolve in organizations. The organizations studied here didn't use organizational learning consultants who imposed their favorite learning techniques on hapless victims. Quite the opposite. These organizations, faced with the challenge of learning or perishing, invented ways to learn that matched their cultures, capabilities, and objectives. What else could they have done? How else could they learn and benefit from learning? These organizations personalized their approach to learning, as much as any organization can be anthropomorphized to reflect the character of a single person. Each found a way to learn and to continue to support and reward and structure learning that worked given its unique history, strategy, and context. In this regard, I hope that what you take away as you read this book is not a new approach to learning or a new organizational design to sustain learning but rather an appreciation for organizational learning as an evolving process. Learning is autopoetic; it is created by the organization but then creates the organization in turn.

I think you'll get a kick out of learning being facilitated by something the authors call *ba*; I know I did. I can hear the remake of an old Beatles tune . . . "All you need is ba." The truth is that organizations need ba and a lot more to learn, which is the message that Shani and Docherty ultimately convey.

Learning requires conscious effort and can be improved if more effort is applied rather than less. Shani and Docherty assert that organizations need to plan how they will learn and how they will sustain learning over time. Organizations that give conscious effort to learning will not only learn more, they will perform better. If they have learned from learning, they will invest part of the increased profits gained from learning in learning mechanisms and structures that make continued learning possible. They will design their human resource development policies to take organizational learning needs into account. They will appoint CEOs who understand and appreciate learning and they will fight against the attempts of those who would slash learning budgets for short-term gains. They invest in the learning capabilities of their employees and create cultures in which employees are not just allowed to contribute ideas, but expected to do so. They view unions as social partners who share an interest in the sustainability of the enterprise and the learning that sustainability requires. They experiment with dialogue, break down boundaries, and create venues where learning can occur. They engage in second-order learning, thereby improving their ability to learn over time.

While it may sound like a lot, it bears repeating that what these organizations did they did by themselves. Paying attention to learning came naturally, in the face of contextual needs and with the help of their own people who grasped intuitively what needed to be done. All of these organizations could have done more and they could have done better; that's not the point. The point is that they did what was right for themselves and perhaps, in a few cases, even a bit more than their leaders might have expected. In no instance was learning confined to a privileged few or a single department. Learning was pervasive, cooperative, and broad in scope.

Leaders who struggle with their ability to influence their far-flung corporate empires should take note that of the many values that they might wish to infuse in their people, learning is perhaps the easiest to seed. As a place to begin, and as a remedy for so many other problems that beset modern complex companies, leaders should consider strongly making a call for learning. As Shani and Docherty note, learning is seldom controversial. Even parties in contention can usually agree to learn. People value recognition for their contributions and see future profit in increasing their ability to contribute. Even stakeholders who are not part of the formal organization may value the opportunity to help the organization learn in ways that could make their own interaction with the organization better or easier.

The wonderful news coming from this book is that learning is not nearly as difficult or mysterious a topic as we once thought. Learning is occurring all the time in organizations. In fact, it may be impossible to stop learning from happening. Yet with focus, planning, and attention, learning can be accelerated and improved. And, with the addition of structures, policies, and procedures to support learning activities, learning can be made more sustainable. It doesn't take years to figure out what needs to be done. As this book shows, most organizations are already doing what is roughly right for them. When the benefits of learning are recognized, they do even more. Learning creates success, which in these cases at least, reinforced the value of learning.

Who can argue the need for more organizational learning? In the wake of recent events like Enron, WorldCom, and Arthur Andersen, there is clear evidence of the need to improve. A few years from now, as you read this, current examples will have been forgotten but others will have taken their place. The factors that drive change and create new challenges won't ever disappear. The need for organizational learning won't subside.

The choice that organizational leaders face is not whether learning is necessary but rather how to influence it. Learning will occur with or without explicit leadership endorsement, funding, and attention. Learning can be accelerated or slowed but not avoided forever. As Shani and Docherty point out, the sensible course of action would appear to be to match learning efforts to the context and needs of the organization. Fortunately, much of this happens naturally. What leaders can do is to recognize this, state their support for learning as a solution, and learn themselves how to be most effective in leading their organizations in learning. Hopefully, this book will provide a map for those who are lost or those who need to reaffirm that they are on the right course in helping their organizations to learn.

Bill Pasmore
New York
July 22, 2002

Preface

The original idea for this book dates back to a seminar that we led at the Stockholm School of Economics during the spring of 1992. The seminar was about organizational learning and change. Coming at the topic from two different disciplinary backgrounds, after an intense decade of independent research in and around learning at the workplace – Peter focusing on human competence and business development and Rami on organizational learning mechanisms and action research methodologies – we joined forces for a set of collaborative research projects, some of which involved other colleagues around the globe. The projects took place in three continents: Europe, Middle East (Israel), and North America. This book is a result of a conscious decision to investigate the theme of learning-by-design in successful companies, from different industrial and service sectors in three different parts of the world.

This book provides up-to-date, state-of-the-art knowledge on building sustainable and competitive human systems and organizations. Our particular interest is in exploring the role and relationships between learning and business sustainability. The literature on learning in the context of work, at the individual, team, and organizational levels, is vast. Yet, despite the fact that many organizations and researchers jumped on the organizational learning bandwagon, the field lacks a coherent framework and practical models for action. This book advances such needed framework and a practical model for action. The framework is used to examine learning at six firms in different industrial and service sectors.

The basic premise of the book is that organizations that prioritize the development and full utilization of their human resources, and simultaneously aim to achieve optimal and sustainable business performance, must explore and implement alternative design configurations. In this book we are taking a design perspective on learning and sustainability. As such, organizations make choices about the design and implementation of specific learning mechanisms that fit their goals, culture, and business context. By "learning mechanisms" we mean formalized strategies, policies, structures, processes, management systems, ICT systems, methods, tools, and routines, and even the design of physical or virtual workspaces that are created for the purpose of promoting and facilitating ongoing learning in the organization. Learning mechanisms may concern formal and informal learning at an individual, team, and organizational level.

This book uses as a point of departure the recent work by Argyris and Schön, Boud and Garrick, Bushe and Shani, Cohen and Sproull, Cross and Israelit, Dibella and Nevis, Dixon, Docherty, and Nyhan, Moingeon and Edmonson, Friedlander, Garvin, Huber, Kolb, Lipshitz, and Friedman, March, Nonaka, Pasmore, Raelin, Senge, and Schein. Our goal was to advance the scientific knowledge about learning at the individual, team, and organizational levels in a comprehensive, interdisciplinary, and action-oriented approach by integrating practices in successful firms around the globe with the existing body of knowledge. As such, we have advanced a new comprehensive framework, at the center of which one can find "learning mechanisms." The theoretical roots for our eclectic framework and proposed model-for-action can be found in business strategy theory, resource-based view of the firm, behavioral theory of the firm, sociotechnical systems theory, organization design theory, human and business sustainability theory, and organization change and development theories.

Students of management and organizational studies, academics, and executives should find *Learning by Design* a valuable resource for learning, inquiry, reflection, and practice. This is a book that can be a source of models, theories, and benchmarks that are built around six successful cases that can help those who are interested in understanding learning in the workplace better, gain new insights. Furthermore, those who are responsible for creating, fostering, and maintaining learning mechanisms might find ideas for reflection and action that can help their organizations be more effective and successful. For organizational researchers, we hope the book stimulates ideas for the much-needed research on learning and learning-by-design.

Acknowledgments

This book would not have been possible without the true research-oriented partnership with the companies whose experiences with learning by design we have studied during the past twenty years. Of the most significant ones, we would like to acknowledge ABB, AstraZeneka, Berol Nobel Industries, Blue Cross Blue Shield, Ericsson, General Electric, Hewlett-Packard, Israeli-American Paper Mill Corporation, Kibbutz Industries Association, Kaizer Permanente, Motorola, Proctor and Gamble, SAAB, Skandia Insurance, Volvo Cars, and United Hospital. Regarding the cases presented here, we would like to express special thanks to the members of the companies who gave generously of their time to interviews in today's intensive work situations.

Many colleagues took part in exploring the topic with us, helping us shape and reshape our understanding of learning in and around the workplace as we continued to share and reflect on our experiences. Rami would like to acknowledge the Case Western Reserve connection and ongoing stimulating discussions about learning in and around organizations – Frank Friedlander, Bill Pasmore, David Kolb, and Gervase Bushe; the California Polytechnic collaborative support and friendship system – Mike Stebbins, Jim Sena, and Dave Peach. The PMO group encouraged and nurtured our initial investigation of learning by design during Rami's one-year sabbatical during 1991–2 at the Stockholm School of Economics, Stockholm – Torbjorn Stjernberg, Peter Docherty, Bengt Stymne, and Jan Lowstedt. The EU "Organovation" research project provided five years' collegial cooperation with Bengt Stymne, Paul Lillrank, and Harvey Kolodny.

The Politechnico de Milano friends – Mariano Corso, Gianluca Spina, Roberto Verganti, and Emilio Bartezzaghi – invited Rami to spend a sabbatical with them during 2000–1 and were willing to listen and offer input as he was struggling with different parts of the book writing. Armand Hatchuel and Albert David from Ecole des Mines in Paris showed great willingness to take the risk of open dialogue about action research and learning by design. Wayne Boss, Eric Goodman, Henrik Larsen, Phil Mirvis, Ken Murrell, Ron Purser, Peter Reason, Peter Sorensen, Gretchen Spreitzer, Bill Torbert, and Chris Worely contributed cooperative hard work and fun during five years of shared experience as elected members on the Organization Development and Change Board of Directors, Academy of Management. Bengt Stymne, Niclas Adler, Flemming Norrgren, Armand Hatchuel, Horst Hart, Sven Kylen, Peter Docherty, Andreas Werr, Alexander Styre, and Mats Engwall have joined in continuous learning and experimentation with alternative doctoral programs and the implementation of different learning-by-design mechanisms at the FENIX program, Sweden. In Israel, special thanks for the continuous support for learning experimentation at the Recanati Graduate School of Business Administration at Tel Aviv University during the last seven summers to Dov Eden and Asya Pazy. In addition, thanks to Yoram Mitki and Victor Friedman for the stimulating discussions about learning mechanisms at the Ruppin Institute.

Peter's first interest in "learning" was kindled by the Swedish Work Environment Fund's program on "New Technology, Work Organization and Management," a six-year effort from 1982 to 1987 with nearly 50 projects. This gave the opportunity for cooperation with such colleagues as Torsten Björkman, Jan Forslin, Sven Åke Hörte, Flemming Norrgren, and Torbjörn Stjernberg. The importance of learning was a key lesson from this program and it was soon followed by the program for Learning Organizations from 1990 to 1996, which involved over 30 projects. This gave the opportunity for stimulating cooperation with Angelika Dilschmann, Per-Erik Ellström, Bo Hedberg, and Arvid Löfberg. Work at IMIT at the Stockholm School of Economics gave the opportunity of working closely with Niclas Adler, Hans Björnsson, Sven Åke Hörte, Jörgen Sandberg, Rami Shani, Bengt Stymne, and Torbjörn Stjernberg. Work at the National Institute for Working Life and the Royal Institute of Technology on organizational development and learning and sustainable work systems has entailed close work with Tomas Backström, Monica Bjerlöv, Marianne Döös, Jan Forslin, Tom Hagström, Marin Kira, Inger Söderberg, and Lena Wilhelmson.

Projects within various European research programs have involved close cooperation with colleagues from different disciplines and different countries. An extended relation with the European Centre for Work and Society in the framework of the Eurotecnet program on new technology and learning involved working with Raymond Pierre Bodin, Ludger Deitmer, Jack Horgan, Christer Marking, Barry Nyhan, Thomas Stahl, Massimo Tomassini, and Dany Wijgerts. In the Leonardo da Vinci program on competence development Peter worked on a project on the relation between HRD strategies and relations between management and unions together with Peter Cressey, Guesseppi Della Rossa, Michael Kelleher, Michael Kuhn, Daniela Reimann, and Christoffer Ullstad. Christoffer played a very important role in the conduct of several of the cases presented here. The European Consortium for Work and Technology has provided the opportunity for close cooperation with Palle Banke, Francesco Garibaldo, Friso den Hertog, and Peter Totterdill.

We both would like to thank The SALTSA Work Organization program project on Sustainable Work Systems which has enabled the development of a network with close interaction with PO Bergström, Monica Breidensjö, Peter Brödner, Peter Cressey, Frans van Eijnatten, Juan Ramon Figuera, Jan Forslin, Bob Hancké, Armand Hatchuell, Annmarie Holsbo, Charlotta Krafft, Michael Kuhlmann, Philippe Lefebvre, Manfred Moldashl, James Sena, and Michael Stebbins.

We also would like to acknowledge each other. This book was a synergistic effort that would not have been completed without a combination of our experiences, energy, and endurance.

The work on the book, including the field work, has been supported financially by grants from the Swedish Work Environment Fund and the European Union's Leonardo da Vinci program. We wish to express our thanks to these research financing authorities as well as to California Polytechnic State University, the FENIX program at the Stockholm School of Economics, the National Institute for Working Life in Stockholm, the Politechnico de Milano, and the Royal Institute of Technology in Stockholm for their support to us in conducting this work. Special thanks goes to Anita Söderberg-Carlsson at the Stockholm School of Economics, our copy-editor, whose ever-cheerful, patient, and constructive support has lightened our work and heightened its quality.

Finally, deepest thanks to our families, our wives Elaine and Elisabeth and children – Talia, Liat, Leora, Noelle, Elinor, and Edward – for their support and their incredible patience in our slow learning curve to achieve what they would regard as an acceptable work–life balance. We hope we're almost there.

chapter 1

The Critical Need for Learning by Design

- Why is learning by design critical in order to sustain organizational performance and competitive advantage?
- What are some of the views on the meaning of organizational learning?
- What are the basic assumptions about organizational learning mechanisms?
- What is the plan of the book?

We have entered a new era in the evolution of organizational life in which all of us can be agents capable of transforming the direction and flow of events. The immense forces of the technological, societal, and global changes resulted in a variety of new terms and labels that attempted to capture the changing work-life reality: post-industrial society, the information revolution, the post-capital society, and the knowledge age, to mention a few. While we may not be able to fully comprehend the magnitude of the changes, organizations and managers around the world are struggling to find the balance between economic performance pressures, managing business transformation, and business and human sustainability.

Over the past decade thousands of companies have seized on a variety of management methods such as empowerment, business process reengineering, self-managed or self-directed teams, sociotechnical systems redesign, and total quality management as a means for improving and enhancing business performance and competitiveness. In many cases their application probably reflects an interest in fashion or what some called "management fads" or "the quick fix" (Abrahamson, 1996, 1999; Gibson and Tesone, 2001). While immensely popular in the business press, there is a growing recognition that these methods have too often failed to deliver on their promise (Beer, 2000). Furthermore, business competitiveness was sustained in only a few of the successful implementations (Stebbins and Shani, 2002). In many cases, the learning potential embedded in the change programs never materialized.

▶ New Management and Learning

One thing is clear: The impacts of these continuous improvement methods, tools, and processes that aim to help organizations to enhance their productivity, quality, and workers' quality of working life are usually very short lived (Lillrank et al., 2001). Furthermore, traditional hierarchical organizations and industrial age notions of management seem to have served their purpose (Purser and Cabana, 1999). In response to the complexity and uncertainty of a turbulent environment, a more innovative and adaptive corporate species is emerging: the learning organization, recognizing the flexibility of its members, the organization, and its relations in the marketplace. This new form of organization did not emerge from nowhere – it has a long evolutionary history that dates back to the early pioneering experiments with self-managing (and learning) work systems conducted in early action research projects such as the sociotechnical work in the British coal mines and Scandinavia.

A careful scanning of the literature reveals that many companies have focused on organization learning and have been engaged in some activities around creating a learning organization with documented impressive results. Some of the companies include ABB, Analog Devices, Bank of America, Blue Cross Blue Shield, Caterair International, Coca-Cola, Corning, Digital, DHL, Electrolux, Ernst & Young, General Electric, Svenska Handelsbanken, Honeywell, Hewlett-Packard, Honda, Israeli-American Paper Mill, MCI, McKinsey, Motorola, Philips, Proctor & Gamble, Reno, Rover, Royal Bank of Canada, SAAB, Shell, Skandia, 3M, Volvo, and Xerox (for a comprehensive list of companies see Marquardt and Reynolds, 1996).

▶ Organizational Learning

The origin of the organizational learning conceptualization is anchored in a synthesis of contemporary theories that include systems theory, sociotechnical systems, group behavior, action research and appreciative inquiry, human development, and individual learning theories. At a very basic level, the literature on individual learning within organizations is considerable and runs through most of the streams of educational, psychological, and organizational behavior research (Friedlander, 1983; Cowan, 1995). At the same time, the literature on organizational learning runs through the organizational sciences, sociological, economics, and organization change and development research (Antal, Lenhardt, and Rosenbrock, 2001). For a synopsis of the growing literature see chapter 2 in this book.

Organizational learning has been described and observed in myriad ways. The following are a few examples of the great variety of possible meanings that can be found in the literature:

■ ". . . is a process in which members of an organization detect error or anomaly and correct it by restructuring organizational theory of action, embedding the results of their inquiry in organizational maps and images" (Argyris and Schön, 1978)

■ ". . . includes both the processes by which organizations adjust themselves defensively to reality and the processes by which knowledge is used offensively to improve the fits between organizations and their environments" (Hedberg, 1981)

■ ". . . organizations where people continually expand their capacity to create the results they truly desire, where new and expansive patterns of thinking are nurtured, where collective aspirations are set free, and where people are continually learning how to learn together" (Senge, 1990)

■ ". . . the intentional use of learning processes at the individual, group and system level to continuously transform the organization in a direction that is increasingly satisfying to its stakeholders" (Dixon, 1999)

■ ". . . is an organization that is skilled at creating, acquiring, interpreting, transferring, and retaining knowledge" (Garvin, 2000)

■ ". . . is a process of inquiry (often in response to errors or anomalies) through which members of an organization develop shared values and knowledge based on past experience of themselves and of others" (Friedman, Lipshitz, and Overmeer, 2001)

Garvin in his recent book (2000) makes a strong case that despite the fact that many organizations have jumped on the organizational learning bandwagon, the field lacks a shared definition and a coherent framework for action and thus is of limited relevance to the practical-minded manager (Garvin, 2000). The variety of theories and perspectives have resulted in few attempts to sort out the field. In chapter 2 we provide three complementary groupings of the current body of knowledge: a) according to the evolution of the stream of research that is placed on a historical timeline; b) first- and second-order learning based on impact; and c) based on level of learning.

This book addresses the challenges presented by Garvin (2000). Building on the seminal work of the founders, and integrating theory and practice, we show in this book in chapters 3 through 8 how leading-edge companies are making major advances by going beyond the different continuous improvement methods, such as business process reengineering (BPR) and total quality management (TQM), to create learning organizations. This book presents in-depth examples from six different companies in different industries and continents that *by design* created organizations that focus on learning. Furthermore, we illustrate how alternative organization design mechanisms can be applied to facilitate learning and to create breakthrough strategies and innovative and sustainable work. Chapter 2 provides a comprehensive articulation and description of learning mechanisms.

▶ Managing Learning: The Place of Design

The basic premise of the book is that organizations that prioritize the development and full utilization of their personnel and simultaneously aim to achieve optimal and sustainable business performance (economic results) must explore alternative design configurations. As such, organizations make purposeful choices about the design and implementation of specific learning mechanisms that fit their goals, culture, and business context. The basic assumption behind the organizational learning mechanisms and methods are that: 1) the development and utilization of human capital requires exploring and thinking through specific organizational design choices of structures and processes; 2) the most effective business strategies and work designs are developed and implemented when employees are involved directly in the redesign process; and 3) achieving sustainability – of continuous competitive economic performance and continuous development of human potential – requires ongoing investment in both the full utilization and the regeneration of human resources.

From an organization design perspective, the learning organization results in a flexible structural alternative to bureaucratic organization, and its power lies in the simplicity of the mechanisms that enable ordinary people to create systemic, fundamental, and sustainable learning processes and actions. The "Design Process-Focus" provides a vehicle for experiential and conceptual learning about the genotypical features of the learning organization alternatives. It is only from people pooling their various knowledge that a learning organization can evolve. When the people involved work out their own designs, they are highly committed and motivated to carry out sustainable and effective implementation.

How do we relate learning to learning mechanisms? Marsick and Watkins (1990) make the distinction between formal and informal learning. Formal learning is typically institutionally sponsored, classroom based and highly structured. Informal learning is not usually classroom based or highly structured and the control of the learning rests primarily in the hands of the learner and is usually deliberately encouraged by an organization (the employer in a workplace context). Company strategies for promoting informal or experiential learning are planning for learning, creating mechanisms for learning, and, as mentioned previously, developing an environment conducive to learning.

Planning makes learning more conscious, better focuses effort, and increases measures of accountability, as long as learning does not become an end in itself with only loose coupling to the work processes. Planning allows people to nurture learning strategically and to take advantage of a wider range of learning strategies that might otherwise be overlooked.

Marsick and Watkins (1997) indicate several difficulties that may hinder informal learning, namely: organizations do not always let people follow their natural inclinations to learn in different ways; people differ in their capacity to seek needed information and skills; there is disagreement as to what learning to learn means and therefore as to how to help people to better learn how to learn; the topic of learning might require the assistance of outside experts. Organizations may not provide clear guidance regarding what people must know and how this will assist them in their career paths.

Learning mechanisms are formalized strategies, policies, guidelines, management and reward systems, methods, tools and routines, systems, information and communications technology (ICT) applications, work organizations, allocations of resources, authority and responsibility, and even the design of physical workspaces that have been designed, formulated, and ratified in order to promote and facilitate learning in the organization. Learning mechanisms may concern formal or informal learning at an individual, group, or organizational level. Learning mechanisms, as we will see later in this book, can be routinized only up to a point. Since learning demands ongoing questioning and inquiry into current and future practices, it can be viewed as a continuous disturbance of existing routines that were developed for the purpose of stability, predictability, and efficiency. Faced with the decision to focus on learning, many managers continue to view the energy, time, and effort spent on learning as wasteful and unproductive (Garvin, 2000; Schein, 2002). Chapters 3 through 8 demonstrate and document the relationship between the different learning mechanisms that were created (by design) and bottom-line results reported on a longitudinal dimension ranging from three to twenty years.

Learning: A necessity or a threat

The work of two social scientists, Fred Emery and Eric Trist, pioneered the movement toward experimentation with alternative work redesigns, different forms of employee involvement, varied degrees of autonomy and responsibility in work teams, participative management orientations, and the development of learning systems, all with deep concerns regarding economic performance (Emery and Trist, 1969). Based at the Tavistock Institute in London, in the early 1950s they introduced a method known as sociotechnical systems design to British industry. Their work is a landmark in the field of organization design, change, and development as it represented the first attempt to introduce flexible learning forms of organization into the world of work.

Recent developments in business and working life have been characterized by the shift from the industrial to the finance economy, by rapid advances in ICT with new technology generations every few years, marked deregulation, and the introduction of management models and methods to "heighten efficiency and effectiveness," such as lean production, time-based management, business process reengineering, outsourcing, downsizing, and contingent labor. For companies the goals have been rationalization and increased flexibility. For personnel the consequences have often been increased work intensity, worse working environments, and decreased personal security (of employment) (Wickham, 2000). Sustained competitiveness at the company level requires competence or capabilities "on the cutting edge," which, in its turn, requires continuous learning. However, the opportunity to learn is not received by many workers as an offer of a generous fringe benefit, but rather as the threat of a "last straw that breaks the workers' back" (to paraphrase a well-known expression). To make things worse, it is not simply that the demands for learning are increasing (for example, manufacturing companies report that in 2001 they have 80 percent of the personnel they will have in 2010, but only 20 percent of the technology), but that the conditions for learning are less favorable. In a study of about 60 companies, Lundgren (1999) found that the demands on the speed of learning had tripled, i.e., time to proficiency had been cut to a third. An important aspect of planning and designing learning mechanisms is that it restores the critical and sensitive balance between company flexibility and employee security – a security that is being established through the development of the concept of "employability."

This book fills a void because there is currently no existing book available that focuses on the design of learning organization mechanisms, experience, and theory. A number of articles and book chapters on learning organization mechanisms have appeared recently. This book uses as a point of departure the recent work by Docherty et al. (2002), Friedman et al. (2001), Garvin (2000), Lipshitz et al. (1996), and Shani and Mitki (2000). We have chosen to study companies that implemented learning mechanisms by design, following a strategic decision to influence the status quo of their companies in their respective competitive markets. Furthermore, while chapter 3 focuses on learning mechanisms at the individual level, chapter 4 focuses on learning mechanisms at the team level, chapters 5, 6, and 7 focus on learning mechanisms at the organizational level, and chapter 8 focuses on learning mechanisms at the network level. As we shall see, in all six companies the efforts were driven by managers, practitioners, and employees and yielded impressive and documented results.

Yet, despite all the energy, time, and money that companies spend on attempts to transform organizations through a variety of change programs, the reality is that few succeed in sustaining the reinventing process (Beer, 2001). Mastering the art of learning in such contexts is not a "quick fix." Our contention is that one of the main reasons for the failure is that most companies do not manage to develop and nurture learning mechanisms that allow them to challenge the basic assumptions about the key/core business processes and as a result are not able to alter their mental models and actions. Developing this kind of managerial and organizational capability requires time, and strong convictions are needed in order to overcome what Schein calls "survival anxiety" and "learning anxiety" (Schein, 2002).

The situation is further complicated for management by the disturbing number of paradoxes relating to learning. Examples of such paradoxes concern the relations between learning, knowledge, and action. Several researchers have taken up the different types of learning that individuals experience at work, which have been termed first-order or second-order learning or single-loop or double-loop learning, or, nearer the worker, learning for production or learning for development (Argyris and Schön, 1978; Ellström, 2001). The production situation requires reaction, using SOP (Standard Operating Procedures), selecting from a repertoire, and valuing stability and safety. The development situation requires reflection, experimentation, new alternatives, and tolerance of risk and uncertainty. Learning requires balancing routine and reflection, the logic of production and design.

In a review of lean production from a learning perspective Berggren and Bengtsson (2001) raise a number of issues coupled to this: is lean production resulting in lean cliques or the generation of knowledge (first- or second-order learning)? Is flexible staffing leading to competence drainage or new knowledge combinations? Is outsourcing leading to less or more competence vulnerability? Is knowledge management usually an example of knowledge retrieval or learning, or exploiting or investing in knowledge (Stymne, 2001)? Other paradoxes are: How are individual and collective learning related to each other? A "chicken and egg" question where knowledge is created in the ongoing joint work commitments and dialogues in, for example, teams (Döös et al., 2001).

The inherent challenge fosters the need for managers and practitioners to have access to, and develop basic understanding of, the ideas and theory behind the learning organization mechanisms, including an understanding of their origins and evolution. Appreciation of the realization that many choices need to be studied and that many design alternatives can be created can help overcome some of the anxiety that seems to hinder successful implementation. The chapters in this book provide a snapshot of the large variety of choices made by executives which resulted in many learning mechanisms that were designed and successfully implemented by companies in Europe, the USA, and the Middle East.

Plan of the Book

The book provides an easily accessible volume for scholarly practitioners that features examples of learning organization mechanisms in six companies. The primary purposes of the book are educative and instructive in nature. As such, each chapter centers on a specific learning theme and a case that illustrates learning mechanisms that were designed and implemented to facilitate and manage learning. Each chapter starts with a few *silver bullets* and theoretical framing of the learning issue. Next, the companies and their stakeholders, strategy, design, resources, and capabilities as well as the learning mechanisms that were chosen and developed in order to help the companies achieve specific strategic goals in a specific business context are presented. Each chapter concludes with *some reflections and key lessons. Chapter 1* provides a broad framing of the relevancy and the need to focus on learning and learning mechanisms if organizations are to sustain competitiveness. As such, the chapter provides the reasons and focus for the book.

Chapter 2 lays out the theoretical foundation. It provides the conceptual framing for the book. Based on the theoretical underpinnings of behavioral, social, and organizational science knowledge, a conceptual organizational framework that links strategy, learning, and sustainability is presented. The position advanced in this book is that the development of learning mechanisms as a business strategy and design choice sets the stage for achieving competitive advantage and sustaining it over time. Next, we provide a brief overview of the field, theories and different perspectives on learning and organizational learning. For the purpose of this book we utilize three complementary groupings of the literature: a) according to the evolutions of the stream of research that is placed on a historical timeline; b) first- and second-order learning based on impact; and c) based on level of learning. Next, we discuss the core concepts of organizational learning mechanisms. Organizations that develop learning mechanisms by design seem to have a central focus of facilitating and managing learning at different levels. As such, in chapters 3 through 8, we provide specific examples of learning mechanisms that were developed within different organizations, each of which focused on designing learning mechanisms at a different system level.

Chapter 3 is built around the Merchant Bank in Sweden. The case provides an illustration of learning mechanisms that were developed for the purpose of facilitating systematic learning at the individual level. The Merchant Bank case illustrates how formal strategies and policies as well as the design choices that were made around learning, work organization, and the management system can promote learning and development for the broad majority of the workforce in order to benefit the competitive and sustainable performance of the organization. The case is of special interest as the company not only made a 180-degree turnaround in its business performance nearly thirty years ago, but managed to continuously improve its position and sustain its competitive advantage.

Chapter 4 is developed around the Automobile Manufacturing Company in Northern Europe. The case illustrates how business strategy and the design choices that were crafted around team learning, work organization, and management systems influenced the competitive performance of the company. The integrated production teams were designed for competence development, learning, and business development. *Chapter 5* is centered around the Telecommunication Services Company in Northern Europe. The company struggled with its transformation from a public utility to a privately owned company.

The turnaround was achieved by integrating business strategy with design choices that were made around structures and processes that will facilitate learning at the individual, team, and organizational levels. For example, learning mechanisms were created to re-skill and outplace people made redundant due to technological advancement (i.e., from electro-mechanical to electronic to digital technology).

Chapter 6 is developed around the Paper Mills Corporation in Israel. The case provides an illustration around learning mechanisms that were developed for the purpose of enhancing development processes within the firm. The Paper Mills case illustrates how the strategic decision to focus on improving the capabilities of key development processes, identified as crucial to the long-term survival and success of the firm, coupled with decisions on and implementation of specific learning mechanisms, influences the competitive and sustainable performance of the firm. The case is of special interest as the firm has managed to continuously improve its performance and sustain its competitive position in its market segment for the past fifteen years.

Chapter 7 focuses on knowledge management processes at a software development firm in North America. In the context of knowledge management processes, organizational learning mechanisms refer to the formal and informal configurations that are created within the firm for the purpose of continuously improving the way the organization creates, transfers, exploits, and manages knowledge. The case illustrates how business strategy and design choices made around mechanisms that can facilitate learning in the context of an intense information technology workplace resulted in the sustainability of the firm in a very competitive environmental context.

Chapter 8 is built around the Medical Services Provider Network in North America. The case involves a company turnaround program that was system-wide, with multiple initiatives. The initiatives were integrated through two different structural learning mechanisms and through the use of external and internal change agents. Thus, the case illustrates design choices and implementations of learning mechanisms in a multi-stakeholder network environment that fostered major improvements in the network's competitiveness and sustainability in a complex regulatory environment.

Chapter 9 provides a focus on integration across the cases and learning themes. Thus, it explores the conditions, structures, and processes for sustainable learning organizations across the cases; it identifies patterns of relationships between strategy, learning, and sustainable performance; it examines the relationships between learning requirements, learning dimensions, and learning mechanisms; and it investigates the relationship between sustainability and the learning mechanisms that were implemented. Some lessons about our model, the sustainability and competitiveness of learning mechanisms, and paradoxes and issues are identified and discussed.

Chapter 10 focuses on implications and issues for practice and suggested directions for future research. As such, the first section proposes a possible roadmap/generic intervention process model that can be used to guide a planned change effort. The second section is devoted to the identification and discussion of some unanswered questions that require further scientific study. The last part of the chapter provides a retrospective conclusion.

References

Abrahamson, E. (1996). Management fashion. *Academy of Management Review*, 21(1), 254–85.

Abrahamson, E. (1999). Lifecycles, triggers, and collective learning processes. *Administrative Science Quarterly*, 44(4), 708–40.

Antal, A. B., Lenhardt, U., and Rosenbrock, R. (2001). Barriers to organizational learning. In A. B. Antal, M. Dierkes, J. Child, and I. Nonaka (eds), *Handbook of Organizational Learning and Knowledge*. New York: Oxford University Press, pp. 865–85.

Argyris, C. and Schön, D. A. (1978). *Organizational Learning: A Theory of Action Perspective*. Reading, MA: Addison-Wesley.

Backlund, T., Hansson, H., and Thunborg, C. (eds) (2001). *Lärdilemman i arbetslivet* (Swedish: Learning dilemmas in Working life). Lund: Studentlitteratur.

Beer, M. (2000). Research that will break the code of change: The role of useful normal science and usable action science. In M. Beer and N. Nohria (eds), *Breaking the Code of Change*. Boston: Harvard Business School Press, pp. 429–46.

Beer, M. (2001). How to develop an organization capable of sustained high performance. *Organizational Dynamics*, 29(4), 233–47.

Berggren, C. and Bengtsson, L. (2001). Produktionens förändrade roll – mager klickfunktion eller kunskapsfabrik? (Swedish: Production's changed role – lean clique function or knowledge factory) In T. Backlund, H. Hansson, and C. Thunborg (eds), *Lärdilemman i arbetslivet*. Lund: Studentlitteratur, pp. 149–76.

Cowan, D. A. (1995). Rhythms of learning: Patterns that bridge individuals and organizations. *Journal of Management Inquiry*, 4(3), 222–46.

Dixon, N. M. (1999). *The Organizational Learning Cycle*. Hampshire, England: Power Publishing Ltd.

Docherty, P., Forslin, J., and Shani, A. B. (Rami) (2002). *Creating Sustainable Work Systems: Emerging Perspectives and Practice*. London, England: Routledge.

Döös, M., Wilhelmson, L., and Backlund, T. (2001). Kollektivt lärande på individualistiskt vis – ett lärdilemma för praktik och teori (Swedish: Collective learning in an individual way: a learning dilemma in theory and practice). In T. Backlund, H. Hansson, and C. Thunborg (eds), *Lärdilemman i arbetslivet*. Lund: Studentlitteratur, pp. 43–78.

Ellström, P. E. (2001). Lärande och innovation i organization (Swedish: Learning and innovation in organizations). In T. Backlund, H. Hansson, and C. Thunborg (eds), *Lärdilemman i arbetslivet*. Lund: Studentlitteratur, pp. 19–42.

Emery, F. E. and Trist, E. (1969). Sociotechnical systems. In F. Emery (ed.), *System Thinking*. Hammondsworth: Penguin.

Friedlander, F. (1983). Patterns of individual and organizational learning. In S. Srivastva and Associates, *The Executive Mind: New Insights on Managerial Thoughts and Action*. San Francisco, CA: Jossey-Bass Inc., pp. 192–220.

Friedman, V. J., Lipshitz, R. and Overmeer, W. (2001). Creating conditions for organizational learning. In A. B. Antal, M. Dierkes, J. Child, and I. Nonaka (eds), *Handbook of Organizational Learning and Knowledge*. New York: Oxford University Press, pp. 757–74.

Garvin, D. A. (2000). *Learning in Action*. Boston, MA: Harvard Business School Press.

Gibson, J. W. and Tesone, D. V. (2001). Management fads: Emergence, evolution, and implications for managers. *Academy of Management Executive*, 15(4), 122–33.

Hedberg, B. (1981). How organizations learn and unlearn. In P. Nystrom and W. Starbuck (eds), *Handbook of Organization Design*. New York: Oxford University Press.

Lillrank, P., Shani, A. B. (Rami) and Lindberg, P. (2001). Continuous improvement: Exploring alternative organizational designs. *Total Quality Management*, 12(1), 41–55.

Lipshitz, R., Popper, M., and Oz, S. (1996). Building a Learning Organization. *Journal of Applied Behavioral Science*, 32(3), 292–305.

Lundgren, K. (1999). Kortare lärotider och ett nytt lärande system (Swedish: Shorter learning times and a new learning system). *Arbetsmarknad och Arbetsliv*, 5(4), 287–302.

Marquardt, Michael J. and Reynolds, A. (1996). Learning across borders. *World Executive Digest*, May, 22–5.

Marsick, V. and Watkins, K. (1997). Lessons from informal and incidental learning. In J. Burgoyne and M. Reynolds (eds), *Management Learning: Integrating Perspectives in Theory and Practice*. London: Sage.

Marsick, V. and Watkins, K. (1990). *Incidental and Informal Learning*. London: Routledge.

Purser, R. E. and Cabana, S. (1998). *The Self-Managing Organization: How Leading Companies are Transforming the Work of Teams for Real Impact*. New York: The Free Press.

Schein, E. H. (2002). The anxiety of learning. *Harvard Business Review*, 80(3), 100–6.

Senge, P. (1990). *The Fifth Discipline*. New York: Doubleday.

Shani, A. B. (Rami) and Mitki, Y. (2000). Creating the learning organization: Beyond mechanisms. In R. Golembiewski (ed.), *Handbook of Organizational Consultation*. New York: Marcel Dekker, pp. 911–19.

Stebbins, M. and Shani, A. B. (Rami) (2002). Eclectic design for change. In P. Docherty, J. Forslin, and A. B. (Rami) Shani (eds), *Creating Sustainable Work Systems: Emerging Perspectives and Practice*. London, England: Routledge, pp. 201–11.

Stymne, B. A. (2001). Kunskapsåtervinning eller lärande? (Swedish: Knowledge retrieval or learning?) In T. Backlund, H. Hansson, and C. Thunborg (eds), *Lärdilemman i arbetslivet*. Lund: Studentlitteratur, pp. 195–214.

Wickham, J. (2000). Understanding technical and organisational change. Chapter submitted for proposed book *Towards a Learning Society: Innovation and Competence Building with Social Cohesion for Europe*. Dublin: Employment Research Centre, Dept of Sociology, Trinity College Dublin.

2

Competitive Strategy, Sustainability and Learning

- How are strategy, learning and sustainability related to each other in an organization?
- What are different perspectives of organizational learning?
- What are some of the core concepts of organizational learning mechanisms?
- How can learning mechanisms help organizations achieve and sustain success?

Recently, it has been argued that the most powerful way to prevail in global competition is still invisible to many managers and companies (Prahalad and Hamel, 2000). A key question for many companies today centers on how companies can exploit their resources and capabilities such that competitive advantage can be achieved and sustained over time. Many companies that have achieved success as measured by economic performance indicators are finding out that maintaining success is a challenging managerial task. Looking at the lists of Fortune 500 companies for the last decade and noting the number of successful startup companies that have disappeared from the scene after a few years of success gives a clear indication that sustaining success might well be more difficult than achieving success (Docherty, Forslin, and Shani, 2002).

The position advanced in this book is that the development of learning mechanisms as a business strategy and design choice can set the stage for achieving competitive advantage and sustaining it over time. In this chapter we develop the conceptual framework for learning by design, anchor the framework in the context of the scientific literature, provide a brief overview of the different perspectives on organizational learning, and discuss the core concepts of organizational learning mechanisms. This is followed by an exploration of the relationship between learning and sustainability. The argument that learning mechanisms are the vital invisible element of a competitive and sustainable organization is advanced.

Strategy, Learning and Performance

The field of business strategy historically focused on the analysis of the industry environment of the firm and its competitive positioning in relation to rivals. Recently, the emphasis seems to have shifted to the interface between strategy and the internal environment of the firm (Grant, 1999). Capabilities are viewed as key elements of the firm's internal environment. At the business level, authors such as Dibella and Nevis (1998) and de Geus (1997) have argued that development and organizing capabilities are the source of competitive advantage. Thus, the key emerging issue centers on matching the firm's capabilities with the opportunities that arise in the external environment. A company can look at an existing business context and examine the current strategy to determine what will make it more successful. Alternatively, the company can look at its existing way of utilizing its capabilities and specify what might be a better way to take advantage of them, or develop internal mechanisms to ensure a continuously successful practice.

If this perspective were generally accepted and these measures were as straightforward as they appear at first glance, we probably would not have seen so many failures in sustaining success as our data and experience indicate. So, what is it about sustainability that makes it such a complicated managerial and organizational challenge? The sustainability literature regarding companies broaches two major areas: the ecological system in which the company operates and the companies' human resources. We are concerned here with the latter topic, the firm's capability to regenerate and extend human and social resources in ongoing processes. According to Moldaschl (2002), sustainability can be examined at three levels:

■ From an individual perspective, a work system is sustainable when it maintains and develops the individual's marketable qualifications and skills, social relations, and personal health.

■ At the group and organizational levels, a work system is sustainable when it maintains and extends the human, social, financial, and institutional resources of the team and the organization.

■ From a societal perspective an organization is viewed as sustainable if it is able to contribute to the generation and regeneration of resources in society.

Business and environmental complexity is one reason that few firms have established close connections between their strategy, sustainability, and learning.

Yet, the argument that we advance in this book is that an essential element in creating business sustainability is the establishment of flexible organizational learning mechanisms. Furthermore, the strategist(s) and the designer(s) have the responsibility of facilitating the creation of the most efficient and appropriate learning mechanisms.

During the 1990s the issue of learning and competence became one of the clearest and most important, and must be considered by management when companies and government organizations design their business strategies. A company's competitive strength and survival demand the complete commitment of all its employees. They must be able to predict changes, adapt to new conditions, and find new solutions and new ideas for products and production processes. This commitment demands not only high personal motivation; the employee must also believe in the company's business idea and work to realize its goals. Many authors contend that learning at all levels in an organization is not only a means for reaching these goals but also a major condition for the long-term success and competitive viability of the company.

A further reason to give special attention to learning and competence development is that it takes a long time to turn a trend – much longer than it takes to solve economic or technological problems. A company may require a few years to turn its economy around, and a technology shift may take somewhat longer. However, it can take much longer to develop new key competencies, not only in individual companies but more especially at the industry level: developing the competence to handle a new technology can take much longer in an entire industry than in the individual leading companies, for example.

In today's business environment, with fragmented markets, worldwide competition, and products with short life cycles, competitive advantage is gained less by a company's product than by how the competition occurs. The core of the strategy is not the static structure of a company's product and market, but the dynamics of its behavior. Howard (1993) and Lillrank, Shani, and Lindberg (2001) concluded that there will have to be a shift in management's perception of its role – less of planner, controller, and decision maker, and more of designer. Managers must also be "ideologists" and create and give form to the organizational values needed to stimulate the commitment, learning, and creativity of the company's employees.

How can organizational learning be linked to strategy and sustainability? As Davenport (1999) pointed out, the three concepts – strategy, learning, and sustainability – are dynamic and multifaceted. A company's strategy must address its current strategic position, or where it wants its strategy to take it in the future. Future strategy involves working within an existing business context that by definition tends to be dynamic. Designing for business sustainability is a challenge for the designer. Assessment of the environmental context allows the designer to identify the "learning design requirements" of the system. Accordingly, "learning design dimensions" are identified that pertain to both performance and sustainability criteria. At the core of the choices around the learning design dimensions the designer needs to investigate the degree of fit between the variety of alternatives for the structural configurations

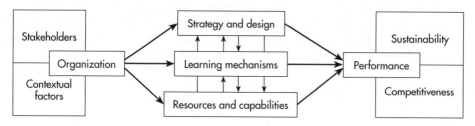

Figure 2.1 Strategy, learning mechanisms, and sustainability

of the organizational learning mechanisms, the firm's strategic objectives, and the firm's internal dynamics and culture.

In order to address this complexity, we advance an integrative framework that is anchored in strategic, sociotechnical systems, sustainability, and learning theories. The framework identifies five clusters of factors that have an impact on the firm's profitability and sustainability. The framework is especially useful when one is attempting to understand an organization's present performance (in terms of both competitiveness and sustainability) and to plan changes that will lead to improved results. Figure 2.1 illustrates organizational competitiveness and sustainability as an outcome of complex relationships between the design choices made around the organizational learning mechanisms, the firm's strategy and design, its resources and capabilities, and the business context.

The environmental context constitutes the elements and forces in the marketplace in which the firm competes. A variety of models can be found in the literature about ways to map out the environmental context of a company (i.e., Daft, 2000; Guns, 1996; Nadler and Tushman, 1997; Pasmore, 1988). For example, Daft (2000) identified ten environmental factors: industry, international, socio-cultural, government, economic conditions, technology, market, financial resources, human resources, and raw material sectors. Each one of the case-based chapters in the book (chapters 3–8) identifies the relevant environmental factors. For example, chapter 3 presents a case in the bank industry that seems to have been influenced by a few dominant environmental factors, such as the economic conditions, governmental regulations, and global financial market.

Stakeholders are viewed as all the relevant partners that have a stake in the firm, such as customers, unions, government agencies, human resources, communities, and other companies that might be suppliers or competitors. Stakeholders and the interaction between them influence the emergence and nature of learning mechanisms. For example, chapter 4 presents a case in an automobile manufacturing company that had the following stakeholders: investors, human resources, unions, suppliers, customers, and community.

The environmental context influences the firm's strategy, the firm's way of organizing (design), the firm's resources availability, and the firm's capabilities. *The firm's resources and capabilities* can be viewed in a variety of ways. One classification differentiates resources based on the units of analysis (i.e., the individual resources of the firm such as capital equipment, skills of individual employees, patents, brands, and so on) (Grant, 1999). An alternative classification differentiates between tangible (i.e., financial, physical), intangible (i.e., technology, reputation, and culture), and human resources (i.e., specialized skills and knowledge, motivation) (Cressey and Docherty, 2002; Segal-Horn, 1998). The firm's capabilities refer to the organization's capacity for undertaking a particular productive activity. The literature uses the terms "capability" and "competence" interchangeably (Hamel and Prahalad, 1992).

The firm's strategy and design choices, coupled with its resources and capabilities, influence the choices that are made by the designers and strategists about the specific design configuration of the learning mechanisms. For example, strategic choice around values, time horizon, flexibility, and readiness for change are likely to influence the specific design orientation. *Learning mechanisms* can be differentiated by their target or unit of analysis (i.e., individual, team, organizational, and network). *The learning mechanisms* are viewed as formal and informal organizational configurations (structures and processes) whose purpose is to develop, improve, and assimilate learning (Bushe and Shani, 1990, 1991; Friedman, Lipshitz, and Overmeer, 2001; Schein, 1993a). For example, Lipshitz, Popper, and Oz (1996) – based on an information processing perspective – used the term organizational learning mechanisms to describe institutionalized structure and procedural arrangements that allow organizations to systematically collect, analyze, store, disseminate, and use information that is relevant to the performance of the organization and its members. As such, learning mechanisms at different levels of the firm serve the critical role of regeneration of resources and capabilities while at the same time having a direct effect on the *business profitability, competitiveness, and sustainability*. Recent studies explored the possible relationships between strategy, learning, profitability, and competitiveness and illustrated the strong causal relationship between them (i.e., Collins and Porras, 1995; de Geus, 1998; Pfeffer, 1998). Just as there are many types of organization designs, there are also various types of structural forms of learning mechanisms (Shani and Mitki, 2000), each of which, and the variety of combinations between any of them, will have a direct but different effect on the firm's performance and sustainability.

▶ Sustainability and Learning

The resource-based view of the firm became the prominent paradigm in strategic thinking in the 1990s (Segal-Horn, 1998). At the most basic level, the resource-based view of the firm advocates that each firm consists of a unique cluster of resources – both tangible and intangible – and capabilities. This will make possible different strategies and different performance.

The increasing focus on the internal resources and capabilities of the firm is rooted in the ever-changing technological landscapes which have a profound impact on the firm and its strategy. Some argue that even the most "bulletproof" product strategies and organizational structures may become obsolete in a short time (Digenti, 2000). As we have stated earlier, the firm's resources are viewed in a variety of ways in the literature. The classifications vary from looking at resources based on units of analysis or on their type, to viewing resources based on products and/or services provided by the firm.

For the purpose of this book we will adopt the classification of resources as tangible, intangible, or human (Grant, 1999; Cressey and Docherty, 2002). Tangible resources, the easiest to identify and evaluate, are the financial resources and physical resources identified and valued in the firm's financial statements. A strategic assessment of tangible resources is directed towards answering three key questions: What opportunities exist for economizing on the use of finance, inventories, and fixed assets? What are the possibilities for employing existing assets more profitably? How can these resources be regenerated and expanded? Over time, tangible resources become less important to the firm in terms of their contribution to value added and as a basis for competitive advantage.

At the same time, intangible resources such as technology (i.e., technological ownership, proprietary technology, patents, copyrights), reputation (i.e., perceived quality and/or customer service, reliability, brand name and other trademarks), and culture are largely invisible. Yet, they seem to be of increasingly important added value for the sustainability of the firm's competitiveness. From a sustainable competitiveness perspective, the key in this context is how the intangible resources can be reproduced and/or extended over time. Since sustainability depends to a large extent on humans, the most critical question needs to center on how human resources can be regenerated, reproduced, and developed on an ongoing basis and not only be consumed by the intense task dynamics at work.

The compilation of the firm's resources strongly influences the organizational capabilities. Organizational capability refers to the firm's capacity, when all the relevant resources are combined, for undertaking a specific productive activity. Yet creating capabilities is not simply a matter of assembling resources. Capabilities involve complex design choices about what resources to use, how to group the different resources, what other tangible and intangible resources will be needed from within and outside the firm's boundaries at different stages of the activity, and how to assess, control, and reward the resource utilization. As such, the firm's resources and capabilities will set the stage and the choices around the firm's design configurations. From a sustainable competitiveness perspective, we view resources and capabilities as the foundation upon which the firm's sustainability and profitability can be achieved, through the facilitation of the flexible learning mechanisms.

One of the essential elements for organizations that are capable of sustaining performance and competitiveness over time is the ability to create and maintain balance between different (and at times competing) stakeholders (Beer, 2001). Maintaining the delicate but necessary balance between economic goals and human development represents a major challenge for managers (Docherty, Forslin, and Shani, 2002). The design, implementation, and management of flexible learning mechanisms can facilitate such needed balance.

▶ Learning Mechanisms – the Vital Link

The resource-based view of the firm emphasized that the key to profitability is not doing the same as other firms – locating in the most attractive industries and pursuing the appropriate generic strategy – but the exploitation of the differences among firms. Since each firm is a unique collection of highly differentiated resources and capabilities, the choices made about the ways to utilize and develop them will determine profitability and sustainability over time. The thesis of this book is that learning mechanisms at and across different levels of the organization are the internal way of organizing, acting on, and developing the firm's differentiated capabilities. Furthermore, we argue that much of the work of managers is likely to shift away from focusing on structure and planning to the creation and facilitation of the type of flexible learning mechanisms that will keep the delicate balance between stakeholders and support corporate differentiated competitiveness, profitability, and sustainability.

The facets of organizational learning

In today's business environment, an organization's internal ability to learn from experience, assimilate new ideas, and translate them into action is a key to achieving and sustaining competitive advantage (Sanchez and Heene, 2000; Schwandt and Marquardt, 2000). Some argue that the firm's ability to learn faster than its competition is a critical source for competitive advantage (Cross and Isrealit, 2000; Dibella and Nevis, 1998). History has shown that to achieve such aims requires focus on a clear business strategy and a learning strategy, the development of the appropriate design and learning configurations, and a distinct set of managerial skills to manage, for example, management support, openness, risk-taking, and tolerating conflict (Cohen and Sproull, 1996; Grant, 1999; March, 1999; Docherty, 1996).

Learning is an integral component of any living system (de Geus, 1998; Brown and Duguid, 2000; Kolb, 1984). At the most basic level, every system must learn in order to survive. Learning is the ability to experience, reflect, adjust, and create new knowledge as a basis for action in a social context. Since without new knowledge or adaptation it is not possible to change, learning is about change. Yet, many of us have been conditioned to think of classroom learning any time we hear the concept "learning." It has, however, been clearly shown that about 80 percent of learning in work life does not take place in formal settings but in the workplace (Marsick and Watkins, 1990; Fox, 2000). However, no one theory of learning in the context of the work is widely accepted (Antal et al., 2001; Burgoyne and Reynolds, 2000; March, 1999; Prange, 1999).

Each discipline seems to have its own conceptualization of organizational learning.[1] The wide range of conceptualizations provides an illustration of many distinct typologies of learning. We attempted to synthesize the different perspectives and summarize them briefly through clustering them into a few different schools of thought that are the basis for the next section of this chapter. Taking the risk of providing a laundry list, the following is an illustration of the conceptual range of learning based on discipline and focus:

■ learning as an individual, group, organizational, inter-organizational, network, and work-based phenomenon;

■ learning as knowledge acquisition, as adaptation, as skill learning, and as development of knowledge base;

■ learning as development of shared assumptions;

■ learning as technical and social processes;

■ learning as content vs. process vs. contextual phenomenon;

■ learning as single loop vs. double loop vs. deutero cycles;

■ learning as adaptive vs. generative processes;

■ learning as cognitive vs. culture vs. action-based phenomenon;

■ learning as an ideology vs. a policy of mobilizing resources vs. a process to manage tension vs. a problem-solving search vs. a discursive practice;

■ learning as organizational change vs. organizational development vs. organizational transformation process;

■ learning as knowledge absorption; and

■ learning as institutional know-how.

An example of learning types with different time horizons includes Schein's (1993b) classification which differentiates between knowledge acquisition and insight (cognitive learning), habit and skill learning, and emotional conditioning and learned anxiety.

A critical element of learning is the need for a space in which learning occurs. The need for "space" for learning – or knowledge creation – was advanced by Nonaka and Konno (1998), based on the concept of *ba* which was originally developed by the Japanese philosopher Kitaro Nishida. *Ba* is defined as a context in which knowledge is shared, created, and utilized, in recognition that knowledge needs a context in order to exist. Recently, Nonaka, Toyama, and Byosière (2001) claimed that *ba* does not necessarily mean a physical space. They suggest that it can be a physical space (i.e., an office

---

[1] For a synopsis of the psychological perspective see Mair, Prange, and Rosenstiel (2001); sociological see Gherardi and Nicolini (2001); management science see Pawlowsky (2001); economics see Boerner, Macher, and Teece (2001); anthropology see Czarniawska (2001); political science see LaPalombara (2001); education see Burgoyne and Reynolds (2000); and history see Fear (2001).

space), a virtual space (i.e., a teleconference), a mental space (shared ideas), or any combination of these kinds of space. A critical aspect of *ba* is space for interaction. As such, *ba* is viewed as interaction between individuals, between individuals and the environment, and between individuals and information, but not necessarily the space itself. In the context of this book, we argue that learning mechanisms provide the space where vital interactions take place and learning gets created.

Schools of organizational learning: A snapshot review

As we stated earlier, many different theories and perspectives about organizational learning can be found in the literature (i.e., Huber, 1991; Lundberg, 1989; Purser and Pasmore, 1992; Marquardt, 1996). A few attempts have been made to group the theories and perspectives. For the purpose of this book we provide three complementary groupings: a) according to the evolutions of the stream of research which is placed on a historical timeline; b) first- and second-order learning based on impact; and c) based on level of learning.

The different streams

The *first stream* grew out of the late 1940s and early 1950s, when the group that worked at the Tavistock Institute in London was preoccupied with the design of systems that would optimize the relationships between the business environment and the technological and social subsystems. The creation of semi-autonomous work teams emerged as one of the key design criteria. At the heart of the work-team learning, clear choices were made about the establishment of mechanisms that would enhance the team's learning. The focus of this stream seems to have been on the shop and office floor. Many of the sociotechnical system school theorists like Hans van Beinum, Fred Emery, Harvey Kolodny, Bill Pasmore, Jim Taylor, Einar Thorsrud, Eric Trist, and their followers continued to refine and define learning at the team and organizational levels within the sociotechnical system-based framework.

The *second stream* began to evolve during the late 1950s and early 1960s when a group of researchers at Carnegie Mellon University, led by Richard Cyert, James March, and Herbert Simon, focused on how organizations make choices and on understanding the phenomenon of decision-making. James March and his colleagues continued the conceptual development work at Stanford and, as an integral part of theorizing about decision-making, were able to articulate new insights and new models of ambiguity, risk-taking, and adaptive learning. In comparison to the first stream, this stream focused on decision makers in the organization.

A *third stream* of research, started in the late 1960s, centered on Harvard and MIT and was led by Chris Argyris and Donald Schön. Their argument was that since organizations are not merely collections of individuals, organizational learning is not merely individual learning. Yet at the same time organizations seem to learn only through the experience and actions of individuals (Argyris and Schön, 1978; Fulmer and Keys, 1998). They advanced a number of important concepts, including the distinction between "single-" and "double-loop learning" and "deutero learning." In single-loop learning, a person learns to do a given task better. New knowledge is integrated with the old, and the person becomes more skilled within the given limits. In double-loop learning, people reflect and question things they used to take for granted. They think about the impact or implications of changes in the given conditions, and how changes in them can lead to other ways to carry out their tasks. Established truths and ways of acting are reappraised. Both require creativity. In deutero learning, people learn to learn better. The quality of learning is improved. Faced with the unfamiliar, people learn to handle it faster and better each time. The process goes more smoothly; sidetracks and dead ends are more quickly recognized and abandoned.

This distinction between single- and double-loop learning has become popular with managers and theorists alike since it maps easily onto models of organization change (Easterby-Smith and Araujo, 1999). While the first rarely leads to significant changes in the firm's basic assumptions, the latter involves the changing of values and beliefs that underlie the errors and thus is likely to result in changing and transforming the firm's culture.

A *fourth stream*, started in the early 1990s, popularized the phenomenon of organizational learning and was led by Peter Senge at MIT. It is widely argued that learning occurs in the interaction between people, and not in the brain of a single individual. Some research programs, such as that led by Peter Senge, William Isaacs, and George Roth at Massachusetts Institute of Technology, have focused on social processes and dialogues between people who are involved in a common learning process (Senge, 1991; Senge et al., 1999; Yeung et al., 1999). Based on the need for dialogue, openness, system dynamics, and other concepts articulated by Argyris, de Geus, Revans, Schein, Schön, and others, Senge's first book was subtitled *The Art and Practice of the Learning Organization*. The book articulates the five disciplines of a learning organization and emphasizes that the organizational learner suffers from several learning deficiencies. Senge suggests that learning in organizations may be thought of as a flow process that often needs to be unlocked or released within individuals and organizations (Fulmer and Gibbs, 1998).

The first and second order of learning

A parallel clustering to the single- and double-loop learning focuses on first- and second-order learning. Two approaches are behavioral adaptation or adaptive learning, and knowledge development or cognitive learning. Behavioral adaptation in a company may comprise changes in the management organization, decision process, work routines, or allocation of resources. This is also called first-order organizational learning. Cognitive learning brings changes in the company's frames of reference, shared mental models, culture, strategy, and/or programs. Such changes are characteristic of second-order organizational learning. These issues are broached in chapters 3 and 4.

The incremental *first-order learning* is brought into play when new routines are introduced into unchanged contexts or situations. In *second-order learning*, both old and new routines acquire new meaning in their context.

When researchers simulate alternative organizational solutions with computer models, they use adaptive learning. These models are usually based on simplified assumptions about how an organization functions, and are often used in complex development projects to test different forms of organization. March, Levinthal, and Lant are researchers on adaptive learning, Argyris, Schön, and Eppie on cognitive learning

Levels of learning

Individual learning is a necessary but not sufficient condition for organizational learning, which is the type of learning needed if an organization is to develop and change with changing conditions. *Collective learning* is then imperative. It is brought into being when groups develop shared knowledge, behavior, attitudes, and values. When employees discuss ideas with each other or work together to interpret assignments or identify problems that need to be solved, the group develops a shared picture of the reality they are supposed to deal with. They acquire a common cognitive map or local theory. This is a theory that is accepted by the group at the workplace and by those in the immediate surroundings. Employees develop a similar way of looking at things. When a new attitude spreads among the employees, from the group to other employees and via them to other groups, the collective learning process has begun. Thus, we can distinguish between individual (see chapter 3 in this book), team (see chapter 4), organizational (see chapter 5), network (see chapter 8), and process-level learning (see chapters 6 and 7).

Individual and collective learning do not automatically imply organizational learning. Both managers and employees can recognize problems, for example, but if this knowledge is not put to use the problems will not be solved. Individual employees and groups can learn and can develop their competence without affecting the organization. Their workplace is not able to benefit from their learning. In organizational learning, information, attitudes, and behavior are spread throughout the organization by the individual and collective learning of the organization's members, and also communicated via changes in the organization's routines, praxis, or products. This does not happen automatically, however. Structures and systems are required that allow the organization to benefit from the insights that have been gained. Management must create good conditions for learning and guarantee that there are meeting places and channels that allow the learning to be integrated into the organization's systems, routines, and praxis. A well-known example of this issue was the debate on learning in car plants. Adler and Cole (1993) maintained that the assembly teams at the Volvo Uddevala plant were an excellent example of individual and group learning, whereas there was little evidence of organizational learning there. The NUMMI plant in California was, however, an excellent example of organizational learning, though there was less individual and group learning than in Uddevalla.

Glynn, Lant, and Milliken (1994) presented a model of the interaction between individual and organizational learning. Two processes, spreading and institutionalization, connect individual learning and organizational learning. *Spreading* means that the new knowledge is communicated between the members of the organization, and *institutionalization* formalizes and legitimizes the company's structure, praxis, and culture. Institutionalization means that information, experience, attitudes, and norms are socially defined as a part of the organization. They are taken for granted. This occurs by development of organizational routines, best practice, regulations, policies, and computer systems to assure that their availability to the organization is not dependent on single individuals (Dixon, 2000).

Ellström (1996) discusses differences in pedagogical perspectives. The cognitive perspective places strong emphasis on formal teaching and verbal instruction, whereas the contextual emphasizes an informal, *experience-based learning* by means such as apprenticeship or active involvement in a community of work. He points out that both *theory-based* and experience-based learning have definite limitations. Theoretical education has been found very difficult to "transfer" or "apply" as a basis for practical action in everyday working life. Experience-based learning, on the other hand, can be extremely context-bound, and thus difficult to generalize and use in new or different situations. There is thus much to indicate that these two forms of learning need to be united. The two perspectives are not mutually exclusive, but complementary. In practice, both viewpoints are probably required for complete understanding of how learning occurs in natural work situations. In a summary of earlier research, Ellström observes that most evidence indicates that a contextual or experience-based perspective is better suited to describe and analyze the work of experienced and skilled workers; work done under time pressure; work in complex production systems; and work in unstructured, unknown, or poorly defined problem situations. This type of learning will be addressed in chapter 4.

In reverse, there is support that a cognitive-theoretical perspective can be used to describe and analyze the work of less experienced skilled workers; handling of abstract information rather than sensory input; work when there is strong pressure to justify decisions to external parties; and work in structured, familiar, and well-defined problem situations. This type of learning will be addressed in chapter 7.

Another level-based typology of learning that is found frequently in the literature, based on Bateson (1992), was developed by Pawlowsky (2001) into three prototypes of learning: *Type I*, the correction of deviations, consists of the detection of performance gaps and their elimination, also referred to as first-order learning or single-loop learning; *Type II*, the examination of the assumptions, frame of reference, and interpretation of why the deviation occurred, focuses on an attempt to correct the assumptions, also called second-order learning or double-loop learning; and *Type III* focuses on the learning-to-learn problem-solving approach, that is "the construction of higher-order rules based on experience and insights" (Pawlowsky, 2001, p. 77), also called deutero learning.

Clearly, the focus on learning and organizational learning is not new. In the context of the work organization, learning is dependent on the integration of multiple and inherently different perspectives and types. For learning to become a dominant character of organizational life it is important that the concept is spelled out at the strategic level and that the activities, processes, and mechanisms are centered on a specific level.

The need to explore alternative learning mechanisms

The popularity of organizational learning has continuously increased and recently its shift to the center stage of organization theory has been suggested (Prange, 1999; Shani and Stjernberg, 1995; Simon, 1991). Ideas of organizational learning have captured the imagination of managers and scholars alike (Garvin, 2000; Edmondson, 2000). Furthermore, an increasing number of organizational scientists and executives are predisposed to understand and adopt the learning organization concept. Some view organizational learning as a comprehensive approach that provides a window of opportunity for assimilating advanced managerial approaches. However, a follow-up study of US organizations that attempted to assimilate new managerial approaches revealed some failures among those that did not have the foresight to construct a suitable mechanism for organizational learning that incorporated processes, tools, and work patterns (Moingeon and Edmondson, 1996). Moreover, the published literature does not provide sufficient knowledge regarding implementation (Popper and Lipshitz, 1998; Raelin, 2000; Stebbins and Shani, 2002; Ulrich, Jick, and Von Glinow, 1993).

The learning mechanism for organizational learning is viewed as a formal configuration – structures, processes, procedures, rules, tools, methods, and physical configurations – created within the firm for the purpose of developing, enhancing, and sustaining performance and learning. Just as there are many types of organizational designs, there are also various ways to design and manage organizational learning mechanisms. The design of a specific configuration is viewed as a rational choice among alternatives based on learning design requirements and learning design dimensions.

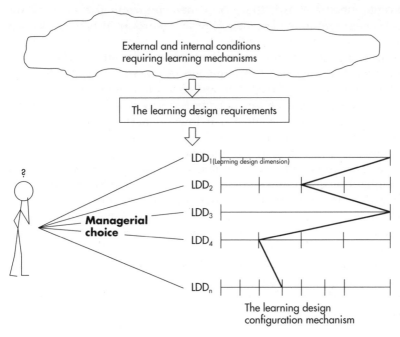

Figure 2.2 Organizational learning mechanisms: a conceptual roadmap for design choices

Our research to date has demonstrated that, in practice, organizational learning mechanisms could be designed and managed in various ways. These "various ways" have been described as a set of learning design dimensions (LDD), each of which fulfills a necessary learning requirement for achieving learning and performance (see figure 2.2). As such, the learning design dimensions are a basic set of alternative solutions that managers can choose from in order to meet the learning design requirements. The range of alternatives needs to be investigated by every organization and could integrate some alternative solutions from the literature as well as benchmarking existing solutions.

The set of necessary but not sufficient learning requirements for achieving learning is referred to as learning design requirements (LDR). Some examples of learning design requirements might include the following: a legitimate forum for exchange of ideas must be created; a specific set of processes that facilitate ongoing dialogue must be developed; a specific set of tools need to be developed and/or adopted that facilitate learning; the design forum and processes must reflect and incorporate the totality of the organization and not just parts of it; goals and objectives that define the direction of the learning efforts must be formulated. Some examples of learning design dimensions (LDD) might include the following: Is learning an integral part of ordinary work or not? Is learning work performed in a permanent working group or in a specially formed task force? Are group members from one or several functions? Are the group members from the same or different levels? Is goal setting made centrally or in the group(s)? Is the process guided or free?

The learning design dimensions represent different possible ways to respond to the learning design requirements. Along each learning design dimension there is a range of choices that an organizational designer can make. The conscious choices could be functionally equivalent ways to achieve the same objectives in a different context. An integral part of the rational decision-making process is to identify the external and internal conditions requiring improvements in the existing learning mechanisms or the decision to create a new one, identify the specific learning design requirements that fit the business situation and business dynamics, and investigate and explore the alternative most appropriate learning design dimensions for the firm.

The chapters that follow – chapters 3–8 – illustrate the learning mechanisms that were developed by a variety of companies in different industrial sectors. The chapters describe the companies and their stakeholders, strategy, design, resources, and capabilities as well as the learning mechanisms that were chosen and developed in order to help the companies achieve specific strategic goals in a specific business context.

References

Adler, P. and Cole, R. (1933). Designed for learning: A tale of two auto-plants. *Sloan Management Review*, 35(1), 85–94.

Antal, A. B., Dierkes, M., Child, J., and Nonaka, I. (2001). Introduction. In A. B. Antal, M. Dierkes, J. Child, and I. Nonaka (eds), *Handbook of Organizational Learning and Knowledge*. New York: Oxford University Press, pp. 1–10.

Argyris, C. and Schön, D. (1978). *Organizational Learning: A Theory of Action Perspective*. Reading, MA: Addison-Wesley.

Bateson, G. (1992). *Mind and Nature: A Necessary Unity*. New York: Bentam Books.

Beer, M. (2001). How to develop an organization capable of sustained high performance. *Organizational Dynamics*, 29(4), 233–47.

Boerner, C. S., Macher, J. T., and Teece, D. J. (2001). A review and assessment of organizational learning in economic theories. In A. B. Antal, M. Dierkes, J. Child, and I. Nonaka (eds), *Handbook of Organizational Learning and Knowledge*. New York: Oxford University Press, pp. 89–117.

Brown, J. S. and Duguid, P. (2000). *The Social Life of Information*. Boston, MA: Harvard Business School Press.

Burgoyne, J. and Reynolds, M. (2000). *Management Learning: Integrating Perspectives in Theory and Practice*. Thousand Oaks, CA: Sage Publications.

Bushe, G. R. and Shani, A. B. (1990). Parallel learning structure interventions. In R. W. Woodman and W. A. Pasmore (eds), *Research in Organization Change & Development*, vol. 4. Greenwich, CT: JAI Press, pp. 193–220.

Bushe, G. R. and Shani, A. B. (Rami) (1991). *Parallel Learning Structures: Increasing Innovations in Bureaucracies*. Reading, MA: Addison-Wesley.

Cohen, M. D. and Sproull, L. S. (1996). *Organizational Learning*. Thousand Oaks, CA: Sage Publications Inc.

Collins, J. C. and Porras, J. I. (1995). *Built to Last*. New York: Random House.

Cressey, P. and Docherty, P. (2002). Feedback, intangibles and sustainable performance. In P. Docherty, J. Forslin, and A. B. (Rami) Shani (eds), *Creating Sustainable Work Systems: Emerging Perspectives and Practice*. London: Routledge, pp. 165–78.

Cross, R. L., Jr. and Israelit, S. B. (2000). *Strategic learning in a Knowledge Economy: Individual, Collective and Organizational Learning*. Boston, MA: Butterworth Heinemann.

Czarniawska, B. (2001). Anthropology and organizational learning. In A. B. Antal, M. Dierkes, J. Child, and I. Nonaka (eds), *Handbook of Organizational Learning and Knowledge*. New York: Oxford University Press, pp. 188–236.

Daft, R. L. (2000). *Organization Theory and Design*. Houston, TX: South Western Publishing.

Davenport, T. H. (1999). Knowledge management and the broader firm: Strategy, advantage, and performance. In J. Liebowitz (ed.) *Knowledge Management Handbook*. New York: CRC Press, pp. 2-1–2-11.

Dibella, A. J. and Nevis, E. C. (1998). *How Organizations Learn*. San Francisco, CA: Jossey-Bass Publishers.

Digenti, D. (2000). Collaborative learning: Core competence for organizations in new economy. *Reflections*, 1(2), 46–57.

Dixon, N. M. (2000). *Common Knowledge*. Boston, MA: Harvard Business School Press.

Docherty, P. (1996). *Läroriket: val och vägval i den lärande organisationen* (Swedish: *The World of Learning: Ways and Crossroads in the Learning Organization*). Stockholm: Arbetslivsinstitutet.

Docherty, P., Forslin, J., and Shani, A. B. (Rami) (2002). *Creating Sustainable Work Systems: Emerging Perspectives and Practice*. London: Routledge.

Easterby-Smith, M., Burgoyne, J., and Araujo, L. (1999). *Organizational Learning and the Learning Organization: Developments in Theory and Practice*. Thousand Oaks, CA: Sage Publications.

Edmondson, A. C. (2000). Learning from mistakes is easier said than done. In R. L. Cross, Jr. and S. B. Israelit (eds), *Strategic Learning in a Knowledge Economy: Individual, Collective and Organizational Learning*. Boston, MA: Butterworth Heinemann, pp. 203–30.

Ellström, P. E. (1996). *Arbete och lärande* (Work and Learning). Stockholm: National Institute of Working Life.

Fear, J. (2001). Thinking historically about organizational learning. In A. B. Antal, M. Dierkes, J. Child, and I. Nonaka (eds), *Handbook of Organizational Learning and Knowledge*. New York: Oxford University Press, pp. 162–93.

Fox, S. (2000). From management education and development to the study of management learning. In J. Burgoyne and M. Reynolds (eds), *Management Learning: Integrating Perspectives in Theory and Practice*. Thousand Oaks, CA: Sage Publications, pp. 21–37.

Friedman, V., Lipshitz, R. and Overmeer, W. (2001). Creating conditions for organizational learning. In A. B. Antal, M. Dierkes, J. Child, and I. Nonaka (eds), *Handbook of Organizational Learning and Knowledge*. New York: Oxford University Press, pp. 757–74.

Fulmer, R. M. and Gibbs, P. (1998). The second generation learning organization: New tools for sustaining competitive advantage. *Organizational Dynamics*, 27(2), 7–20.

Fulmer, R. M. and Keys, J. B. (1998). A conversation with Chris Argyris: The father of organizational learning. *Organizational Dynamics*, 27(2), 21–32.

Fulmer, R. M. and Keys, J. B. (1998). A conversation with Peter Senge: New developments in organizational learning. *Organizational Dynamics*, 27(2), 33–42.

Garvin, D. A. (2000). *Learning in Action: A Guide to Putting the Learning Organization to Work*. Boston, MA: Harvard Business School Press.

Geus, A. de (1998). *The Living Company*. Boston, MA: Harvard Business School Press.

Gherardi, S. and Nicolini, D. (2001). The sociological foundation of organizational learning. In A. B. Antal, M. Dierkes, J. Child, and I. Nonaka (eds), *Handbook of Organizational Learning and Knowledge*. New York: Oxford University Press, pp. 35–60.

Glynn, M. A., Lant, T. K., and Milliken, F. J. (1994). Mapping learning processes in organizations: A multilevel framework linking learning and organizing. In C. Stubbart, J. R. Meindl, and J. F. Porac (eds), *Advances in Managerial Cognition and Organizational Information Processing*, vol. 5. Greenwich, CN: JAI Press.

Guns B. (1996). *The Faster Learning Organization*. San Francisco, CA: Jossey-Bass Publishers.

Grant R. M. (1999). *Contemporary Strategy Analysis*. Malden, MA: Blackwell Publishers Inc.

Hamel, G. and Prahalad, C. K. (1992). The core competence of the corporation. *Harvard Business Review*, 68(3), 79–91.

Howard, R. (1993). *The Learning Imperative*. Cambridge, MA: Harvard Business School Press.

Huber, G. P. (1991). Organizational learning: An examination of the contributing processes and a review of the literature. *Organizational Science*, 2(1), 88–115.

Kolb, D. A. (1984). *Experiential Learning*. Englewood Cliffs, NJ: Prentice-Hall.

LaPalombara, J. (2001). The underestimated contribution of political science to organizational learning. In A. B. Antal, M. Dierkes, J. Child, and I. Nonaka (eds), *Handbook of Organizational Learning and Knowledge*. New York: Oxford University Press, pp. 137–61.

Lillrank, P., Shani A. B. (Rami), and Lindberg, P. (2001). Continuous improvement: Exploring alternative organizational designs. *Total Quality Management*, 12(1), 41–55.

Lipshitz, R., Popper, M., and Oz, S. (1996). Building a learning organization: The design and implementation of organizational learning mechanisms. *Journal of Applied Behavioral Science*, 32(3), 292–305.

Lundberg, C. (1989). An organizational learning: Implications and opportunities for expanding organization development. In W. A. Pasmore and R. Woodman (eds), *Research in Organizational Change and Development*, vol. 3. Greenwich, CT: JAI Press, pp. 61–82.

Mair, G. W., Prange, C. and Rosenstiel, L. (2001). Psychological perspective of organizational learning. In A. B. Antal, M. Dierkes, J. Child, and I. Nonaka (eds), *Handbook of Organizational Learning and Knowledge*. New York: Oxford University Press, pp. 14–34.

March, J. G. (1999). *The Pursuit of Organizational Intelligence*. Malden, MA: Blackwell Publishers Inc.

Marquardt, M. J. (1996). *Building the Learning Organization*. New York; McGraw-Hill.

Marsick,V. J. and Watkins, K. E. (1990). *Informal and Incidental Learning at the Workplace*. London: Routledge.

Moingeon, B. and Edmondson, A. C. (1996). *Organizational Learning and Competitive Advantage*. Thousand Oaks, CA: Sage Publications.

Moldaschl, M. (2002). A resource-centered perspective. In P. Docherty, J. Forslin, and A. B. (Rami) Shani, *Creating Sustainable Work Systems: Emerging Perspectives and Practice*. London: Routledge, pp. 52–64.

Nadler, D. A. and Tushman, M. L. (1997). *Competing by Design*. New York: University Press.

Nonaka, I. and Konno, N. (1998). The concept of "ba": Building a foundation for knowledge creation. *California Management Review*, 40(3), 40–54.

Nonaka, I., Toyama, R., and Byosière, P. (2001). A theory of organizational knowledge creation: Understanding the dynamic process of creating knowledge. In A. B. Antal, M. Dierkes, J. Child, and I. Nonaka (eds), *Handbook of Organizational Learning and Knowledge*. New York: Oxford University Press, pp. 491–517.

Pasmore, W. A. (1988). *Designing Effective Organizations*. New York: Wiley.

Pawlowsky, P. (2001). The treatment of organizational learning in management science. In A. B. Antal, M. Dierkes, J. Child, and I. Nonaka (eds), *Handbook of Organizational Learning and Knowledge*. New York: Oxford University Press, pp. 61–88.

Pfeffer, J. (1998). *The Human Equation*. Boston, MA: Harvard Business School Press.

Prahalad, C. K. and Hamel, G. (2000). The core competence of the corporation. In R. L. Cross, Jr. and S. B. Israelit (eds), *Strategic Learning in a Knowledge Economy: Individual, Collective and Organizational Learning Process*. Boston, MA: Butterworth Heinemann, pp. 3–22.

Prange, C. (1999). Organization learning – desperately seeking theory? In M. Easterby-Smith, J. Burgoyne, and L. Araujo (eds), *Organizational Learning and the Learning Organization: Developments in Theory and Practice*. Thousand Oaks, CA: Sage Publications, pp. 23–43.

Popper, M. and Lipshitz, R. (1998). Organizational learning mechanisms: A structural and cultural approach to organizational learning. *Journal of Applied Behavioral Science*, 34(2), 161–79.

Purser, R. E. and Pasmore, W. A. (1992). Organizing for learning. In W. A. Pasmore and R. Woodman (eds), *Research in Organizational Change and Development*, vol. 6. Greenwich, CT: JAI Press, pp. 37–114.

Raelin, J. A. (2000). *Work-Based Learning*. Upper Saddle River, New Jersey: Prentice Hall.

Sanchez, R. and Heene, A. (2000). A competence perspective on strategic learning and knowledge management. In R. L. Cross, Jr. and S. B. Israelit (2000). *Strategic learning in a Knowledge Economy: Individual, Collective and Organizational Learning*. Boston, MA: Butterworth Heinemann, pp. 23–37.

Schein, E. H. (1993a). On dialogue, culture, and organizational learning. *Organizational Dynamics*, 22(2), 40–51.

Schein, E. H. (1993b). How can organizations learn faster: The problem of entering the green room. *Sloan Management Review*, 34(2), 85–92.

Schwandt, D. R. and Marquardt, M. J. (2000). *Organizational Learning: From World-Class Theories to Global Best Practices*. New York: St. Lucie Press.

Segal-Horn, S. (1998). *The Strategy Reader*. Malden, MA: Blackwell Publishers Inc.

Senge, P. (1991). *The Fifth Discipline*. New York: Doubleday.

Senge, O., Kleiner, A., Roberts, C., Ross, R., Roth, G., and Smith, B. (1999). *The Dance of Change: The Challenges to Sustain Momentum in Learning Organizations*. New York: Currency Doubleday.

Shani, A. B. (Rami) and Mitki, Y. (2000). Creating the learning organization: Beyond mechanisms. In R. Golembiewski (ed.), *Handbook of Organizational Consultation*. New York: Marcel Dekker, pp. 911–19.

Shani, A. B. (Rami) and Stjernberg, T. (1995). The integration of change in organizations: Alternative learning and transformation mechanisms. In W. A. Pasmore and R. W. Woodman (eds), *Research in Organizational Change and Development*, vol. 8. Greenwich, CT: JAI Press, pp. 77–121.

Simon, H. A. (1991). Bounded rationality & organizational learning. *Organization Science*, 2(1), 125–34.

Sitkin, S. B., Sutcliffe, K. M., and Schroeder, R. G. (1994). Distinguishing control from learning in Total Quality Management: A contingency perspective. *The Academy of Management Review*, 19(3), 537–64.

Stebbins, M. and Shani, A. B. (Rami) (2002). Eclectic design for change. In P. Docherty, J. Forslin, and A. B. (Rami) Shani (eds), *Creating Sustainable Work Systems: Emerging Perspectives and Practice*. London: Routledge, pp. 201–12.

Ulrich, D., Jick, T., and Von Glinow, M. (1993). High impact learning: Building and diffusing learning capability. *Organizational Dynamics*, 22(2), 52–66.

Yeung, A. K., Ulrich, D. O., Nason, S. W., and von Glinow, M. A. (1999). *Organizational Learning Capability*. New York: Oxford University Press.

Individual Competence Development, Learning and Performance

- How can individual development in work be integrated with business development?
- How can managers shoulder responsibility for Human Resource development?
- What are effective Human Resource development mechanisms and practices?

A historical perspective on individual competence development

Attitudes towards personnel and their personal development in organizations have changed radically in the past forty years. In the 1960s the main term used when referring to personnel development, especially for non-professional staff, was "training," and this usually referred to occupational training in the form of vocational training such as apprenticeship schemes. The term "learning" came to be used in the mid-sixties in the context of "learning technologies" in the early attempts to use programmed books and computer programs to support self-paced individual learning. The inappropriateness of the early technology was a major reason for the disappearance of this product/service from the market. The term "learning" remained in a "personnel development" debate as the antipode to "training." In the 1970s the debate was broadened to cover the issue of "tacit knowledge," its importance for effective performance in most work situations, and difficulties in defining and rewarding it (Polanyi, 1973). The 1970s also saw the emergence of the term human resource management (HRM) for the personnel function in organizations and "training" became "human resource development" (HRD).

At the turn of the 1970s–80s a study in the Organization for Economic and Co-operation and Development (OECD) identified three main streams in personnel development strategies: the mobility, the elite, and the HRD strategies (Bengtsson, 1985). The "mobility" strategy defined individual development as the primary responsibility of the individual concerned and was to be pursued outside of working hours. This strategy was mainly to be found in the Anglo-Saxon cultures. Organizations applying the second, "elite" strategy confined their development activities to personnel in prioritized specialist and management categories. Broad groups of personnel, especially those on the shop and office floor, received no planned development. For example, a study by the Commission for Electronic Industry Development in Sweden in 1982 found that the typical employee in "training" in Sweden was a male business or engineering graduate who was 30–35 years old. This led the Swedish TUC to demand that the government legislate that workers had a right to at least two days' training a year. This "elite" strategy was found in the majority of OECD countries. The third, HRD-intensive strategy entailed recruiting qualified personnel and ensuring their continual development through planned measures throughout the individual's (lifetime/extended) employment. This strategy was mainly associated with the Japanese economy at that time.

In the 1980–90s the European Commission showed strong interest in competence development coupled to the rapidly increasing utilization of information and communication technologies (ICT) in business and industry. It launched competence-oriented R&D programs such as the Eurotecnet and Leonardo da Vinci programs. In a Eurotecnet project Docherty and Nyhan (1997) noted that in the most successful cases of the implementation of new technology in European industrial companies management pursued a "vision-based" strategy. This entailed management giving clear priority to the goals and interests of both the social partners, i.e., the business interests of the company and the interests of its employees. Management worked in close cooperation with the personnel and their unions in the design of the work organization and of the competence development programs required by the new sociotechnical systems. Berger, Hart, and Lindberg (1996) have reported similar strategies regarding the implementation of continuous improvement systems.

These developments emerging in the mid-eighties, not least in the Nordic countries, were based on the realization by management that the delegation of goals, decision discretion, and planning and control functions to broad groups of personnel on the office and shop floor could lead to marked improvements in performance. Thus it was natural to integrate their interest in business conditions with an interest in conditions of work. From a union perspective it was gratifying to see that the scope for employees' personal initiative, autonomy, and meaningfulness at work increased. Such goals had already been formulated by many unions, e.g., in the Swedish Metal Workers' Union's congress report "Rewarding Work" in 1985.

At the turn of the 1980s–90s the learning debate had developed to refer to the entire organization. The knowledge and skills of the members of a company and their organization were designated as its most viable means of competition (de Geus, 1988). Learning was seen as a key process for an organization's dynamic efficiency and effectiveness (Docherty, 1996). The growth in the interest in learning and learning organizations was almost exponential in the nineties. Practitioners from different walks of life and academics from different disciplines became deeply interested in the area. There were and are marked differences between the definitions given of the concept of the "learning organization," as has been outlined in chapter 2. We find that of Pedler et al. (1991) most appropriate for our use in this context, namely:

> A learning organization is one that facilitates the learning of all its members and which continuously transforms itself in order to achieve its strategic aims. Pedler (1991, p. 128)

Pfeffer (1997) reports that American experiences of companies that have succeeded in realizing the needs and ambitions of both the investors and the employees are characterized by employment security, selective hiring of personnel, the use of self-managing teams, and decentralized decision-making as basic principles of organizational design, comparatively high compensation contingent on organizational performance, extensive training, low status distinctions and barriers, and extensive sharing of financial and performance information.

A feature of the Japanese "human resource development" strategy that has become a political slogan in Europe is "lifelong learning", not simply for an individual's career development with their current employer but also to maintain their employability. Employability means that individuals' knowledge and skills are such that they will be able to find employment outside their current employer. In fact, politicians give the term "lifelong learning" an even wider meaning; not simply leading to employability, but also active citizenship to exercise rights and duties in society. It entails the integration of general education, vocational education, and learning in and at work. Learning also entails learning to learn and to adapt to change in and outside the workplace.

The case on individual development has been chosen to illustrate a number of the important points of departure that have emerged in recent decades, namely that individual learning concerns all employees and not simply an elite; learning is not simply personnel-oriented, it is also business-oriented; it is not simply course-based training, but also includes learning on the job and at the job. This means that learning that is usually informal is now subject to systematic planning. There is often considerable cooperation between management and personnel and their unions on these issues. Learning activities are supported through the organization of work and the design of management systems and policies.

The case presented is of a merchant bank in Sweden. It illustrates how formal strategies and policies as well as the design of the work organization and the management system can promote learning and development for the broad majority of the workforce to benefit the performance of the organization. The case is of special interest as the company made a 180-degree turnaround in its business performance nearly thirty years ago through radical changes in its culture, organization, and business strategy and has since maintained its position as the most profitable bank in the country. Since the relatively recent independent sectoral surveys of "customer satisfaction" started, the bank has also topped the list from the start of the 90s even in this area.

▶ Recent Developments in the Financial Sector

The 1980s saw some significant deregulation of banking activities in many European countries (Morgan and Knights, 1997). In some cases, it was not a question of easing regulations, but of taking them away altogether. Deregulation was one factor that contributed to the rapid developments in the real estate market which collapsed in the early 1990s. This led to the Swedish government deciding to rescue many banks from bankruptcy (Engwall, 1997).

Deregulation has also fired the trend to consolidation via mergers, and acquisitions were a distinct characteristic of Nordic financial markets in the 90s. At the same time, deregulation has also led to a blurring of the boundaries between different parts of the financial services sector, for example between insurance and banking, and between retail and investment banking. Banks have entered insurance by diversification or acquisition. Insurance companies have entered banking mainly by diversification. The development of IT has spurred the creation of niche telebanks with a few branch offices concentrated on major cities. Successive deregulation has allowed companies outside the financial sector to establish business in the financial transaction sector. Retail chains such as J. C. Penney in the USA and ICA and the COOP in Sweden are typical examples. Given the marked similarity in the strategies of key players in the sector, the acquisition and development of skills and knowledge and their organization may be expected to play a central role in a bank's success in the marketplace.

These developments are leading to the emergence of the "financial supermarket," a one-stop-service store offering the full range of financial services that complement and extend the basic services provided by the welfare system. Advantageous package solutions will entice the customer to become a full-service customer, loyal to a single financial institution. This development increases the competence demands on personnel. The role of the bank office employee has been changing from being basically a teller to being a seller to being a professional financial advisor. These roles also demand more commitment, empathy, and initiative in creating tailor-made solutions for customers.

This has also meant that there is a differentiating of the service accorded customers or clients depending on their value to the business. Parallel with this development, banks are extending their use of ICT as a means to rationalize transaction costs through extending customer self-service. This has taken the form of telephone banking, call centers, and the Internet. Many experts forecast that the need to visit branch offices will decrease significantly, though studies show that these electronic communication channels mainly replace paper-based communication, e.g., via giro (Sannes and Steneskog, 2002).

The Merchant Bank

The basic organization

The Merchant Bank aims to be an *universal bank*, i.e., a bank which offers its private and business clients the full spectrum of banking and financial services. Examples of such services are loans, real estate financing, payments, investment banking, trading, factoring, and leasing and insurance. Besides offering a broad spectrum of services, the provision of a large network of branch offices is considered as being a basic component in its concept of a universal bank. In fact the *extensive branch office network* is seen as this bank's most important competitive advantage and not just an alternative channel.

The Merchant Bank's basic idea is that the client should be its central focus and not its products. To achieve this, the bank has implemented a *marked decentralization* of the bank's business to its branch offices. The local branch office has total responsibility for a coordinated and qualified service to each of its individual customers. It is individual contact persons in the local office who make all the decisions regarding their customers. This principle was introduced in the bank in the early 1970s and is regarded by management as its most important source of stimulation and personal development for personnel.

In the late 1990s asset management assumed a prominent strategic role in the bank. The 1990s saw the rapid automation of routine transactions from about 20 percent to over 70 percent. This has led to more and more qualified tasks being delegated to branch offices. The work at branch offices is increasingly made up of giving advice concerning investment and payments and granting credit.

Self-services via the Internet were launched in the late 90s with the aim of reducing the volume of routine payment and deposit/withdrawal transactions in the bank office. This released personnel for the more qualified services requiring the design of specific solutions to the client's needs. These developments in business activities require significant developments both in the knowledge and skills of office personnel and in their support functions and systems.

The company's value base

A company's value base is a key component in creating a positive commitment, harmony, and feeling of security in the workplace. Maslach and Leiter (1997) found that dissonance between an employee's value base and that of the firm in which he or she worked could lead to considerable stress and even burnout. Meglino et al. (1989, 1991) explicitly define organizational culture in terms of values and the concept of strong culture in terms of value congruence among organizational members. Value homogeneity among members allows managers to make safe assumptions about the likely behaviors of their subordinates when first-order control mechanisms (such as rules) or second-order mechanisms (such as direct supervision) are not present.

The Merchant Bank's culture is based on a number of clearly formulated values, maxims, and principles that guide how the members of the company do business and how the company is run. This is, in itself, not an uncommon phenomenon in the business world. What is special in this instance is the extent of the diffusion of the values in the organization and the degree of acceptance of and adherence to the values by personnel. It is to all intents and purposes 100 percent in each case. These value principles outline the company's relationships to its key stakeholders: investors, customers, and personnel. Concerning personnel, the bank may be regarded as exceptional in its expressed aim to offer its employees secure employment. No one, for example, has been made redundant on account of insufficient work in the past hundred years – a record in stark contrast to many competitors, not least in the early 1990s when 10,000 jobs were eliminated in the bank sector in Sweden (Arvedson, 1997). Extended employment, in its turn, requires very special attention to recruitment and to competence and career development – points that are made explicitly in the company's value document.

The management system

The basis of the management system is a strong company culture, clear company policies, and an effective economic management and control system. The basic idea is that the branch offices have full responsibility for the customers in their district, be they humble private clients or major international companies. It makes all decisions regarding the utilization of its resources and has full responsibility for its economic results. The branch offices themselves are often organized in teams, for example tellers, private customer service, investments, and company service. Specific performance goals are set at the office, the team, and, in certain areas, the individual level.

The bank's competence development strategy is based on the full-service customer concept and the conviction that *all* the staff at a branch office will be actively conducting business with their own customers. A major development in the bank that is well under way is the "own customer responsibility" (OCR) system by which branch office staff members are made personally responsible for the bank's business with a number (200–250) of specifically identified customers. It will be a number of years before the system will be fully implemented. Current ICT developments in the bank are also geared to supporting this development by providing an integrated information system facilitating an overview of a customer's total business with the bank.

The development of "individual competence" practice at the bank

General competence development principles

Having defined personnel competence as a key means of competition, the Merchant Bank decided to meet the challenge of the "global collapse of the real estate bubble" in 1992 by renewing its competence development strategy. It formed a joint management–union competence council. The goal of the program was to produce "a generally accepted description of the career and development paths in the corporation, which would be easy to understand and follow and which would stimulate personnel to further development in the whole corporation."

All development activities (business, organizational, technical, and personnel) at the bank have always been characterized by two features. The first is that development activities are seen as an essential opportunity for the development of the bank's personnel. Thus the bank has always had a very restrictive attitude to the utilization of external resources in the form of consultants and researchers. The second is that development work has always had a very practical and pragmatic base. Thus the point of departure in this competence development study was to develop a number of practical models and tools which would enable the branch office personnel to take immediate and powerful measures to better their competence.

A key goal in the program was therefore to make all the staff personally aware of their responsibility and need for their own learning and competence development. The work was also primarily designed to involve the personnel in general in the development of tools to be used locally, rather than to develop centrally in the project a system of tools that dovetailed to include all job categories in the company.

Competence development models

To involve personnel in the new competence drive, they were involved in the development of a series of competence models or matrices. A matrix is depicted

Level		Work-content:			Authority and responsibility
	Competence	Payment	Investment	Finance	
D					
C					
B					
A					

Figure 3.1 The basic structure of the matrix regarding competence development

as a two-dimensional figure: the vertical axis depicts the different job demands and competence requirements at the different levels, while the horizontal axis represents different dimensions in a person's job (see figure 3.1).

The same basic two-dimensional model is used throughout the company. Every part of the company was encouraged to get involved in applying the basic concepts to their own particular situation. There was a broad and positive response from personnel to this initiative. As all groups were invited to engage in this development activity, the project has resulted in roughly fifteen different specific versions, which form a fairly comprehensive overlapping system. However, intellectual parsimony was no goal in this context and a certain overlapping or redundancy was acceptable, given the considerable psychological and goodwill gains of involving everybody in the exercise. We will present here examples from three matrices to indicate how they have been developed in some cases to dovetail and how they may differ from each other.

The matrices are divided into four levels or steps – A, B, C, and D (see figure 3.1). New employees are placed in level A and work their way up. Thus:

- *Level A* corresponds to basic competence, a minimum level that *all* personnel must reach. On reaching this level, an individual has a basic grasp of the work carried out at the office so as to be able to deal with a customer's requests. This is equivalent to being able to carry out c. 30 percent of the tasks conducted in a branch office. To master level A takes at least two years' experience.

- At *level B* the individual is the bearer of the bank's policies and culture and must be able to perceive a customer's needs as a whole and carry out c. 50 percent of the tasks conducted in a branch office. It entails discretion to grant private customers credit. Mastering level B takes a further two years at the office after level A.

- *Level C* entails the individual being a broad generalist who is competent enough to be able to develop a customer's business from the bank's perspective. Individuals at this level can seek the information they need to handle a case/task. They have full personal responsibility for designated customers (200–250 in number), both private and company customers. Many offices choose to allot individuals either private or company clients. Level C personnel can carry out *c.* 70 percent of the tasks conducted in a branch office and require about two years' experience beyond level B.

■ *Level D* is reserved for individuals who are very competent generalists with long and broad experience who have also developed competence in specific areas requiring advanced knowledge, skills, and experience. At this level staff must be able to take care of both private and company customers with complicated and demanding business. This requires specialization in certain specific groups of customers or types of customer needs, for example investments or international trade. The need to maintain generalist competence, however, remains. A person at level D can carry out roughly 85 percent of the tasks conducted in the office and requires a further two years to reach this from level C.

These four levels are divided into three different areas: work content, authority and responsibility, and competence. The work content field in the branch office model is divided into three subareas: payments, investments, and finance. It defines which products and task elements should be mastered and to what extent, e.g., initiating, doing business, and administrating for each development step. The "authority and responsibility" section has similar specifications, not least related to the OCR system. Thus at level B, individuals are responsible for getting to know their customers' needs in their total context. Level C, however, entails a specific responsibility for given customers. The matrices do not define any clear limits for customer responsibility. OCR responsibility develops gradually from level B to full responsibility at level C.

The competence section includes the specification of a series of areas which have continually developed in the specification and ranking since the system began. The current "competence fan" includes nine dimensions: company culture, initiative and goal-orientation, communication, cooperation, ability to change, ICT competence, knowledge about products and services, understanding and knowledge on profitability, and, lastly, company routines and regulations.

The first five competencies concern cognitive and social skills. The others concern technical skills related to the company's business area, financial services. The same competencies appear at the different levels in the matrices or levels but the focus shifts in the different stages of development. At level A the focus is on "the business we're in": products, routines and regulations, and technical tools, systems, and support. At level D the focus is more on culture, social networks, and experience.

Key competencies

We have already referred to the special position the company culture has in the Merchant Bank. This is underlined by its position in the competence hierarchy. It constitutes the value base for doing business and in particular the relationships to key stakeholders: staff, investors, and customers. These values are clearly stated in a value document originally formulated about thirty years ago and revised every five years. The revisions usually entail the reformulation of a single principle or the addition of a further one, plus nuancing, clarifying, and updating the interpretations of the principles in the light of business and societal developments in the preceding period.

Investor values and business skills

The primary focus regarding investors is profitability. Business transactions and decisions must generate profit. Economic result orientation permeates the management control system. As a branch office is responsible for its economic result, it has considerable degrees of freedom in the conduct of its business, including how it uses its economic resources. The office staff is intimately involved in the planning of the business at the office and participates in regular business follow-up meetings. They receive detailed information on economic and business performance and are well aware of their office's performance in relation to other offices in the bank and the bank's performance in relation to other banks.

Client values and relationship skills

The client is the primary focus in all planning, actions, and decisions in the business. A good relationship with a client must be built on mutual understanding and respect, entailing honesty, sincerity, and empathy. These may well be expressed through advising against the client's wishes, recommending alternative solutions to those they envisaged. This is essential for long-term credibility. Sustainable service requires in turn that the bank's personnel are highly competent, more so than their colleagues in other banks.

The customization of services to individual clients naturally requires the delegation of full responsibility and discretion for clients to the branch office. The clients must know they are dealing with a decision maker and not a messenger. It is the person responsible for the client that decides the conditions pertaining to the service.

In collecting data for the case a survey was carried out among the customers of two branch offices, 600 per office; 69 percent replied. The questionnaire was based on previous research into customer relationships. The results of the survey show very clearly the impact of customer relationships on customer satisfaction and on the attitudes and behavior on the part of the contact persons that are of import for the customers.

Table 3.1 shows the number of items or survey questions contributing to each factor or index and the measure of the reliability of these indices (Alpha coefficient). All of the indices are very robust. It also shows how these indices are correlated to customer satisfaction. The majority of the relationships are

Table 3.1 Relationships with customer satisfaction for predominantly branch office and Internet customers at the Merchant Bank with respect to the attitudes and behavior of the contact person to the customer (* $p < 0.05$, ** $p < 0.01$)

Factor (Index)	No. items	Alpha coefficient	Satisfaction B.O. customer	Satisfaction Internet customer
Customer: Satisfaction	7	0.90		
Economic activity	5	0.82	0.18**	0.11*
Switching propensity	4	0.79	−0.16**	0.14
Personal relationship Customer/Contact person (CP)	5	0.92	0.64**	0.53**
CP's perceived competence	2	–	0.63**	0.47**
CP's mutuality	4	0.87	0.60**	0.44**
CP's customer orientation	6	0.78	0.54**	0.49**
CP's informed communication	3	0.80	0.48**	0.38**
CP's responsible behavior	4	0.85	0.60**	0.50**
Contact person behavior	19	0.93		

Table 3.2 Regression analyses of customer satisfaction against customers' economic activity and perceptions of their relationship with their contact persons at their bank branch office

Analysis of satisfaction	Constant	Coefficient pers. relnship	Coefficient CP behavior	Coefficient econ.activity	R^2
Total sample	2.0	0.22	0.33	–	0.400
Branch office	1.9	0.22	0.37	–	0.457
Internet	2.0	0.21	0.31	0.11	0.332

significant at the 1-percent level. The individual behavioral indices have also been combined to form a contact person behavior index. A statistical regression analysis shows that the customers' satisfaction is explained to a very high degree by the two indices: a) personal relationship between customer and contact person, and b) contact person's behavior towards the customer (see table 3.2).

The customers' satisfaction appears to be highly dependent on the attitudes and behavior of their contact person at the bank. This is probably enhanced by the current practice at many offices that the customers choose their own contact person. The index "personal relationship" concerns the contact person's involvement and commitment, empathy, and responsiveness for the customer. This "Trust" constitutes a coordinating mechanism based on shared moral values and norms supporting collective cooperation and collaboration within uncertain environments. Allan Fox (1974, pp. 67–8) argued that the essential character of all trust relations is their reciprocal nature. The financial services can be said to be in, or even to be, *the* business of trust. The creation and maintenance of trust relations is a fundamental condition of their existence. Financial services are dependent on the establishment and sustenance of a climate of public trust in financial institutions and their representatives (Morgan and Knights, 1997; Dodd, 1994).

"Perceived competence" concerns professional trust and respect. "Customer orientation" concerns behaviors related to analysis, adjustment, monitoring, and planning. "Informed communication" concerns initiatives for information exchange in situations of special interest to the customer. "Mutuality" concerns understanding and responsiveness with the aim of creating "win–win" solutions, and "responsible behavior" concerns a moral professionalism.

Thus the survey results presented here exemplify and nuance the social and cognitive skills mentioned above and underline the weight given to relationships in the bank.

Professional values and moral competence

The "OCR" system is implemented in practically all branch offices. It entails each client's personal contact person being responsible for the bank's service and the client's "financial health."

There is a strong and growing public interest in professional behavior in the financial services sector following erratic stock exchange behavior and exceptional "irresponsibilities." Bank personnel share this interest. Recent serious shortcomings in the public welfare systems are making private sector alternatives more important, especially in long-term economic spheres. Brytting (2000) has minted the term "moral competence" in this context. Two important aspects of this concept are the personal shouldering of responsibility and the competence embedded in the formal organization. Moral competence in working life is the ability to handle situations of moral concern. It entails taking responsibility for our own and others' welfare even in a long-term perspective. Burnout is often caused by the absence of reasonable moral commitments that give meaning to work (Martin, 2000, p. xi).

More and more companies are endeavoring to create common values as a means for integrating, guiding, and managing businesses conducted in decentralized forms (Brytting and Trollestad, 2000). Moral competence includes some form of memory function that ensures continuity and learning. It may be more or less formalized; to maintain and develop moral competence requires suitable arenas, i.e., places that provide the opportunity to exercise the communicative ability in dialogue that promotes the development of moral competence.

Career paths

What are the possible next steps for branch office staff beyond level D? Two alternatives are either to enter management by becoming a branch office manager or to continue professional specialization. The matrix tools and methods provide guidelines for the long-term development of staff but there remains much to do regarding long-term career development. Many staff members have no long-term career plan – a situation which is somewhat aggravated by the increased recruitment of academics. Some regions have special plans for potential managers.

Branch office manager

The managerial roles are many: employer, leader, coach, and banking professional. The bank makes a clear distinction between being a leader and being a manager. Leadership concerns *how* one works, management *what* one does regarding 1) administration, 2) economy, 3) personnel, and 4) sales management. Company guidelines lay out clearly what is expected of new and experienced managers, respectively, regarding a) these four functional task areas and b) their abilities regarding the areas: goal orientation and ability to perform, cooperation, communication, and visionary ability, as well as c) their personal maturity and analytic ability.

The company regards the will to lead, to handle different situations, and to be able to see the consequences of different decisions as the basis for leadership. The manager's key task is to draw up a business plan together with the branch staff, and to ensure that this is realized by working within the framework of the company's guidelines and policies in agreement with regional management. Coaching and maintaining a continuous dialogue with office staff are very important. The company emphasizes the experiential learning cycle in all situations, even for managers, encouraging them to seek feedback for reflection. As managers' skills as managers and employers increase, they will have more resources available for developing staff and the business.

The company is almost "Japanese" in approach with its extensive preparation of potential managers for their position. Applicants who usually have *c.* four years' experience in the bank are assessed. An individual development plan is made for successful applicants. This includes formal courses, on-the-job training, and on-the-job learning. Planned experience takes place at their local branch offices, with regular follow-ups. Special attention is given to social and cognitive skills, such as identifying goals and getting staff to accept and commit themselves to attaining them, and to the use of tools for "contingent leadership," holding "difficult" and personnel development interviews. Those with no previous managerial experience may expect their first position within three years.

Professional specialization

As mentioned before, there are about fifteen different competence matrices in the bank. All modules have the same basic structure of being divided into competence levels and columns for work tasks, authority and responsibilities, and competencies.

A relevant matrix for branch office staff is the "payments" matrix, Cash Management (CM), namely the use of bank services or combinations of bank services, in order to improve the efficiency and effectiveness of client companies' routines for cash flow and liquidity management. CM specialists can be attached to branch or regional bank offices or head office. Cash Management includes over ten different types of task dealing with different payment channels and payment types. The work tasks concern initiating, designing, and executing cases and services for business or product support. Authority and responsibility are highly differentiated at the different competence levels. New competence areas arising are business politics, law, and foreign languages, as well as new dimensions in negotiations, salesmanship, and advising.

Another relevant matrix is Accounting and Economic Management. The basic conditions are the same as the "Cash Management" case regarding its positioning (regional bank offices or head office) and competencies, though it only has three competence levels and the work tasks concern initiating, analyzing, reporting, and administrating.

▶ Developing Competencies: Integrating Learning in Work

A common feature of the first five cases (chapters 3–7) is their strong focus on experiential learning (Kolb, 1984). Thus, the Merchant Bank's competence development strategy prioritizes "learning on the job" rather than learning in formal courses. The competence matrix is an established concept for all the staff and they express themselves in such terms as "I am a full B." The matrices function both as a steering mechanism and as a measuring tool. It is possible to show graphically how far each individual has come. It is also possible to visually aggregate competence at the branch office and regional level, and to assess competence in the same way at all the offices, in fact in the entire bank.

The original competence matrix, model 1992, was an excellent working model or vehicle for launching the bank's strategic program on individual competence development. It succeeded in making people conscious of their personal need for training and development, moving between competence levels and areas. However, it did have some drawbacks. Firstly, the traditional banking work task areas were easily associated with products. Secondly, many individuals confused learning with training and regarded their development as needing to be coupled to the pursuit of specific courses.

These drawbacks were tackled through several developments. Firstly, the competence development planning process was clearly integrated into the business development process. Competence needs were then directly related to business needs at the branch office level. Secondly, as there are continual

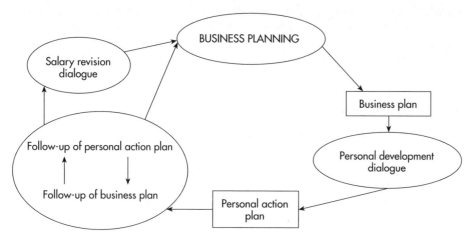

Figure 3.2 The integration of the business planning cycle and the personnel development cycle

follow-ups of business progress during the year, this enables continual follow-ups of competence development, instead of a once-a-year exercise coupled to the annual personal planning meeting between each individual and the branch manager. Thirdly, the competence areas were less closely coupled to specific banking tasks and more directly related to "business competence." (It is the later development of competencies that was presented above.)

The business development cycle (figure 3.2) is something that is conducted in *all* the branch offices. The analyses are conducted from the perspective of the customers. The personnel in the branch office participate in the development of the business plan for the branch office. The results of this planning form one key basis for the personal development interviews. The other key elements are the assessment of how the previous year's personal development plan has been realized and a current competence analysis of the individual's competence needs and ambitions. This analysis is supported by a questionnaire in which each competence dimension is assessed. These interviews are also conducted from the viewpoint of the customer, together with the evaluation of what has been achieved. The personal development programs are focused on "individual learning" and are adapted to individual learning styles. The monthly follow-ups of the business plans at branch offices also give the opportunity to check up on each individual's personal development, especially the strengthening of each person's responsibility for their own development. This is regarded as a marked improvement on the "annual interviews" as supporting individual development. Salary adjustment interviews are held before the new business plan is drafted, clearly separating them from the development interviews.

The distinct aim of the competence development program is that all individuals should be offered the opportunity to progress through the levels in the matrix – at least the first three levels. Presently, up to 75–80 percent of the visits by customers to many branch offices are for the purpose of depositing and withdrawing money from different accounts. Thus some offices have tended to specialize certain personnel as cashiers to deal with these tasks. This is, however, against the spirit of the competence development program and hopefully these cashier positions will become "circulation positions."

The development of *business competence* with its customer focus has been facilitated by a "Customer in focus" campaign on "need-oriented relationship-based sales," i.e., the object is to identify but *not* to create needs in the customers. This has formed a key issue in the development of branch office staff at levels C and D and of the "marketing" topic developing coaching skills for office managers. The case method is used. The cases describe situations, for example cash management situations, in which the bank/customer relations are not good. After the first course, the students practice what they have learned at their branch offices. Key issues are: What is best for the customer? Why do customers say "no"? If the customer does not understand the offer, the deal should not be closed.

Business competence is also oriented to acquiring "full service" customers. This process in itself, from being responsible for some elements of a customer's economy to expanding it to cover all facets, takes considerable time. Courpasson (1997, p. 71) points out that trust and the model of social competence are reinforced by the length of time over which the commercial relationship exists:

> First the trust is reinforced by the amount of time over which there occurs a mutual investment and common experiences which can confirm the solidarity of the link. Time also reinforces the banker's "social learning" and competence.

The bank employee may be regarded as having full responsibility when they initiate business with their customers, e.g., suggest renewing loans, taking out insurance or placing money. Today 30–40 percent of the branch office personnel have reached this level. The "own customer responsibility" system is still under development.

Experiential learning

It is in the day-to-day work that the best opportunities for learning arise and this forms the basic point of departure for the bank's adult pedagogics.

This is illustrated by an interview with a manager on this topic:

> We have a training center but focus mainly on tutors or coaches at the branch office. Most learning takes place at the office and is complemented by a few days' intensive training or workshops. Staff conduct practical on-the-job "live" exercises with new cases with customers at the office. They have the responsibility for dealing with the new case. As manager, I identify cases of suitable difficulty and support the learning process as they do the job. After a while the staff can study the basic principles

behind the cases with a CD on their home computers and take part in a course or workshop in which they have their own experiences as a basis for discussion. Learning by doing is our best method.

We have come quite a long way since we introduced "OCR." Important areas at my office are investments and asset management, professional support to SMEs, and ICT solutions for companies, specially offering customized solutions to individual clients. It demands considerable training and practice to shoulder responsibility for a customer and we train in real time with real customers. I accompany my staff on company visits. We prepare the visits together and go through the customer meetings afterwards. The "live situation" makes my feedback more effective than in a classroom situation. Positive closure on a business deal gives even greater reinforcement.

People feel much more secure with a coach at the office and their development horizon is both short term (this year's plan) and medium term (the matrix model). Development is based on creating "rich occasions for learning" and opportunities for the exchange of experience. People get responsibility for their own development.

IT and CD-ROMs are beginning to play a much more important role via e-learning. Staff must pass the company's "computer driving test" to use the new IT systems at the office.

In addition to many "real cases" the bank has a number of clients who are prepared to assist in the customer role in "training exercises" and who provide the bank with feedback for the trainee on the meeting. Meetings may be videotaped so that staff member and coach can go through them at the branch office. This basic approach is used throughout the bank.

Leadership and organization

There is an ongoing organizational development that is strongly coupled to the personnel development. Individual development always takes place in an organizational framework. This may be schematically described as:

- development from position A to position B,
- development from a position to working in a team,
- development from a position in a team to working in a value-creating process/ organization.

The first is the basic model at the bank, although there are discussions at some regional banks of the second model of the application of "group and leadership" training using models and exercises with roots in the armed forces. Teamwork is emerging as the dominant model for branch office work. There are even ongoing discussions on the relevance and applicability of different value creation models to retail banking (Stabell and Fjeldstad, 1998; Docherty et al., 1999).

▶ Discussion and lessons

The bank has a very positive reputation in its field – a reputation that extends far beyond its national boundaries. It aroused curious attention in its first radical efforts to put its house in order nearly thirty years ago, for example by disbanding its marketing function and discontinuing traditional budgeting procedures. These were followed by formalizing a company value base as the cornerstone of a new culture and a profit-sharing system for the personnel, which gave them the same dignity as investors as company stakeholders. Top management regarded its actions as achieving a positive course in the short term. Careful management has, however, succeeded in maintaining the company's sustainability over nearly thirty years, so that in 2001 the CEO of a major competitor even admitted that other banks could learn something from it. It is its sustained competitiveness that makes the case so interesting.

The bank has maintained its sustained competitiveness during decades that have seen considerable changes, mainly following deregulation, the impact of ICT developments, and the globalization of the financial market, which has increased almost exponentially. The turnover in the global financial market increased by a factor of 42 between 1972 and 1995 and daily trade is in the order of trillions of dollars (Wikman, 2001). One element in keeping up with these changes is a learning orientation in the organization, with changing perspectives on how business should be conducted, organized, and managed, and the nature of work and the role of learning in work. In this context Cressey and Docherty (2002) refer to a number of perspective shifts in the assessment of sustainable work systems. We are moving:

- from simple jobs in complex organizations to complex jobs in integrated organizations,

- from solely financial evaluation to holistic, multidimensional evaluation,

- from solely an investor perspective to a multi-constituency, stakeholder perspective,

- from being primarily outcome-oriented to being outcome- and process-oriented,

- from primarily focusing on the management function to including partnership and learning functions.

The bank has experienced these shifts with, broadly speaking, positive outcomes. When approaching the role of learning in its "sustainability story" we underline the company's general approach to learning. There is no precise and measurable conception of learning at work that adequately accounts for the range of influences upon it. This is one reason why we are among those who argue for the *promotion of "learning environments"* as a key element in the promotion of learning. This is coupled to the idea that people learn more effectively by moving from the concrete to the abstract and that there should be mentors and coaches in the workplace to provide guidance and support.

Table 3.3 Learning requirements, design dimensions, and learning mechanisms at the bank

Individual learning requirements	Learning design dimensions	Learning mechanisms
Business-focused work	Involvement/understanding in the business A "management cycle/process"	Management dialogue through business plan Joint goal setting Regular feedback, follow-up sessions
Customer identification	Strong relationships Full responsibility Professional behavior	"Own customer responsibility" "On-the-job" learning methods Coaching by office managers E-learning as homework "Experience exchange" workshops Office development projects
Company approach	Corporate social	Secure employment Clear value guidelines (Culture)
On-the-job learning	On-the-job learning	Coaching and office meetings

The individual's own experience is extremely important as learning is embedded in the structures and processes in the workplace. Boud et al. (1993) outline a number of assumptions that underlie learning from experience, namely:

■ experience is the foundation of and stimulus for learning;

■ learners actively construct their own experience;

■ learning is a holistic experience;

■ learning is socially and culturally constructed; and

■ learning is influenced by the socioemotional context in which it occurs.

Table 3.3 shows our analysis of the bank case with respect to the learning requirements, learning design dimensions, and learning mechanisms. The underlying learning requirements for the staff employed at branch offices concern basic dimensions of the character of the work. Firstly, the sound business focus of fulfilling the investors' goal of sustainable profitability, secondly, establishing an understanding, empathy, and commitment to the needs and ambitions of the branch office's customers, and thirdly, to attain a professionalism in relation to dealings with all parties coming in contact with the branch office. These factors are related to the design dimensions. Business dimensions concern the involvement in and understanding of the planning, production, evaluation, and development processes regarding branch offices' business. It also concerns the attitudes and behavior towards customers. A good relationship with a client must be built on mutual understanding and respect, entailing honesty, sincerity, and empathy. It also requires due care and concern for the needs and ambitions of the clients within a professional and ethical code of norms. Formal ethical norms do not exist as yet in the Swedish banking sector in the way they do, for example, in some sectors of the US financial sector. Basic professionalism in the bank is covered by the company value statement, which has the character of a "corporate social accountability" statement as it outlines the company's basic norms in relation to its main constituencies, investor, customers, and personnel.

The detailed description of the character of experiential learning also indicates the basic learning requirement of the bank for at- or on-the-job learning, in which managers play a key mentor and coach or tutor role – a role that may sometimes be problematic, given the power dimension in the relationship.

▶ Learning mechanisms

To achieve individual learning for all members in an organization, based on personal responsibility for both work and performance, and personal and business development, requires clear, robust, understood, and accepted learning mechanisms at all levels in the organization – top management, middle management, and the "front line," branch office staff. Those are illustrated here by the strategy and policies, by the work organization, and by the management system. This must function in the individual's situation, embedded in work, via informal or experiential learning in production and development.

Strategy and policy statements

From a sociotechnical systems (STS) theoretical perspective we may say that top management has adopted the minimum critical specification principle. Rules and regulations are kept to a minimum but those that exist are very important and great effort is made to ensure that everyone in the company knows, understands, accepts, and applies them. Some of these are:

The value base statement. The document is the cornerstone of the corporate culture. Every employee has received a personal copy with her/his name on it. The document confirms the dignity of the primary constituencies, investors, customers, and personnel. The constituencies also have equality in sharing the value created in the company – the personnel through allocations to a reserve fund. It also confirms the importance of personnel as a resource, aiming to offer all secure employment – an ambition they have managed to hold for the past hundred years. This also confirms competence and career development – positions being filled in the first instance by internal recruitment.

The value statement is revised every five years. An aim of the value statement is to create conditions for a high trust culture for the organization, both between management and staff and between personnel and customers.

The HRD policy and practices. This is an example of the very positive relations between management and staff and their unions (as is often the case in Sweden, c. 95 percent of the staff are unionized). The recent competence development drive has been planned by a joint committee between the social partners. Even internationally, some union leaders are envisioning new roles for unions that emphasize partnership, collaboration, and consensus-building, and they see learning as central to their new focus (Field and Ford, 1985). The HRD policy involves:

- an annual personal development plan for every employee following an interview with her/his immediate superior;
- branch office HRD plans are attached to the annual business plans sent to senior management;
- general models, tools, routines for planning and following up these activities have been developed and are continuously under revision;
- personnel development activities are primarily focused on experiential or informal learning at the workplace, often together with customers;
- a major task for managers at branch offices is to be advisors, coaches, and mentors to their personnel.

Traditional management training has been oriented to managers "getting things done" rather than "helping staff learn." This means that managers' new supportive roles must receive a prominent position in their development work. There are complex relationships between staff (employees/learners) and their managers who double as their superiors and as teachers/advisors/ coaches/mentors. This means that performance and learning outcomes and power and surveillance are more aligned and the activities of employees are being made more accountable than ever before (Garrick, 1999). Lennerlöf (1986) has also illustrated the dysfunctional impact that power may have on what is learned in the workplace – it can well lead to "learned helplessness" or alienation.

The personal development entails multiskilling to include business, technical, cognitive, and social skills.

A further area mentioned by the personnel interviewed in the course of writing this case is professional ethics. The customer's contact person at the branch office often feels a strong sense of responsibility for the financial health of the customer in the short and long term. The value base gives only a few guidelines in moral issues. These are, however, very important as research indicates that ethical reasoning is governed more by the immediate business context than the individual's character (Fraedrich et al., 1994). Here the company's *moral ethos* – a hidden moral curriculum which comprises the spoken and unspoken norms, prohibitions, social pressures and incentives, and typical operating principles into which members are socialized is of great importance for the development of business practice – a factor recognized by this company (Jackall in Snell, 1997, p. 192).

Work organization

Here again there have been several central decisions that have strongly contributed to creating a positive learning environment:

- *A marked decentralization of resources, responsibility, and authority.* Head office and regional staffs are kept to the minimum required to maintain strategic planning and coordination and sufficient expertise for development and branch office support. Branch offices have full control over their business. They may utilize their resources as they wish in order to realize their goals. They are not subject to central marketing functions and they determine to what extent they participate in central development projects.

- *Own customer responsibility.* On having reached a certain proficiency or competence level, branch office personnel are made responsible for "full service" business with specified customers. This requires multiskilling, increased responsibility and discretion, expert support, and personal business and personal development goals.

- *Team development.* Many branch offices are implementing a team organization, which will have their own goals, planning, and follow-up procedures.

- *Development processes.* The branch offices are responsible for their own business processes regarding business, organizational, personnel, and techniques, and initiate and conduct their own development in these areas. They are also expected to participate in regional and central development projects. This work is regarded as a key opportunity for "double-loop learning" for office staff.

Management system

Branch office business plans

The staff at the branch offices participate in the drawing up of business plans and the monthly follow-up meetings. The business plan forms an important input to the personal development interviews between management and staff. These meeting are in themselves important learning events providing opportunities for feedback, reflection, and revised planning.

Thus there are robust mechanisms in the critical areas. Learning is encouraged and accepted on the whole. The bank has the feeling that it is on the right track, though not all 400 branch offices are moving ahead at the same rate. Not all the above features are functioning 100 percent across the board. Similarly, there are variations within the offices on such points as the level of skills, the penetration of the "OCR" reform, the degree to which teams have been introduced, the interest in professional ethics, the degree of rationalization, and the penetration of the Internet. At the same time the "performance bar" is being steadily raised in the name of maintaining competitiveness. The delicate balance between sustainability and competitiveness becomes all the more important to understand and to maintain. Vital challenges remain if one is not to rest on one's laurels.

Though the bank is taking steps toward the introduction of teams regarding private client and company services and placement services, the focus today is primarily on individual competences, especially in relation to clients for whom the contact person has personal business responsibility: business is on a one-to-one basis. In the next chapter we present a case in which there is a key team dimension. The team is responsible for the quality, cost, and timeliness of products leaving the team. Individual development is strongly coupled to group needs and many skills are related to interpersonal behavior in the team.

References

Arvedson, L. (1997). *Downsizing: När företag bantar* (Downsizing: When companies slim). Stockholm: Trygghetsrådet.

Bengtsson, J. (1985). *Human Resource Strategies in the OECD*. Presentation to the Swedish Work Environment Fund Workshop on New Technology, Management and Working Life, August, 1985.

Berger, A., Hart, H., and Lindberg, P. (1996). *Ständiga förbättringar: Ännu ett verktyg eller en del av arbetet i målstyrda grupper?* (Continuous improvement: Another tool or part of the work in goal-steered groups?) Stockholm: National Institute for Working Life.

Boud, D., Cohen, R., and Walker, D. (1993). Understanding learning from experience. In Boud, D., Cohen, R., and Walker, D. (eds), *Using Experience for Learning*. Buckingham: SRHE and The Open University Press, pp. 1–17.

Brytting, T. (2000a). *Att vara som Gud: Moralisk kompetens i arbetslivet* (Being like God: Moral competence in working life). Stockholm: Liber.

Brytting, T. and Trollestad, C. (2000). Managerial thinking on value-based management. *International Journal of Value-Based Management*, 13.

Courpasson, D. (1997). The French Deposit Bank: Managerial professions between rationalization and trust. In G. Morgan and D. Knights (eds), *Regulation and Deregulation in European Financial Services*. Basingstoke: MacMillan Press, pp. 66–85.

Cressey, P. and Docherty, P. (2002). Feedback, intangibles and sustainable performance. In P. Docherty, J. Forslin, and A. B. (Rami) Shani (eds), *Creating Sustainable Work Systems: Emerging Perspectives and Practice*. London: Routledge, pp. 165–78.

Docherty, P. (1996). *Läroriket – vägar och vägval i den lärande organizationen* (The world of learning: Ways and crossroads in the learning organization.) Stockholm: National Institute for Working Life.

Docherty, P., Fredriksson, O., Sannes, R. and Steneskog, G. (1999). *Informationsteknologius påverkan på baukontoreus kunder och medarbetare* (Swedish: *The impact of information technology on bank district offfices customers and personnel.*) Stockholm: IMIT working paper.

Docherty, P. and Nyhan, B. (eds) (1997). *Human Competence and Business Development: Emerging Patterns in European Countries*. London: Springer Verlag.

Dodd, J. (1994). *The Sociology of Money: Economic Reason and Contemporary Society*. Cambridge: Polity.

Engwall, L. (1997). The Swedish banking crisis: The invisible hand shaking the visible hand. In G. Morgan and D. Knights (eds), *Regulation and Deregulation in European Financial Services*. Basingstoke: MacMillan Press, pp. 178–200.

Field, L. with Ford, W. B. (1985). *Managing Organizational Learning: From Rhetoric to Reality*. Melbourne: Longman.

Fox, A. (1974). *Beyond Contract: Work, Power and Trust Relations*. London: Faber and Faber.

Fraedrich, J., Thorpe, D. M. and Ferrell, O. C. (1994). Assessing the application of cognitive moral development theory to business ethics. *Journal of Business Ethics*, 13(10), 829–38.

Garrick, J. (1999). The dominant discourses of learning at work. In D. Boud and J. Garrick (eds), *Understanding Learning at Work*. London: Routledge, pp. 216–31.

Geus, A. de (1988). Planning as learning. *Harvard Business Review*, March–April, 70–4.

Jackall, R. (1988). *Moral Mazes: The World of Corporate Managers*. New York: Oxford University Press.

Kolb, D. (1984). *Experiential Learning: Experience as a Source of Learning and Development*. Englewood Cliffs, NJ: Prentice-Hall.

Lennerlöf, L. (1986). *Kompetens eller hjälplöshet: Om lärande i arbete: en forskningsöversikt* (Competence or helplessness: On learning at work – a research overview). Stockholm: Arbetarskyddsstyrelsen.

Martin, M. W. (2000). *Meaningful Work: Rethinking Professional Ethic*. New York: Oxford University Press.

Marsick, V. J. and Watkins, K. E. (1990). *Informal and Incidental Learning*. London: Routledge.

Marsick, V. J. and Watkins, K. E. (1997). Lessons from informal and incidental learning. In J. Burgoyne and M. Reynolds (eds), *Management Learning: Integrating Perspectives in Theory and Practice*. London: Sage, pp. 295–311.

Marsick, V. J. and Watkins, K. E. (1999). Envisioning new organizations for learning. In D. Boud and J. Garrick (eds), *Understanding Learning at Work*. London: Routledge, pp. 199–215.

Maslach, C. and Leiter, M. P. (1997). *The Truth about Burnout. How Organizations Cause Personal Stress and What to Do about It*. San Francisco: Jossey-Bass Publishers.

Noble, D. (1978). *The Design of America*. Cambridge, MA: The MIT Press.

Meglino, B. M., Ravlin, E. C., and Adkins, C. L. (1989). A work values approach to corporate culture: A field test of the value congruence process and its relationship to individual outcomes. *Journal of Applied Psychology*, 74, 424–32.

Meglino, B. M., Ravlin, E. C., and Adkins, C. L. (1991). Value congruence and satisfaction with a leader: An examination of the role of interaction. *Human Relations*, 44, 481–95.

Morgan, G. and Knights, D. (eds) (1997). *Regulation and Deregulation in European Financial Services*. Basingstoke: MacMillan Press.

Pedler, M. (1991). The need for self-learning organizations as part of an overall business/ management strategy. In B. Nyhan (ed.), *Developing People's Ability to Learn*. Brussels: European Interuniversity Press, pp. 128–40.

Pfeffer, J. (1997). *The Human Equation: Building Profits by Putting People First*. Cambridge, MA: Harvard Business School Press.

Polanyi, M. (1993). *Personal Knowledge*. London: Routledge & Kegan Paul.

Sannes, R. and Steneskog, G. (2002). *The Adoption of Internet: Customer channel choice in retail banking*. Göteborg: IMIT Working paper.

Snell, R. S. (1997). Management learning perspectives on business ethics. In J. Burgoyne and M. Reynolds (eds), *Management Learning: Integrating Perspectives in Theory and Practice*. London: Sage, pp. 182–98.

Stabell, C. B. and Fjeldstad, Ø. D. (1998). Configuring value for competitive advantage: On chains, shops and networks. *Strategic Management Journal*, 19, 413–37.

Wikman, A. (2001). *Internationalisering, flexibilitet och förändrade företagsformer* (Internationalization, flexibility and changes in company structure). Stockholm: National Institute for Working Life, Report series "Work life in Transition", 2001.

4

Designing Business-Focused Teams

- What is the role of the Human Resource strategy for competence development at the team level?
- How can competence development at the team level be achieved?
- How is competence development at the team level related to that at the individual level?

▶ Learning at the Team Level

How much of learning is a social process? The social perspective focuses on learning as a component of a person's daily life. This perspective regards learning as context-bound, woven into a social and cultural pattern. It implies that people, by interacting with those they work with, adopt a way of thinking, a culture, and a way of acting that characterizes the group. Group belonging is determined by occupation, workplace, or work team. Learning is regarded as a socialization process in which people obtain or develop professional competence as a part of their occupational role or occupational identity.

> The individual's learning is inextricably bound up with the limitations and opportunities characteristic of the job, in such forms as established occupational identities, relationships, and institutionalized ideologies and traditions. (Ellström, 1996)

Collective learning occurs when groups develop shared knowledge, behavior, attitudes, and values. When several employees work together with ideas, interpret assignments, or identify and define problems that are to be solved, the group develops a shared picture of the reality they are supposed to deal with. They have a common cognitive map, or local theory. The group develops similar ways of seeing things and similar behavior. Collective learning is enhanced if the members of the group have the same goals, share the same culture, are prepared to take risks, feel mutual trust and support, and can tolerate conflicts. It also stimulates the collective learning process if they can influence each other's behavior and obtain reliable, clear, and relevant feedback on the results of their actions. Obviously, learning also depends on the way authority and tasks are distributed, and the way the work is organized may easily create situations that make learning more difficult (see Edmonson, Bohmer, and Pisano, 2001a, 2001b).

"Teams" is a term that has become popular in the literature and in many instances simply is a synonym for "work group." Researchers have sought to differentiate the terms. Hackman (1990) differentiated teams into seven categories with respect to the type of work they do. Orsburn et al. (1990) identified eight increasing levels of employee involvement and expected levels of action at each level, of which the two most advanced levels concerned the team's discretion for self-direction. These levels required partial or full restructuring of organizational systems to support such teams. High decision discretion is a key variable in European definitions of teams. Using this criterion a recent European study found that "teams were useful, but not used" in production in most European Union countries (Benders et al., 1999). Other characteristics of internal team dynamics include common goals, team roles, the inevitability of change, high workloads, and time pressures.

Considering learning in teams, the output of learning can be useful new knowledge or the application of knowledge to achieve organization, team, and individual goals. Döös et al. (2001, p. 59) found that formal "learning meetings," i.e., meetings called specifically to promote the exchange of experiences, were hardly ever reported by workers in their study. But, when interviewed on what and how they work, the mutual collective emerges as they make up each others' working environment and prerequisites for learning – talking, questioning, working together, giving and taking. Each person's task is, in a way, a collective task. They were all working in the same technical context which may be seen as a common arena for action. It is the informal conversations, the discussions arising from personal interest, that convey useful knowledge available for later use. Such team aspects are also reported by the workers in the paper mill (chapter 6) and on the software projects (chapter 7).

A typical group in working life is the natural working group in production. These have a stable membership and do the same jobs for long periods. In order to meet environmental pressures, in the form of international competition, shifts in customer demands, and accelerating technological advance, functions and levels must be more integrated, and the borders between them must be broken down. To reduce lead times in production and product development, authority and responsibility have to be distributed in new ways. A typical way of meeting these challenges is to form multiskilled semi-autonomous groups or teams. The action sphere of the worker is systematically expanded. The worker progresses from simple tasks to taking care of maintenance, planning, quality control, solving production problems, and participating in product development.

Mass production in the organized market economies is a negotiated affair, for two fundamental reasons. Taylorized lines have in many cases been replaced by "multiskilled teams along the line," especially in Northern Europe (Karlsson, 1996; Kuhlmann, 2002). Over and above the workers' technical skills, this system relies on a host of "social" or "organizational" skills in these economies: working in teams, discussing production processes with engineers, early involvement in product and process engineering, highly effective but idiosyncratic systems of quality control and conflict resolution. In short, the workers have a series of both technical and non-technical skills which make them indispensable to management.

In an international research program on group work and teams in the automobile industry, Durand et al. (1999, pp. 412–15) consolidated their observations regarding such factors as the nature of tasks and the role of supervisors into three models of teamwork: the Fordist, the Japanese/Lean Production model and the "Kalmar" model (from Volvo's plant in the town of that name). The traditional Ford model allows the workers very little discretion. The Japanese model gives much more, due probably to such contextual factors as the high educational level of the workers, company unions, and meritocracy. The Kalmar model of semi-autonomous teams also may be related to the special relations between unions and management at the local level and the favorable political and labor market climate in Sweden over several decades (Cole, 1985). The main reasons given by management in Sweden for introducing team-based participation are improving productivity and quality of working life. Team-based participation is seen as clearly the most effective form of direct participation for reducing costs and throughput times, improving quality and increasing output, as well as decreasing sickness and absenteeism.

This chapter describes the introduction of autonomous teams into a large plant in a North European automobile manufacturer and the competence development programs associated with this development. The case describes the long-term dimension of the development process which reflects the development of a trustful cooperation between management and unions built up during several decades of organizational and competence development. It also describes the character of the integrated production teams introduced in the company and the learning mechanisms implemented to facilitate their smooth development. Essential aspects of the case are the interplay between a) the long-term and the immediate with respect to time and b) the macro- and the micro-scale, with respect to the company's actions together with other stakeholders at the regional level on the one hand and with respect to the teams and their members on the other.

The Integrated Production (IP) Teams at the Automobile Manufacturing Company (AMC)

Some key characteristics of the Northern European car manufacturing industry

Europe is well known for its automobile manufacturing industry. In Northern Europe the automobile manufacturing industry is an important sector of the economy in Belgium, Germany, the Netherlands, Sweden, and the United Kingdom. There has been an effort to consolidate in the industry in recent years. American manufacturers have acquired companies in Sweden and the United Kingdom, and German ones have acquired companies in the UK and the USA. To date, however, there has been considerable sensitivity in integrating different businesses and labor cultures. National companies have been given leeway in the running of their businesses, e.g., in their organizational and competence strategies, as long as they continue to meet business goals.

AMC is an actor in a global branch characterized by growing overcapacity, keen competition, and increasing demands for safety and for environmentally friendly performance. It competes with companies in the high-end value product range. It is a producer with process and product development. It offers a growing mix of products and services with scale and flexibility advantages in development, purchasing, production, and distribution. It has roughly 30,000 employees and produces about 400,000 automobiles a year. AMC's main markets are Western Europe, North America, and Japan. Its main production units are in Northern Europe.

The late 80s–early 90s were a period of severe economic crisis, especially in the financial sector. But for AMC the picture was no less unpleasant. From 1988 to 1992 car sales in a number of key markets dropped alarmingly by 20–40 percent. In addition, the company had a number of personnel problems concerning recruitment, turnover, and absenteeism. The issue of whether to continue car production was raised and 50–60,000 jobs were in danger. The Japanese car industry was seen not only as a major competitor but also as a major influence organizationally. The AMC formed a task force to a review car production, including work organization and competence profiles, for the 1990s. The task force developed the idea of integrated teams to meet the expected challenges in the industry.

▶ AMC's Resources and Capabilities

Partnership capability

From the beginning of the 1970s the company sought to establish a social dialogue with the unions where the social partners act on the basis of the highest common denominator in their interests and values. Investing in such a strategy depends to a large extent on the social partners' trust in each other, their readiness to take risks, and their ability to handle their relations with their main constituencies. Management's concern to involve the unions in the development of the company through ensuring their presence in many fora where vital product and production process issues were discussed met with a positive response from unions who adopted a very positive attitude to organizational change and the introduction of new technology. The assignment of priority to relations between the social partners emerges as a key feature of strategic development in five of the six cases presented here (chapters 3–6 and chapter 8).

The idea of guaranteeing workers' security of employment within the individual company evolved in the 1990s to guaranteeing regional or market employability within a known population of companies. People who are deemed to be redundant are not dismissed but are outschooled, i.e., retrained and outplaced in a job in another company without losing a day's paid work. The concept of value creation is no longer solely applied externally (to owners and customers) but also internally (to employees). Similarly, the goals of world class performance and rewarding work are no longer regarded as alternatives reflecting the individual management and union perspective but form complementary joint goals for both parties.

Trust has been systematically built up in a series of development projects during the 1970s–90s. This is reflected in a series of new work forms of conducting the social dialogue. The steps involved in the progression may be defined in the following terms from a union perspective:

■ Unions participate in negotiation arenas with management.

■ Unions are involved with management in broad decisions within the company.

■ Management and unions conduct major joint projects, e.g., the development of a new car model.

■ Union-appointed workers participate in general project organization at subproject or more basic level.

■ Finally, union-appointed workers participate as resource persons in the line organization, e.g., as competence analysts.

"Social responsibility" capability

There has been a clear management goal to seek to improve personnel's quality of working life in a series of development projects concerning work organization and competence development. Since the early 1970s the company's sights have been systematically raised from the workers' health and safety to their well-being and then their personal development. About the same time, AMC adopted the design strategy of safety regarding the design and performance of its products. This was later complemented by an environment-friendly dimension. The company's proactive strategy in these areas has resulted in positive effects for the company in terms of goodwill from the employees and their unions and from the market and the authorities.

Referring to social responsibility, it is important to point out that in the 1990s the number of employees at AMC's main plant was reduced by 6,000 people without a single person being "laid off" in the traditional way. This is mainly due to the development of the concept of "employability" within the manufacturing industry at the regional level. This is a key concept which entails the company being at the cutting edge (state of the art) regarding business-relevant competencies at the same time as it entails the highest security for the individual and the greatest flexibility for the company.

Learning and development capability

AMC's management perceives that the effective utilization of new technology to meet, amongst other things, the new demands being made by customers and suppliers requires the delegation of goals, freedom of action, planning, and control possibilities to broad groups of personnel. They regard it as a natural development to integrate their interest in conditions for good business with personnel's interest in good conditions for work. From a union perspective the enhancement of the employees' degrees of freedom, autonomy, and meaningfulness in work is seen as positive. Such goals had already been formulated by the metal manufacturing workers' union in the mid-1980s in a congress report, "Rewarding Work."

The concept of "employability" is central to AMC's competence development strategy. It means that an individual's competence development plan may lead either to up-skilling to meet new challenges within AMC or to outschooling to a job in another company. No one is laid off. The competence development program for an individual is based on a gap analysis and defined together with the manager. The implementation of the development program is coordinated by a development administrator within the company.

At a company level there are two main competence-related systems, which for the sake of simplicity we may call the macro and the micro. The macro-system concerns the automobile company in its greater context: partly as the hub in a complex network of companies, mainly suppliers, producing an automobile, partly the major company in the societal network of the economic region. In the first aspect of the macro-context, AMC has an active policy of competence quality assurance for the personnel involved in all supplier companies, which entails the company actively checking the competencies of the individuals in the supplier companies: e.g., What tools and methods do they use? How are they trained?

In the second aspect of the macro-context AMC has been working with a regional competence development coalition. The stakeholders in this coalition are the regional offices of the metal manufacturing workers' union, the manufacturing employers' confederation, and the major manufacturers in the region such as AMC. Important public sector stakeholders are the Regional Labor Market Board (LMB), the Regional Educational Authority, the Regional Business Development Authority, the Regional SME Association (small and medium-sized enterprises), and important training bodies. It is this competence analysis, training, and follow-up system that runs the off-the-job training for the manufacturing companies in the region.

Within AMC itself, there is a pressing need to establish a competence culture in the company, not least to keep pace with technological developments. The company is well aware that it already employs 80 percent of the workforce it will have in 2010. However, 80 percent of the technology in the workplace in the year 2010 does not exist today. The key trio in the competence development or learning system for the individual worker is made up of the individual him-/herself, his/her manager and his/her union representative. Each worker has a personal competence development program that is reviewed every year. The actual program may involve participation in on-the-job learning projects, practical workshops (which are also characterized by experiential learning), courses, supervision by internal tutors, multimedia, and other learning within learning centers in close proximity to the workplace (Klimecki and Lassleden, 1998). All elements in the development program are followed up in the competence quality assurance drive.

▶ The AMC Strategies

The development of the work organization strategy

There has been a marked increase in the complexity and sophistication of the strategies within AMC's different functional areas, which in turn has been matched by a growing complexity in the structure of the cooperation and joint negotiation mechanisms and work forms. Since the best selling book *The Machine that Changed the World*, the concept of lean production may be regarded as having taken "pride of place" as a management school in the manufacturing industry. In areas where the global market functions, the advocates of "lean production" maintain that this technological paradigm prevails due to its demonstrated ability to improve efficiency and effectiveness. It may almost be regarded as exercising "technological determinism," implying that the basic principles of lean production must be applied with their consequent reduction in the degrees of freedom available for the design of the work organization. All too often "lean production" is misused as a synonym for "downsizing" and the result is a one-year improvement followed by further (worse) problems. In lean production, the production process is characterized by production to order, zero fault and just-in-time, horizontal and vertical integration, and the extended use of information systems. There is a steady integration of functions between product development processes and production processes. The integration of functions characterizes design for manufacturing, product development with suppliers, and support functions integrated in the production line organization. Further challenges to the organization and its members are the erosion of company boundaries, the network as the managerial unit, globalization, outsourcing, integration engineering by the OEM (original equipment manufacturer), integrated work tasks, regional competition, and the need for capital. If the rationalizing that lean production promises can be combined with innovations in work organization, new technology, and learning, then positive results may well emerge (Ellström, 2000; Schumann, 1998).

Figure 4.1 shows the development over time of the production philosophies at AMC in response to the emerging managerial issues. In the 1970s the need

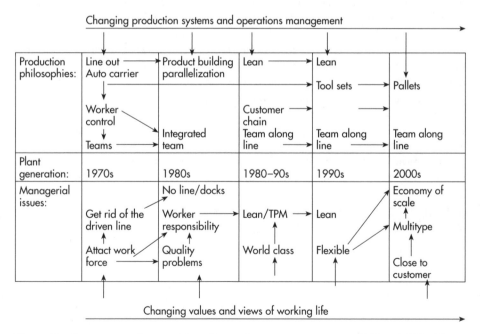

Figure 4.1 Dominant production philosophies and management issues in AMC in 1970s–90s
Source: Karlsson, 1996

to attract the workforce to the automobile industry led to AMC's elimination of the driven line in a newly built plant. This included auto carriers between docks and increased worker control. In the 1980s the issues of quality problems led to giving workers increased responsibility through the formation of integrated teams. At the turn of the 1980s–90s there was a focus on world class performance, which in turn led to the introduction of lean production and total production management. Docking was replaced by teams along the line with the concept of customer chain and AMC's Integrated Production teams with full business responsibility for their own static and dynamic effectiveness and efficiency.

Considering the past thirty years, from the late sixties when the unions became strongly interested in participation and industrial democracy, top management in AMC had a very strong interest in involving the workers in the activities of the firm. Since the beginning of the seventies the unions have been highly involved in management's development of the production processes, especially at the club level but even at the central level.

The macro-organized training programs: Upgrading and outschooling

We have already presented in chapter 2 our reasoning on formal and informal learning and the difference between them (table 4.1). We referred to formal learning as training and informal learning as experiential learning. In the previous subsection we have also spoken of macro- and micro-contexts in which AMC is conducting learning programs (table 4.1). Workers in production are influenced by both the formal and informal ways of learning and the macro- and micro-programs. The macro-programs are regionally oriented and motivated by the goals of employability and an upgrading of personnel to work with new automobile models with more advanced production technology. The micro-programs are oriented to improved competence for improved performance. Table 4.1 indicates that AMC has a complex HRD strategy. To simplify the presentation, we start by presenting the plant-wide programs that have been carried out by management and unions together with other stakeholders.

Table 4.1 Systematic learning activities in different contexts for different purposes

Forms of learning	Formal (training)	Informal (experiential learning)
Macro-context (Employability) (World class workers)	Off-the-job training EDP programs for re-entry, outschooling	
Micro-context (Improved performance) (World class performance)	On/at-the-job training Planning of individual/team development	Work dialogues, joint action Production meetings Continuous improvement Development projects

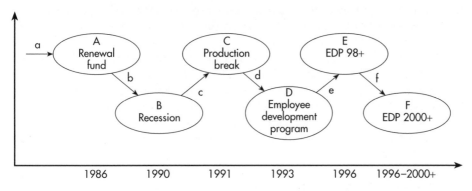

Figure 4.2 The evolution of competence development in the AMC

In the mid-1980s a series of competence development programs was implemented, whose aims and sophistication also increased through time. Figure 4.2 shows the major events in the evolution of the competence development strategy based on broad training programs. Experiences from each step have influenced subsequent steps:

1. The current strategy stems from AMC's handling of a government decision to regulate an overheated economy in the mid-1980s by making companies allocate 10 percent of their profits to a so-called "Renewal Fund." The company decided to use this fund for a six-year in-company training program which was available to all personnel. Up to then it had focused primarily on vocational training, i.e., training in the technical skills needed to produce a car. The utilization of the Renewal Fund was a joint venture between management and unions and this led to a new or different direction in the program. Early school leavers received training in the basic subjects of Swedish, English, and Mathematics. This was the company's first step in a new strategy: it shouldered a responsibility for both the employability of the workers outside AMC as well as their individual growth within the company.

2. The early 90s saw a recession and a fall in the demand for cars. AMC was forced to cut down one shift at its main plant. This meant that 850 workers were potentially redundant. The situation was delicate. The national labor legislation on security of employment prevented management from choosing which workers to retain. Furthermore, company experts estimated that the demand for automobiles would rise again within one or two years. AMC contacted the regional LMB and negotiated a broad educational program which would be subsidized by the LMB and entail keeping on personnel while participating in the program. Some of the people would be retrained to "re-enter" the company in "new" jobs. The others would be helped to find jobs outside the company. The program covered subjects outside AMC's specific competencies and entailed building up relationships with external educational organizations – both private and public. The main goal of the project was improved employability.

The main lessons of the partnership at this stage were that training is an excellent alternative to laying people off and that training can be much broader than simply vocational training.

3. The "Production Break" project arose in a one-year production drop between two car models. The production of one model stopped one year before the production of the new model started at its main plant, the old paint shop there was closed, and two smaller plants were also closed. This meant that 1,100 people had nothing to do for 12 months. This was almost the number of people required to produce the new model. At the same time unemployment had begun to grow sharply in the labor market in general. A new significant negotiation took place between AMC and the LMB on a second jointly financed training program. This time the focus was skills required to build an automobile in a highly developed technical environment. The city educational department joined the network to help design the program to meet the company's needs. After the program the majority of the participants returned to the plant. The others either went to new jobs/occupations outside the company or continued their studies.

The project resulted in AMC building up a network with public educational planners and public and private educational organizations in the region. The labor market actors in the region had modified their mental models and values from regarding the public sector's role as one of simply meeting the needs of unemployed people and of companies anxious to recruit, to encompassing the issue of developing people in employment to maintain their employability.

One important lesson from the "Production Break" project was that training alone is insufficient for improving work and efficiency. Participants who returned to the same working situation they had left a year earlier did not benefit from the training. On the other hand, participants who joined a new team based on the principles of job enlargement and job enrichment benefited a lot.

4. The "Employee Development Program" (EDP) was "the next logical step," a joint venture between the major companies in the region, the SMEs in the motor vehicle industry, the LMB, the city educational department, the local universities, the local unions, and the employers' confederation. It is a future-oriented project to improve the region's possibilities of successfully developing the competence and employability of people in the manufacturing industry. One aspect of the project is to produce tools and methods concerning competence demands now and in the new millennium:

- models for the learning organization;

- pedagogics for adult learning, e.g., utilizing multimedia;

- prerequisites for competence development;

- models for cooperation between actors on the labor market.

The three EDP projects were carried out after the formation of the Integrated Production (IP) teams. The workers who were to work in these teams were key candidates for the three projects. The EDP project's basic goals were to develop the organization and functioning of the "off-the-job" training network and to develop the tools, methods, models, and pedagogics for use in the individual companies participating in the network. It may be said that the results went beyond a simple training organization to a learning organization.

The EDP 98+ project, which started in 1996, is the first project within the EDP-theoretical framework. Cost reduction necessitated the retraining and outplacement of 600 workers. Two hundred needed to be retrained to switch from the body shop to the assembly shop, and 2,400 were retrained for re-entry into the company's IP teams. The project was occasioned by a decline in the demand for cars. After negotiations with the unions the parties agreed on yet another competence development program. The project had a "motto": "It is not enough that we have world class products, we must have employees with world class competence."

The education was broad and basic, with subjects such as Swedish, English, and Mathematics. These were combined with specific technical subjects and an extensive program in the skills of working in teams. The project used the EDP analysis tools and developed individual development plans for each worker involved, not only in the "retraining program" but also in factory production as a whole. Each participant in the retraining program was aware that the program would lead either to a new job within AMC or to a job in another company. Thus one stream in the program addressed a broad orientation on possibilities in the labor market.

A clear lesson from the EDP 98+ project was the importance of individual development plans based on matching competence analyses with personal needs, expectations, and aspirations. Another was the importance of conducting a joint venture between different actors. It was clear that some participants would re-enter Volvo and that others would leave, but it was not clear who would choose which. People made their choice gradually during the program. In a sense the program was process-oriented rather than goal-oriented.

The EDP project entails a shift from training as such to the learning organization and the learning society. Another very important lesson was that individuals must take responsibility for their own future, must participate in designing their own educational program, and must be motivated to participate. This entails having a clear idea of what comes after the program.

The industrial project EDP 2000+ is oriented to the competence development of employees in the region's manufacturing industry. During 1998, roughly 200 persons per month were retrained to work with a new car model. The main innovation in the project was to focus on developments in competence and work organization through cooperation between SMEs and large companies in the automobile manufacturing sector. High priority was given to participants with little or dated formal training. One of the main aims of the project was to develop methods for custom-designed change-oriented training for suppliers and subcontractors. The project utilized a radically new method for the analysis of production systems. This was developed following the insight that the formal training available from the public educational system did not meet the current demands for renewing the knowledge and skills workers in industry. This was related to the increasing rate of change in the sector and to the decline in the numbers of young, well-educated workers entering the sector.

Change and renewal must therefore be focused to a greater extent on those already employed in the industry.

The development of the industrial relations strategy

At the present time, there is a national tendency toward more decentralized systems of social dialogue and industrial relations. The tendency became noticeable in the mid-1980s. A number of disturbing problems had arisen in the old-established industrial relations model, among them wage drift in certain sectors, which led to relatively high inflation rates (Olsson, 1991). In the 1980s there were even political aspirations among workers to reduce the influence of the Trades Union Congress (TUC) over wage formation at the national level (Brulin and Nilsson, 1991).

The close cooperation between management and unions in the work, with the introduction of new technology, new forms of work organization, and competence development programs, has resulted in a trustful relationship between the social partners that characterizes industrial relations in the company. However, there has been some shift in the relationships between the levels of contact with the union organizations outside the company, from the national to the regional level. The relationship between the social partners has become more of a regional relationship centered in the region with the company's major plant.

It should also be pointed out that it was only the metal manufacturing workers' union and the supervisors' union that had been invited by management to participate in the EDP program. The professional unions for technical and clerical staff and for professional engineers have not been invited on account of their more traditional relations with both management and the other unions. Management's decision to maintain a more distant relation to these unions is based on the judgment that these unions would oppose many of the organizational changes taken as unacceptable blue-collar infringements of traditional white-collar tasks and responsibilities.

▶ The Integrated Production Teams: The Focus of Learning in the Micro-Context

The forming of the teams

The task force review process that started in 1991 led in 1993 to the decision to organize the production function at all the plants in integrated production teams which would, among other things, be responsible for quality, delivery precision, and economy of their output. These teams would have greater autonomy, engaging in continuous improvement of the product and the production process. The main final assembly plant had a production manager, with five production workshop managers, c. 50 production leaders and roughly 1,500 workers.

The company's current basic work organization policy is that the IP-team model should be customer-driven, with a holistic perspective, goals-steered, simple and clear, comparable with the best, and capable of continuous improvement (Ahlstrand, 2000; Nilsson and Brulin, 1999). The idea of quality was developed in the 1980s to entail work being right-first-time, i.e., zero defects, with a clear customer–supplier relationship and with feedback from the customer. Delivery precision entails contingency-free business, just-in-time delivery, reduced lead times, and flow efficiency. The demands on economy require business- and flow-oriented management and control, capital rationalization, management by key ratios/indices, and activity management. This work organization had an underlying sociotechnical system approach, which was characterized by leadership, active team-member communication, and teamwork, matching the flow and competence development. The technology utilized was chosen for its appropriateness, being simple, flexible, and environmentally safe. Most of the workers in the IP teams had gone through the EDP-training programs, which gave a good "topping-up" on general education and many specific courses in technical, cognitive, and social skills required by the teams.

The integrated production teams consist of about ten members with several rotating team leaders. They are self-regulating, participating in change and development projects, planning and following up production, recruiting, training, conducting problem- and conflict-solving, and in daily contact with customers and suppliers. Roughly 10–20 percent of the work in the teams is classed as intellectual work. The reward system includes a basic component, individual and group competence components, and individual and group performance components.

Management gives priority to the formulation of project work for developing and applying knowledge and skills. The teams have responsibility for goal fulfillment and problem-solving, and for taking part in the development of processes and products, often via their own personal initiatives. Continuous improvement activities have flow process and result goals (cf. the teams in the paper mill, chapter 6). This organization is aimed at facilitating and enhancing on-the-job learning.

The vision for the teams is to be able to function in plants producing several car models with world class performance with a good plant environment and utilizing the workers' full competence. Goals for the teams are very clear; for example, the quality goals of J. D. Power's index of 40 faults per 100 cars. Typical delivery goals are 97 percent precision, lead times 19 days, production times 2 days, and materials delivery 7 days. Economic goals are 10 percent cost reduction per year for manufacturing, distribution, and product development. Personnel are expected to take a holistic perspective in their work, to show high commitment, and to be oriented to creating customer value.

The "team along the line" is designed to include a number of tasks which allow both job enlargement and job enrichment. Enlargement ranges from simple tasks, such as machine work and simple assembly, to complex tasks, such as re-tooling and control and line adjustment. Job enrichment ranges from administrative and budget tasks to work improvement and production engineering (doing their own line balancing). Those team members engaged in the administrative and production engineering tasks are referred to as resource persons, as distinct from operators. Each group has at least one personal computer which is used, among other things, for daily communication with customers and suppliers, for budgeting and production scheduling, and for capital rationalization calculations.

The IP-team strategy entails the workers being responsible for the results of their work. The groups must be skillful enough both as "customers" and "suppliers" in the company's customer–supplier relations. Many work groups are responsible for the recruitment of new personnel (which is otherwise done by the production leaders) and training. They are also responsible for contacts with subcontractors regarding materials delivery, e.g., regarding the quality and number of parts delivered. Statistics on "waste" are also maintained. There are also team follow-up routines related to the goals of the groups regarding quality, output per unit of time, flaws per body, degree of scrap, staff times, and material consumption. The teams' self-control of quality has resulted in an 80 percent reduction in the number of inspectors and final adjusters. Team members also participate in work groups engaged in product (new car models) and production development projects.

The teams may be said to function as small companies with their own goals and local discretion. The teams exhibit business, technical, organizational, and social skills. Collins (1988) refers in this context to "internalized control" which leads to voluntary self-motivated compliance (with management's ambitions). Grønning (2000) points out that "internalized control" is based on such "indirect" or "soft" controls as preselection and socialization, implementing order-giving and promotion possibilities, and ritual participation.

The IP teams aim at achieving a high degree of internalized control normally associated with medical, scientific, religious, and educational organizations. The management of work through such involvement is tending to spread in working life due to generalizations of pressures on individuals to respect prescribed standards of organizational behavior and work. The personnel-related responsibilities within the functional work description for the teams leave a great deal of discretion, responsibility, and self-regulation at the team level. This is also the case regarding being "able to change plans in case of changed circumstances."

The team members were highly dependent on each other in their work situation. Each member was qualified to conduct several functions or tasks in the group. The team leader was primarily responsible for the planning and coordination of the work, but this was a rotating position and the other team members were also involved (Marsick and Watkins, 1990). This was also the case regarding development work, problem-solving and learning. Functioning within the team as well as with the other teams on the shopfloor and with suppliers and customers outside the company required social skills, including negotiation and conflict resolution. The company asked the union to select over one hundred workers for training in conflict resolution.

Regarding learning in the teams, individuals develop strategies in order to draw on the collective knowledge and experience, such as building networks (within and outside the team), working with others, and noting others' experience. Apart from reflection, conversations, and dialogue, "joint action," doing things together, is communicative action and is important for learning (Döös et al., 2001, p. 47). In teams in which reflection and dialogue are combined, a collective dialogue emerges which is the motor for collective learning. Important prerequisites for this to happen are common tasks and arenas for action, common technology, terminology, and language, the opportunity to test and work with others' solutions, and personal curiosity and the will to learn. The organizational prerequisites were all present in the IP teams.

The competence development program for the individual team member may entail:

- on-the-job learning, through extending the mix of tasks the individual carries out in the coming year;

- on-the-job training, i.e., training arranged in the worker's "near environment" via learning centers, workshops, and specific courses with internal tutors; or

- off-the-job training with the purpose of a) complementing the individual's basic education to enable him or her to be able to cope with the training for the more qualified tasks in the group, b) more extensive theoretical and practical training for new tasks in his or her present group, in a new group in the company (e.g., in a similar group but with a new car model), or, if a decision has been made on "outschooling," for a job in another company.

Informal learning in the teams: Working together

On-the-job learning is mainly arranged by planned job rotation coupled with on-the-job training in the execution of ordinary assignments. The character of the team development is illustrated in figure 4.3. The "administrative group" is characterized by the members of the group having individual tasks, physical proximity, and job rotation. The organization of the group is functional, centralized, and hierarchical. The "goal-steered group" is characterized by the members having group tasks and joint responsibility. It has a decentralized and flow-orientated organization. Finally, the "learning group" is one in which the members have a responsibility for the group's tasks and development. The group as such is a central actor in the business process. As is shown in the figure, as one moves from the administrative to the goal-steered to the learning group the number of separate tasks in the group increases rapidly.

Work group's level of development		Group's organizational context	Main meaning of the competence concept	
Extensive administrative/ planning tasks	Development and improvement	**Learning group** with responsibilits for the group's tasks and development. A central actor in the business process.	Social competence: support cooperation, shared vision, acceptance	Theoretical competence: reflection and learning
Execute and maintain operative tasks			Practical competence: assignment oriented	
Few administrative/planning tasks		**Goal-steered group** with group tasks and joint responsibility. Decentralized and flow-oriented organization.	Social competence: support and cooperation	
Execute and maintain operative tasks			Practical competence: assignment oriented	
	Execute and maintain operative tasks	**Administrative group** with individual tasks, physical proximity and job rotation. Functional, centralized and hierarchical organization.	Social competence: support	
			Practical competence: assignment oriented	

Figure 4.3 The work group development in terms of organizational contact and competence context
Source: Hart, Berger and Lindberg, 1996, p. 17

The continuous dialogue in the groups around different plans, projects, and problems to be solved is fundamental to the development of the team's "community of practice" (Wenger, 1998).

The second main form for on-the-job learning in a development context is the team members' participation in the continuous improvement activities in the group. The introduction of "continuous improvement" (*Kaizen* in Japanese) was integrated into the basic education provided for the groups when the IP-team system was introduced into the factory. The system was introduced in a series of seminars. Firstly, a management group seminar was held at which the overall goals for the plant and the internal relationships between "customer–supplier" chains within and external to the company were discussed. This was followed by a seminar for production leaders, who are the development managers immediately above the teams. The third step was to hold team member seminars in which action plans for the development of the teams were discussed.

After the seminars a number of "driving meetings" were held within the teams in order that they should discuss the development of the processes within the teams, their roles and ambitions, and which individuals would be most suited to be team leaders. When selected, the team leaders were sent on a special training program. Some months after the teams had been put into action, the follow-up program was designed with separate meetings for management, product leaders, and team leaders. The groups discussed the results of attitude surveys, analyses of the customer–supplier processes, and experiences from the workplaces. The development in terms of the J. D. Power's indices was analyzed and discussed. Finally, new action plans were developed. Further iterations of these seminars have been devised.

On-the-job training in the teams

The competence development strategy required the development of tools, methods, and models that were basic to the company's needs for both on-the-job training and off-the-job training. This common effort is described here. The systematic development of the skills of the individual employee entailed considerable development efforts, which included:

- Defining the client companies' needs. In this context both AMC and the other companies participating in the "off-the-job" training program are regarded as "client companies." Many of these companies are in fact suppliers or subcontractors to AMC.

- The focus is on "competence," defined as the ability to handle situations arising in the workplace. Key situations must be identified and described. It also involved developing new partnerships between the companies, e.g., to identify common key competencies.

- Developing tools to determine the individuals' competencies in relation to those needs (a gap analysis). Again the tools are to be used not only in AMC's main plant but also in SMEs which are its suppliers.

- Developing new learning methods, including interactive methods.

- Developing a model for the learning organization, including creating future competence pools and dealing with the intriguing problem of integrating the lean production paradigm and other management paradigms with the learning organization paradigm.

The systematic development of competencies is based on the balance between individual and team needs. These processes must be integrated. Assessing individual needs begins with the individual personal development interview between a team member and his or her manager around his or her work situation. Before the planning interviews special "competence analysts," often appointed by the unions, conduct competence gap assessments of the team members using the tools developed in the joint project. The important documents for the discussion are 1) the team member's own competence (gap) analysis, 2) an analysis of the main competence areas in the team as a whole, and 3) the administrative records of the individual's development since the previous interview. On the basis of these meetings a team development plan and individual plans are drawn up, discussed, and ratified. Individual wishes must be balanced between the different team members, and, more importantly, against the needs of the team as a whole. For example, the team needs another person qualified in quality control, yet nobody has shown any interest in this topic. This issue must be resolved.

The specific character of "on-the-job" training is that it is arranged in a "near environment." The worker may arrange with his or her colleagues to leave the workplace for a short period (several hours) in order to participate in one or more of several activities. These include personal tutoring sessions, workshops on specific topics with other workers, or visiting a learning center adjacent to the factory to carry out some IT-mediated teaching module. All such activities and facilities exist at the production plant. There are also special tutors/administrators who serve as advisors to the workforce on the most suitable way for them to plan their competence development activities, e.g., how to mix theoretical and practical activities, or the best way to plan theoretical studies regarding methods, blocks, and choice of methods. The metal manufacturing workers' union also has a subsidized scheme for its members to purchase computers at home, which brings the alternative of self-study with IT-based training programs at home within the economic reach of most members.

The IP teams' reward system as an incentive to learning

The IP teams have their own reward system. The more assignments a worker performs and the more difficult they are, the better the pay. On top of that, there is a group bonus on the work quality performed by the group as a whole. That part can amount to a maximum of 10 percent on average basic wages. A third part of the ladder consists of an individual part and can also amount to a maximum of 10 percent of the average basic wages. This part is determined by the production leader and depends on such factors as the operator's level of activity at work, his or her willingness to cooperate or to take the initiative in changes. At the very top of the system, there is a bonus that depends on the company's financial results. This bonus is the same for all employees.

The aim of the model is to motivate the workers to widen their areas of competence and to take initiatives. There is a certain risk that some individuals will endeavor to master all available assignments as soon as possible, while others will be satisfied with mastering one or two. The "team competence" development plan is the basis for the competence plans for the individual members. There are norms for the number of members in each team who master each assignment, e.g., quality control. In order to facilitate a broader interest in multiskilling, *all* members of the team receive a certain team-skill allowance when the number of members mastering an assignment reaches the team norm. For example, if the norm is that three persons in a team should be formally qualified in the quality control methods, then all the members of the team who are not qualified in this area get a "team competence allowance" when three members are qualified. The three get an "individual competence allowance."

Reflections and Lessons

As described above, the IP teams are multiskilled with broad business responsibilities in relation to customers in a radically upgraded technical environment. The IP teams constitute a new strategic platform for competence and business development. They are based on shared value premises between the unions and management on the need for and relevance of social responsibility in the company and the critical importance for the company of both providing rewarding work and achieving world class performance. Furthermore, it is based on a "we-spirit" which entails management's and unions' joint identification with the local region and the joint venture/cooperation/alliance between management and unions.

Two key management values which have facilitated developments in the company are:

■ *The identification of the value of an employee to the company, which is expressed in the form of "employability."* Management and unions have shouldered responsibility for arranging for the retraining and outplacement of individuals who are made redundant. This has shown itself not to be a severely controversial position in relation to top management and the owners. On the contrary, it has facilitated developments for the company by retaining the motivation, initiative, and creativity of the workforce whose unions are important partners in development, rather than opponents looking to block management's every idea.

■ *Management's and unions' identification with the region.* This has strengthened existing alliances and created new ones. Possibly the most important new alliances are those between the company and institutions in the public sector. The latter have provided both extensive professional know-how and resources in the formal educational programs and essential financial resources by substantially underwriting the costs of maintaining redundant workers within the company while under training.

The project as a whole is a good example of a "Win, Win, Win" situation for management, personnel, and society.

The developments of AMC have been facilitated by the continuous new development of the company culture, as illustrated in figure 4.4. The 1970s were dominated by a production culture. The 1980s saw the development of a quality culture strongly influenced by the Toyota experiences. The latter part of the 1990s into the present decade is characterized by the competence culture. Key elements and premises in the strategy EDP 2000+ project reflecting the competence culture were:

■ defining member companies' needs;

■ developing tools to determine individuals' competencies in relation to those needs, a so-called gap analysis;

■ developing a model for team learning and even the learning organization;

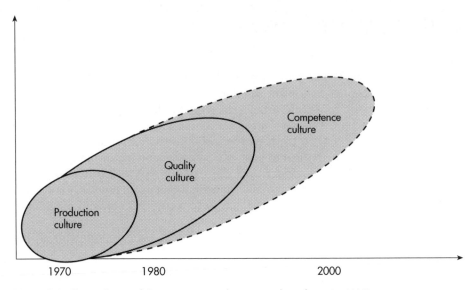

Figure 4.4 The evolution of the perspectives dominating the cultures in AMC

■ establishing an alliance with local business and industry including SMEs, the school authority, and the labor market authorities.

Team learning and sustainability

The company feels that the establishment of the competence culture and the continuous regeneration of its personnel resources are essential to individual, group, and company sustainability. Today's workforce will need to be continually retrained. As noted earlier, 80 percent of the workforce in the year 2010 is already employed today, while 80 percent of the technology in the workplace in 2010 does not exist today.

There is a very close interaction between the functioning of the IP teams and the EDP 2000+ competence development project. Competence development in the production process has now been established as an institutionalized iterative process. There is a constant group competence revision cycle being conducted, in which current competence levels are compared with required competence levels by managers and team members within the framework of planning interviews and the analysis of the main competence areas in teams. These analyses lead to team and individual development plans. The action taken on the basis of the gap analysis is evaluated and recorded as the basis for the next iteration in this ongoing process.

The teams function practically as small companies and their work has the character of joint communicative action. Their conversation and dialogues concern production planning and follow-up, problem-solving, continuous improvement and development work, HRM, teaching and learning, and negotiation and conflict resolution. These develop a community of practice and culture within the group and with shopfloor management. The learning and the joint culture, with a common value base, are key factors strengthening sustainability at the individual and group level (Maslach and Leiter, 1997). The teams constitute a high trust organization. The "local theory" or common frame of reference regarding the functioning of the team and the technology will also promote productivity and effectiveness in the work and thereby support competitiveness. However, the issue of balance is as critical in the group context as it was shown to be in the individual case. The groups have considerable decision discretion, but have scarce resources. There are also risks that different group members focus on different issues and that real conflicts may arise, eroding sustainability.

The metal manufacturing workers' union has accepted the principles of lean production partly under the threat of relocation but mainly in return for the proactive policy of employability (security of employment with re-skilling) and the development of teamwork in line with the union ambitions of increased worker autonomy and multiskilling. There are different schools of opinion within the union, but the company union as a whole supports the current practice of the election of team leaders and the rotation of workers between jobs which rapidly increases the range of skills they master. Though the implementation of the union's ideas on "rewarding work" has created more meaningful and stimulating jobs for its members in the IP teams, it has also created new problems for the union. The staffing levels in the plant with "teams along the line" are considerably lower than on the traditional assembly line, i.e., the implementation of the union policy has "put c. 25 percent of its members out of work." At the same time there is a constant struggle to maintain the delicate balance between intensive work forms and sustainable work forms when lean production is introduced in self-managing teams with "internalized control with management's values." There are distinct signs that the regional union offices are re-evaluating the union's role and are planning to be more active (and proactive) in the area of human resource development for their members, working with the tasks of placement and competence development (Berggren and Brulin, 1998).

Learning Requirements, Learning Design Dimensions, and Learning Mechanisms

Learning requirements and design dimensions

Table 4.2 shows the learning requirements, learning dimensions, and learning mechanisms regarding the integrated production teams at the AMC plant. Considering the requirements, the teams needed in practice all the skills required by a business unit. The teams were to all intents and purposes small companies. The exceptions were legal and taxation responsibilities, bank relations, and marketing. They needed cognitive, technical, social, business, and teaching skills. In their marketplace they had to maintain good "business" relations with the other teams and staff groups at the plant regarding their own production, and with corporate development projects regarding products and production processes. They had similar relations with suppliers and customers outside the company. The need for social and cognitive skills, especially reflection and communication, is very high within the team.

There is also a requirement for a "competence overcapacity" in order for the team to be robust and flexible. The team must be able to function, at least for a certain time, with lower than normal staffing levels. There is much planning, development, and training (as participants and tutors) work, for individuals and groups, involving action and discussions. Norms exist for the number of qualified individuals needed for each function.

Learning also requires the availability of learning processes for "on-the-job" and "at-the-job" learning. The "lean production" philosophy in the plant requires this – people cannot be excused from the plant for lengthy courses. Learning centers adjacent to the plant and many mini-workshops, exercises, and tutorials are arranged in the plant. Team learning is, as stated earlier, highly dependent on the dialogue created within each team and even between teams in different networks. A difference must be made here between the less suitable, consciously organized dialogue structure and the facilitation of the more appropriate, emerging organic structure. Formal structuring of the reflection process can destroy it.

Table 4.2 Learning requirements, learning design dimensions, and learning mechanisms at AMC

Team learning requirement	Learning design dimensions	Learning mechanisms
Total range of "business unit" skills	Cognitive, social, technical, business, and teaching skills	Tools, methods, routines, and organization for the assessment of individuals' skills Competence reward system Competence development/training system
Competence "overcapacity"	Minimum required status per skill dimension	Team member development programs Team development assessments Dialogue on team vs. individual development priorities
"On-the-job" and "at-the-job" learning processes	Appropriate methods and organization for the different skills	Learning centers adjacent to the production line. Tutors in the workplace Learning sessions in the workplace Development assessment tools E-learning courses for homework

Learning mechanisms

At the *strategic level* the company had evolved a number of practices, some of which were institutionalized or formalized in agreements but which created a climate of trust, commitment, and understanding that was supportive for the plans and ideas regarding team and individual learning. These included the following:

■ *A high level of trust between the management and the unions representing plant personnel.* These unions had over several decades worked closely with management regarding the development of workplace design, work organization, and competence development. This cooperation had taken the form of conducting innovative experiments in these areas, in which the company was often a prime mover in the automobile manufacturing industry.

■ Management had a close relationship with the national and regional authorities and could persuade them to join in institutional experiments regarding the retraining of workers threatened with redundancy.

■ Management introduced the *concept of employability* and has followed this for over a decade. On their part, the unions have accepted the *"lean production"* model for the main plant.

As regards *work organization,* the following mechanisms have been implemented:

■ *Integrated production teams* responsible for the planning, execution, and follow-up of production, the human resource management in the team, and for contacts with in-company and external customers and suppliers. The team is also responsible for participating in development work via the continuous improvement system in the plant and in development projects initiated by management regarding product and production process development. They also participate in learning as teachers and tutors.

■ *A management system* for planning and following up the performance of the team in such areas as production output, team costs, HR data, quality control data, delivery precision data, and follow-up of the individual and team development programs.

As regards *Human Resource Development,* the following mechanisms have been implemented:

■ tools, methods, routines, and organization for assessing mainly cognitive and technical skills of team members;

■ routines for following up the individual and team development programs;

■ an HRD development infrastructure and program.

The team skills development in terms of the development of new knowledge and its transfer within the group is facilitated by the feedback provided via the Team Management Information System and the separate discussion arenas outlined for the teams for performance follow-up, development follow-up, and continuous improvement. The teams have coaches/advisors at their disposal for advice on the facilitation of team dialogues, partly related to conflict resolution and partly to learning. In addition, specific learning mechanisms are the learning centers, the organization of learning sessions in the workplace, and e-learning for learning at work and at home.

Even in this case there is a very fine knife-edge to balance in order to maintain sustainability and competitiveness. The lean production model leaves very little organizational slack at the same time as the business demands made on the teams are many, and all very tight. Apart from the differences that may arise between team members regarding the priorities they allot different goals, there is very little flexibility or resources available to the group to solve mismatches or conflicts.

This case presents a continual and radical change program over decades. The teams are probably more integrated and multifunctional than those in the paper mill and software house. However, the changes have not been as radical and as contextually precipitated as in the next case, the telecommunications services provider, which we regard as a clear example of an organizational transformation.

References

Ahlstrand, R. (2000). *Change in Participation in Production: Examples from Final Assembly Plants in Volvo*. Lund: Dept. of Sociology, Lund University, Ph.D. thesis 31 (in Swedish).

Benders, J., Huijgen, F., Pekruhl, U., and O'Kelly, K. (1999). *Useful but Unused: Group Work in Europe: Findings from the EPOC Survey*. Dublin: European Foundation for the Improvement of Living and Working Conditions.

Berggren, C. and Brulin, G. (1998). *Goda arbeten och utvecklande regioner: Metall på två ben* (Swedish: Rewarding Work and Developing Regions. Metal on two feet). Stockholm: Svenska Metallarbetareförbundet.

Brulin, G. and Nilsson, G. (1991). *Mot en ny svensk modell: Arbete och förhandlingssystem i förändring*. Stockholm: Rabén & Sjögren.

Cole, R. E. (1985). The macropolitics of organizational change: A comparative analysis of small-group activities. *Administrative Science Quarterly*, 30(4), 560–85.

Collins, R. (1988). *Theoretical Sociology*. San Diego, CA: Harcourt Brace Jovanovitch.

Durand, J.-P., Stewart, P., and Castillo, J. J. (eds) (1999). *Teamwork in the Automobile Industry: Radical Change or Passing Fashion?* London: MacMillan Business.

Döös, M., Wilhelmsson, L., and Backlund, T. (2001). Kollektivt lärande på individualistiskt vis – ett lärdilemma för praktik och teori (Swedish: Collective learning in an individual fashion – a learning dilemma). In T. Backlund, H. Hansson, and C. Thunborg (eds), *Lärdilemman i arbetslivet*. Lund: Studentlitteratur, pp. 43–79.

Edmonson, A., Bohmer, R., and Pisano, G. (2001a). Speeding up team learning. *Harvard Business Review*, 79(9), 125–33.

Edmonson, A., Bohmer, R., and Pisano, G. (2001b). Disrupting routines: Team learning and new technology implementation in hospitals. *Administrative Science Quarterly*, 46(4), pp. 685–718.

Ellström, P. E. (1996). *Work and Learning*. Stockholm: National Institute for Working Life (in Swedish).

Ellström, P. E. (2000). Lärande och kompetensutveckling i "mager organizationer": problem och möjligheter (Swedish: Learning and competence development in 'Lean Organizations': Problems and possibilities). In L. Lennerlöf (ed.), *Magra organizationer i arbetslivet: Avveckla eller utveckla?* Stockholm: Swedish Council for Work Life Research, pp. 136–57.

Grønning, T. (2000). Control and co-determination: An assessment of the Volvo QDE system. In *Comparative Studies on a New Industrial Model between Sweden and Japan*. Kyoto: Dept. of Social Science, Ritzumeikan University.

Hackman, J. R. (1990). *Teams that work (and those that don't)*. San Francisco: Jossey-Bass.

Hart, H., Berger, A., and Lindberg, P. (1996). *Continuous Improvement: Yet Another Tool or Part of the Work in Goal-Steered Groups?* Stockholm: National Institute for Working Life (in Swedish).

Karlsson, C. (1996). Radically new production systems. *International Journal of Operations and Production Management*, 16(11), 8–18

Klimecki, R. and Lassleden, H. (1998). Modes of organizational learning. Indicators from an empirical study. *Management Learning*, 29(4), 405–30.

Kuhlmann, M. (2002). Group work and democracy. In P. Docherty, J. Forslin, and A. B. (Rami) Shani (eds), *Creating Sustainable Work Systems: Emerging Perspectives and Practice*. London: Routledge, pp. 126–38.

Marsick, V. J. and Watkins, K. E. (1990). *Informal and Incidental Learning in the Workplace*. London: Routledge.

Maslach, C. and Leiter, M. P. (1997). *The Truth about Burnout. How Organizations Cause Personal Stress and What to Do about It*. San Francisco: Jossey-Bass Publishers.

Nilsson, T. and Brulin, G. (1999). The Swedish model of Lean Production: The Volvo and Saab cases. In J.-P. Durand, P. Stewart, and J. J. Castillo (eds), *Teamwork in the Automobile Industry: Radical Change or Passing Fashion?* London: MacMillan Business.

Olsson, A. (1991). *The Swedish Wage Negotiation System*. Worchester, MA: Dartmouth.

Orsburn, J. D., Moran, L., Musselwhite, E. and Zenger, J. H. (1990). *Self-Directed Work Teams: The New American Challenge*. Homewood, IL: Business One Irwin.

Schumann, M. (1998). New concepts of production and productivity. *Economic and Industrial Democracy*, 19(1), 17–32.

Swedish Metalworkers' Union (1985). *Rewarding Work*. Stockholm: Swedish Work Environment Fund.

Wenger, E. (1998). *Communities of Practice. Learning, Meaning and Identity*. Cambridge: Cambridge University Press.

5

Transformation and Learning

■ What role can learning mechanisms play during total system transformation?

How can learning mechanisms at the individual, team, and organizational levels facilitate the accomplishment of business strategy and performance?

What are some of the learning mechanisms that foster the balance between the need for economic performance and the sustainability of the business and human development during system-wide transformation?

▶ Organizational Transformation

It is not an unusual state of affairs that an organization is seen to need radical, systemic change to avoid or solve critical problems or to realize promising opportunities. Radical systemic changes are often referred to as "transformations." Kochan and Useem (1992) point out that such changes usually involve four interdependent activities: strategic restructuring, using technology to strategic advantage, redesigning structures and boundaries, and using personnel as strategic resources. The challenges involved in personnel development include upgrading the knowledge and skills of the workforce, valuing differences and diversity in the workforce, sustaining a high level of participation, and supporting the transformation of both the industrial relations and human resource management policies, practices, and traditions. Top management must also institutionalize the different constituencies' or stakeholders' commitment to these new principles. This requires that all relevant stakeholders are included.

There are a number of paths that may be chosen for this organizational transformation (Useem and Kochan, 1992). One is to adopt the "rationality" of a current political model. This played a part in the Merchant Bank's choice to become a universal full-service bank (chapter 3) and in AMC's choice to adopt "lean production" (chapter 4). It was also relevant in the case to be presented here, a public utility, which took the step to become a limited company. Another path is management discretion. New CEOs have been recruited many times to achieve a rapid turnaround in a failing company. They have the power to change, for example, core values, and management and reward systems. The courses they choose can differ widely. In Dunphy and Stace's (1990) study of Australian organizations, success was achieved by autocratic CEOs' coercive actions, as distinct from close cooperation between the social partners.

However, a third approach that Useem and Kochan (1992) note is to establish a learning organization to engage systemic change on a continuing basis. This approach enables the engagement of many constituencies or stakeholders. Flexibility and innovativeness may be heightened by decentralized decision-making and networks over boundaries. The formation of a learning culture can promote openness, risk-taking, tolerance of conflicts and differing perspectives, and the management of diversity. In fact, the main conclusions from their anthology are that:

- organizational change should be systemic;

- while management cannot create the systemic change on its own, it plays a critical role in defining the organization's vision;

- other organizational stakeholders, whether shareholders, employees, customers, or public-policy makers, face the same critical choices;

- continuing systemic change depends on the building of a permanent learning capacity across as well as within organizations.

The transformation case presented here is that of a public utility struggling to establish itself in a deregulated market economy as a limited company at the same time as the basic technologies in the sector are changing rapidly. This entailed determined efforts to establish a learning organization at the same time as the company had to change its business strategy, its organization, its technology, and its relations towards its employees and their unions. Action taken throughout the organization, from top management to the shop and office floor, involved changes in all of these areas that acted to promote learning and the emergence of a learning organization.

▶ A Public Utility Becomes the TeleCom Services Co. Ltd (TCS)

The 1990s were a turbulent decade. Factors which contributed to this were the growing globalization of the world economy, the shift in relative import-ance from the industrial market to the financial market, deregulation, and technological shifts, especially regarding information and communication tech-nologies. The telecommunications net has been rebuilt twice since the 1950s: first with automatic exchanges in the 1960s and then with digitalization in the 1990s. Both technical shifts have had dramatic effects on the staffing levels in telecom organizations. Companies' and other organizations' reactions to the economic crisis in the 1990s to a large extent took the form of measures for cost reduction, slimming resources, and reducing the numbers of personnel. The growth and development optimism of the 1980s in which "personnel are the company's most important resource" had been exchanged for a more timid and sometimes cynical handling of employees as an exchangeable production factor.

The 1990s were a revolutionary period for TCS. The decade has seen them change from a state-owned monopolistic public utility to a limited company, though still owned by the state. The country was one of the first telecom markets to be opened to international competition and had one of the lowest price levels in the Organization for Economic and Cooperative Development (OECD). By 1997 there were thirteen companies in the country with permis-sion to offer telecom services and several more awaiting permission to do so. By 1997/98 the majority of national telecom monopolies in the European Union were deregulated and an agreement had been reached by 69 countries in the World Trade Organization (WTO) to successively liberalize the basic telecom market and not let geographical boundaries interfere with telecom-munication. With the increased price pressure, customer bases and services ranges had to increase to maintain profitability. A Leonardo da Vinci com-parative study reported that the number of radical innovations, not simply technological but also organizational, in the telecommunications sector was greater than the sum of those reported in the banking and car manufacturing sectors (Cressey, 1998).

In meeting these challenges TCS had reduced its personnel from 47,000 to 30,000 by 1994. But this was only the beginning. Further rationalization was necessary to meet national and international competition. The impacts of such technological developments as mobile telephony, the Internet, intranets, and Mobitex had only just started. The initial downsizing strategy on which TCS had embarked had followed the existing labor market legislation. The "law on protection of employment" (LPE) stipulates basically a "first in, last out" principle. The law allows people to be dismissed if there is insufficient work, but it is those who have been most recently employed who must go first. In addition, employers are also bound to offer first those recently dismissed the option of being re-employed when new recruiting takes place. The dismissals had resulted in dramatic demographic consequences for the company:

■ There was no one over 60 as a result of early retirements.

■ There was no one under 30 as a result of the "last in, first out" principle.

■ The average age of those remaining was 49–50.

■ The average employment time was 19–20 years as a result of low mobility.

Management felt that it had downsized itself into a corner. Repeated downsizing had also led to a very strained relationship between management and employees and their unions. The unions felt that management was mainly interested in reducing their influence. The unions had adopted a reactive strategy to minimize the negative effects of rationalization for their members. An adversarial climate existed. A radical transformation was necessary that could not be achieved by simple shrinkage. A new strategy was necessary.

Pfeffer (1998) points out that the considerable research indicating the economic efficacy of the implementation of what are variously called high involvement, high performance, or high commitment management practices is being generally ignored. The trends in actual management practice are, in many instances, moving in a direction exactly opposite to what a growing body of scientific evidence prescribes. A number of management practices or doctrines being adopted are applied in a way that emphasizes their rationalization capabilities while involving negative consequences in other key areas of the companies' overall effectiveness. Two such methods which have been widely applied in the 1990s are downsizing and outsourcing. Research shows that the impact of downsizing is dependent partly on the set of measures implemented in a development program. Simply downsizing does not usually result in improved productivity. The stock market's reaction to downsizing is both short-lived and dependent on the motives given to justify the measure (Morris et al., 1999; Arvedson, 1998).

A Restart in the Relations between Management and Unions

In 1994 the public utility became a state-owned limited company. The new CEO appointed a new head of business and competence development, a new position that was responsible for integrating business and competence processes and development in the company and headed the group designing and implementing the new HRM strategy and policies. The new management had a clear value base for the organization, including the employability principle (which was also a central value at AMC in chapter 4). A new "Vision 2001" project was initiated in 1995. The company aims to have a leading position in the Nordic telecom market, including a number of important information services related to Internet, cable-TV and interactive broadband and mobile technologies. The company is organized in eight business areas and four marketing areas. A shift in the staffing of several key top management positions was followed by changes in TCS's personnel and industrial relations policies. TCS discarded its traditional personnel administrative (PA) approach and adopted a Human Resource Management (HRM) perspective in the face of the new business realities and the demographic composition of the staff. It was quite simply no longer possible to manage personnel development in the corporation with traditional PA methods and tools. The view of HRM can be illustrated by two quotations. The first is taken from TCS's director for business and personnel development:

> HRD at the corporate level has no function today. It is a relic from an old view of personnel development. The sole task of personnel managers is to get line managers to shoulder their responsibility for the development of their staff. We shall have total leadership in the line organization.

Line managers should have responsibility for all issues related to personnel – from recruitment to competence switching, mobility, and possible outplacement. The HRM function's role is to create appropriate conditions for the total leadership. The second quotation is taken from TCS's annual report 1996:

> A factor that is of growing significance in (a customer's) choice of supplier is "image." TCS's decision to invest in the development of customer's quality of life, milieu, and competitiveness must go hand-in-hand with corresponding investments within TCS.
>
> TCS aspires to create the conditions for competence development where every employee knows the company's goals and business direction and the expectations and demands these entail for him- or herself so that he or she may take responsibility for his or her own competence development.

These quotations illustrate TCS's view of their personnel – or human resources – before the shift to the second half of the 1990s. An indication of the direction that HRM was taking in TCS in 1996 can be seen in the measurement tool regarding different aspects of "the development of human capital" which the company was using as part of a Balanced Score Card approach to management. "Human capital" is measured every year using an extensive survey questionnaire which is sent to all employees. The overall results are reported as a Human Capital index in which the answers are combined under a number of headings, such as values and culture, competence, motivation, responsibility and initiative, leadership, cooperation and process, organizational effectiveness.

The second major change concerned new conditions for the social dialogue. The new management underlined that cooperation, commitment, and development were the values that would permeate the organization. The new values gave the unions the opportunity of breaking with the culture of negotiating about rights which had prevailed between the parties, in favor of a partnership in which the issues of business and competence development dominated the agenda.

In the mid-90s the social partners in TCS signed *two local joint agreements* that manifested the new direction in their joint efforts. The first was a co-operation or development agreement that regulated the formal work practices between the parties and emphasized their mutual interest in creating the best possible conditions for development processes – both business and com-petence development processes. In short, it may be said that the agreement was based on cooperation and not negotiation as the main method of working. The participation system was harmonized with the decision structure in the company, which meant including the shop stewards in decisions. Agendas which had been based on formal rights and obligations were to a large ex-tent replaced by ones based on mutual interests in development. Instead of negotiating on the consequences of different employer suggestions, the parties discuss possible developments of mutual interest.

The second local joint agreement of significance was a change and security agreement. The social partners agreed on a three-year moratorium in order to create favorable conditions for a massive transformation program. During the three-year period all personnel were guaranteed security of employability on the condition that management could transfer people who were in danger of being declared redundant to a newly formed and temporary "personnel development division" (PDD). The social partners agreed to utilize the three-year period for competence development and to increase personnel's mobility and employability. The shift from industrial relations to partnership is experi-enced by both management and unions as a success.

Transformation to a Learning Organization

Means of management

Management and the unions drew up two joint agreements to make a con-certed effort to realize a learning organization. This was to embrace all mem-bers currently in the organization – even those who were to be regarded as redundant. Competence development plans were to be made for all. General policies, methods, and routines were to be drawn up for the company as a whole, but with due respect to the different character of its various business units, the units were allowed considerable degrees of freedom in the applica-tion of these principle solutions to their particular contexts. Several means were used to steer the transformation process towards realizing a learning organization.

Steering with culture and values

The corporate culture in this case, as in the cases of the Merchant Bank (chapter 3) and AMC (chapter 4), has been highly influenced, not to say created, by a charismatic leader and has been maintained and reinforced by his successors. The current culture in TCS is characterized by cooperation, commitment, and development. As in the previous cases, "personal development" holds for *all* employees. Everyone has a personal development plan. The concept of "employability," which also holds for everyone, answers for the basic security everyone may feel in the company. The company will ensure that those who get the opportunity to switch competencies will have a future within this or another organization. This security is coupled to an acceptance by individuals and their unions of greater mobility and flexibility, built on trust, respect, and cooperation, rather than negotiation, and on mutual perceptions of the company's position. People interviewed in the company speak of a "win–win–win" situation for the individual, company, and society. It is a matter of company ethics that entails TCS taking responsibility for reschooling and outplacing that other companies leave to the state. The company has a social responsibility and acts as such in the regional and national context. How responsible behavior brings its own rewards is taken up later in this chapter.

Steering with language

The introduction of HRD and the new organization and working routines has also been accompanied by a change in the language used. This has been subtle and not prescribed. However, the language conveys the new values and perspectives. Some examples are: "training facilities" are now referred to as "learning rooms," "workplaces" are now referred to as "meeting places," specialists and superiors are referred to as "coaches" or "tutors." Training programs are referred to as "learning programs" and are often held at "training camps" instead of the TCS school. TCS are in favor of "on-the-job training," which they call "learn-where-you-are." Similarly, they adapt learning programs to personal learning styles, which has been given the name "learning-as-you-are." The language is a considerable help in focusing competence development as a strategic issue in the company. But not only that, the language underlines the form of learning and competence development of import in the company.

Steering with organizational networks

Given that the basic technology in the organization is ICT, networking is an everyday activity in TCS. Creating human networks ought to be the next natural step in this organization, and this appears to be the case. The separate business, market, and production companies are independent and have full responsibility for their own development, including competence development. At the same time, all these organizational units participate in a corporate competence network.

The corporate network has a double function. Its main function is to be the support group to top management regarding the drawing up of policies and guidelines concerning competence development. Another task is to identify and diffuse best practice between the different parts of the organization. The basic concept in the HRD strategy is that each unit should find its "own path to the learning organization" within the joint frame of reference in the corporation. This pluralism aims to foster innovative approaches that can be a source of inspiration to all members. To quote an interview from TCS Net:

> They are extremely clever at using Intranet and interactive learning at TCS Retail. We have a lot to learn from them. I spoke to their competence manager who was interested in working with us. She is interested in our exercises which are based on practical cases instead of more theoretical cases when we develop our learning profiles and in how we work with individual learning profiles (Myers–Briggs).

The competence network replaces to a large extent the central personnel department. Cooperation and joint ventures can be seen in the meetings between people from different units. Such meetings and "dialogue opportunities" are a *method* for competence development. The company builds support resources, coaches, tutors, mentors, instead of specialists in competence development. Managers have a specific responsibility for competence development and receive special training to be coaches (cf. The Merchant Bank, chapter 3; AMC chapter 4). Even the line organization is characterized by working methods that result in on-the-job learning. TCS Retail is an excellent example of such a way of organizing the work and the physical work space for learning.

Steering with mental models

In order to facilitate the development of good practice and the exchange of experience within the corporation, the company developed a standard frame of reference and basic routines that applied to the entire organization. These included four components: 1) a competence development process that applied to the whole organization, 2) a common competence model, 3) a common way of describing the competence profiles, and 4) a common management "company competence" evaluation process as a dimension in the corporate Balanced Score Card system. Competence development was thereby integrated with business development.

The competence model aimed to ensure balance between the technical, business, and social competence. That this happens is checked by TCS's measurement tools. The content of the competence framework can be varied for different professional groups, functions, teams, and individuals. The competence scale allows assessments of the company's competence needs in a few years' time plus assessments of current competence of individuals or teams. These form the basis for gap analyses. The methods help clarify diffuse competence concepts and create a common language in the company.

Integrating "learning" in the management system

There is a strong belief in the company that competence development is primarily the responsibility of the line managers and their staff, although this does not mean that management has abdicated. Direct control has been replaced by several systems, of which the more important are:

- A Balanced Score Card (BSC) system with focus on economy and finance, market and customers, human capital, and development and innovation. Every manager and many teams have BSCs.

- Measurement tools and schedules coupled to the BSC system.

- A reward system that is coupled to the BSC system, with considerable weight attached to the human capital dimension. A manager's performance regarding long-term efforts on competence development, integration of competence and business development, recruitment of competence, and handling redundancy (over-staffing) is assessed.

▶ # Examples of Different Business Units' Application of the Learning Strategy

As previously stated, these general policies, guidelines, methods, and tools are adapted and applied in the various divisions to deal with the specific issues confronting each division's situation. We present three short cases to illustrate the various approaches used in different divisions, namely: TCS PDD, TCS Retail, and TCS Net.

Personnel Development Division (PDD): Re-skilling personnel at risk

The PDD was formed in 1995. All those in the company in danger of being redundant in the period 1995–8 were referred to the PDD for re-skilling and placement in new jobs within as well as outside the company. In a three-year period, 1996–8, a total of 6,550 people were placed in this division for shorter or longer periods. During the same period over 2,000 new employees joined the company. When the company was closed at the turn of the year 1998/99, there were roughly one hundred people remaining that had not been found new jobs. The average time spent by an individual in the division was 7–8 months, which can be compared with the lead time for traditional dismissal, which can be up to 18 months.

The three-year project cost TCS roughly 600 million euros. This may be compared with the traditional dismissal process which would cost about 435 million euros. TCS regards the difference as an investment in a broad competence improvement program, the creation of considerable goodwill both within and outside the company, and, not least, a significant improvement in the change climate in the company. A research project conducted by the School of Business at Stockholm University estimated a net profit for TCS of 146 million euros through investing in competence development and outschooling instead of traditional downsizing (Hansson, 1999).

PDD was a joint venture between management and the unions. Its point of departure was their common values to achieve or create security, competence-switching, employability, and increased mobility, both internally and externally. This massive transformation process did *not* entail a stop in recruitment in TCS at this time. The parties were in agreement on the need for the company to recruit key competencies. The figures below are a summary of the flow of people in and out of the division in its second year:

Number of people in the PDD on January 1, 1997   2.367

New jobs within TCS   726

Outplacements   354

Pensions   829

New transfers to PDD   563

Number of people in PDD on December 31, 1997   1,039

The partnership between management and the unions aimed at creating a winner–winner–winner situation. Both the company and the individual employee have something to gain from the competence strategy. In addition, TCS had the goal of societal responsibility.

The partnership showed itself to be successful, even if the experiences were not wholly positive. Given hindsight, three years was somewhat generous to accomplish this transformation. A shorter time for the project would have increased the pressure on the participating individuals to take personal responsibility for their own learning. Success also had its price for the unions. Many felt that the unions spent too much time protecting their older members and had little to offer younger members who were starting their careers. A problem that both parties encountered was that middle managers and union representatives had difficulty in playing their roles in the new participation system which was based on working with their mutual interests. They had difficulty in acting proactively and in taking the offensive, instead of simply reacting to the other party's position in a negotiation. Old habits die hard and it was difficult to cooperate.

In the crisis in the early 1990s, the union carried out its own development study, formulating a vision for the future. This had a clear value-added character and was change oriented. Management had done a similar exercise and produced its Vision 2001. The similarity between the two documents was striking. The "shared mental model" formed the basis for the new developments in which the competence transformation and business development would form two parallel tracks that were coupled to each other. TSC took great pains to create positive conditions to support both business and competence development.

Development of employability at TCS

It was important that the PDD was a specific program for a three-year period. It underlined the important aim of preparing the organization for "*Total Leadership*" which is characterized by managers who have acquired the prerequisites for handling the entire range of personnel issues.

Values played an important part in the role of the division. One value was "*We will* not *pay people not to work*," a value which meant that the company did its utmost to avoid the traditional early retirement (with 72 percent salary). (One alternative was to be "on call" at home for 75 percent salary and receive 100 percent salary when called upon to come to work.) Another value was to seek to create "*winner–winner–winner*" *situations*, i.e., the work of the division should create value for the company, the individual staff member, and society in the form of reduced unemployment. A third value was that "*the individual must take responsibility for his or her own development and employability*." The division's task was to support the individual in finding new employment within or outside of TCS.

The division's way of going about its work is best conveyed by briefly describing some of its projects or strategies/methods. These are available in the organization today via the HRM internal consultancy unit.

The PDD conducted competence analyses in the same fashion as every other division. Business plans were collected from all the divisions and were analyzed to ascertain the competence of the organization in the future. On the basis of these, *key professions* were identified and suitable training programs developed. Examples of such professions were IT/network technicians, programmers/ systems analysts, work with validating and quality assurance. The training programs were carried out, but with poor results, to the extent that the line organization responded with a very weak demand for the participants in the courses when the courses were completed. This illustrates the difficulties with the central planning of competence development in such rapidly changing sectors as telecommunications.

An adjustment allowance, a specific sum of money, was made available to each PDD individual to be used either for competence development for a job outside the company or for personal subsistence during an adjustment period. The sum was calculated individually and had a maximum value of 17,000 euros. The grant was highest on joining the PDD and decreased continuously each month that the individual remained in the division. This was intended to be an incentive to the individual to take personal responsibility for his/her situation. In practice this meant that a TCS employee could contact another employer and, apart from his/her current qualifications, even offer to finance the further training that might be needed to suit a position in that company. The grant was coupled to the individual but its use could be discussed with the new employer.

A *guide* or supervisor was appointed to each individual employed in PDD with the task of providing information on different job opportunities both within and outside TCS. The guides had extensive external networks, e.g., with *"job brokers."* PDD had contracts with about fifteen companies around the country that functioned as job brokers. The companies represented a broad spectrum of businesses, from local/regional IT companies to further education companies, service companies, and recruitment companies. The job broker received the sum of 5,600 euros for each person placed in a job. This sum is very modest compared with the fees demanded by outplacement consultants and, moreover, their results were much more satisfactory than such consultants, according to TCS. An important motive for the job brokers was of course that good relations with TCS usually had special value for these companies, apart from the recruitment fees.

PDD had a contract with one of the major *contingent labor intermediaries* in Sweden. The contract offered PDD employees permanent jobs in this intermediary. TCS guaranteed the employees their current salary for three years. After the guarantee period the employee continued his/her employment with the intermediary but on its normal conditions, which are a market wage and a minimum of 75 percent of their wage in periods with few assignments. The intermediary often functioned as a bridge for the individual to permanent employment in a company that had utilized the intermediary. For some individuals the arrangement meant an extended separation from TCS with plenty of time to prepare a new career. For others the three years meant a period to adjust their private economy and a way to arrange their life in the long term in accordance with the conditions associated with the intermediary.

PDD also came to play the same role of an *internal intermediary*. This could involve appointing a temporary substitute or a permanent replacement. The advantages are obvious. Those responsible for recruitment could come in contact with relevant candidates at short notice and be sure that they were well acquainted with the company. For the individual it meant being able to try a new job and possibly find a new niche in TCS, or otherwise to return to PDD if the job did not match his/her knowledge, skills, experience, needs, or aspirations. It was mainly during the first year that PDD was a source of personnel to TCS itself. The internal mobility decreased markedly after a year as the line organization achieved the staffing it desired. PDD's activities then became focused more on external mobility.

PDD cooperated with the company's suppliers, offering people employment in one of its suppliers or subcontractors. This could be arranged at the same time as TCS signed a new contract with the supplier. TCS could offer to outsource certain activities to the supplier if the supplier agreed to take on personnel from TCS in the process. The contract could also stipulate, not only that certain personnel would be taken on from TCS, but also that further non-TCS personnel should also be employed (social responsibility).

PDD had an entrepreneur school which offered an eight-month course for those wishing to *start their own firm*. This was coupled to an offer of mentor support for a five-year period. An example in this field was cooperation with McDonald's, the fast food company, which offered the opportunity of getting a franchise. That arrangement involved one year's training with salary.

The individuals could also be offered lifetime employment in the company under special circumstances. People who were born no later than 1944 and who had worked for at least 25 years in the company could be contracted for permanent employment on the following conditions:

- The individual could be placed in a more or less temporary job within or outside of TCS. The job should be in line with the individual's work experience and may involve some travelling.

- A guaranteed salary of 75 percent of the normal wage would be paid when the individual was not hired out. When on assignment, the individual received full salary and even a bonus.

- The company saved the costs of office workplaces as the employee was either at home or at a customer's premises.

- The project gave great freedom to engage in seasonal work in another sector or some leave in which to seek another job.

- This solution also offered some possibilities for training to take on new tasks or to change profession.

What is the situation from 1999?

When the division was disbanded at the end of 1998, its responsibilities were taken over by the ordinary organization, i.e., each business unit has the responsibility for ensuring the employability of its personnel. Thus the same policy applies, but it now forms part of each manager's "total leadership." For support in this particular task there are a number of internal consultants attached to the central HRM unit who are experts in the methods and tools used by the PDD and who can advise managers as to the most suitable strategy to be applied in individual cases. The unit is staffed by people who previously worked in PDD and is financed centrally. These consultants have a very good name in the labor market and receive many requests for help from outside the organization.

Radical solutions at TCS Retail

TCS Retail's main task is to coordinate business between the corporation's different business areas and the firm's numerous distributors and agents outside the corporation, establishing long-term relations with them. It is a relatively young company, which means that that it is not weighed down by custom and tradition. It has *c.* 300 employees organized in four regions. It serves about 15,000 people working at *c.* 10,000 workplaces. Distributors are made up of four categories: distribution chains, wholesalers and suppliers, independent chains with up to eight outlets, and system integrators.

The application of business process engineering at TCS has made flow thinking dominant at the firm. This applies also to TCS Retail which has complicated contacts within and outside the organization. The company has a rather unusual organization, which may be illustrated as a flow (see figure 5.1). To the left in the figure are the business area managers who are each responsible for one of the business areas. The Resource House has all the specialists regarding sales, production, and marketing. This unit has no responsibility for customers but is responsible for the competence development of its staff. The Function House has an administrative service role and also gives business and sales support. On the right-hand side are those who are responsible for the customers. The four managers are each responsible for a business sector and together they are responsible for sixteen teams.

The organization has a shared responsibility for results (customer responsibility) and personnel (Resource and Function Houses). The head of the Resource House has as his/her main task to develop the staff's competence. There is a dialogue between the manager and the personnel section who provide specialist support. Staff can work in several permanent teams as well as on

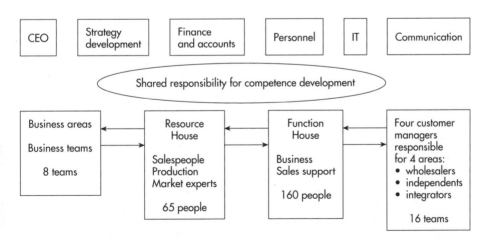

Figure 5.1 Organization of TCS Retail

temporary assignments. There are internal market mechanisms as the customer managers are anxious to secure competent staff for the current needs of their own customers. The Resource House must continuously align the competence development to the demands of the "marketplace."

The learning role of the intranet

The organization is connected to all the links in a value chain from TCS's business areas to customers and customers' customers. The company strives to strengthen that value chain. Its most important tool in that context is an intranet. This net is basically accessible to all agents and distributors. It contains product information, campaign support, and, above all, interactive e-learning. The net has high customer value and binds the distributors more closely to TCS. The net enables TCS customers to increase the value for the end users. The net also allows the certification of distributors, by which TCS gains quality assurance of its distributors.

The spatial layout of a learning workplace

The entire workplace is designed for learning. They have imported many of the ideas from Digital Equipment's "virtual office." The main office has 140 staff, 100 workplaces, and about 70 staff are in the office at any one time. The rest are either visiting customers, working at home, or traveling. No one has a personal workplace, not even the managers. The company lives as it preaches and is extremely IT-oriented. Using IT has almost become an end in itself and is justified by heightening staff's tacit knowledge and establishing the ICT media as the basis for business. (We asked to see the annual report and were given a CD-ROM. Similarly, when we asked for documentation on competence models and courses we were given access to their intranet.)

The physical workplaces take very little space and are arranged in circles, dominated by cables for plugging in equipment. On the other hand, there is plenty of room for spontaneous meetings of different kinds – with other colleagues or team members, with customers or stakeholders. There are closed meeting rooms but most arenas are open oases in the open space office, for coffee discussions, team meetings, ad hoc conferences. The aim has been to create a milieu that allows, in a natural way, cross-functional contacts between different units or teams.

The workplace breathes learning. The manager of the Resource House is in practice a "competence manager." In addition, there are learning coaches with special responsibility to support learning. The office has a learning center for on-the-job learning, so that "dead time" between tasks or assignments may be used for personal competence development. In addition to the computers there is a library and expert helpdesk.

Making the learning ideas practical and concrete in TCS Retail

All the ideas and models making up the company's framework for competence development are included in TCS Retail's intranet, accessible to all and edited to meet local conditions. This material opens with a presentation of the basic points of departure or values behind the strategy:

Three factors for success:

Associates: A company's most important resource and success factor is its associates (staff) and their competence. Competence is the key to success, satisfied customers and staff.

Cooperation: Another success factor is the ability to cooperate. This means both internally and externally through alliances with large and small companies. By using a common model for competence we can develop a common idea on how we need to retain and develop competencies.

Learning: Learning is yet another success factor. Our common structure and language give us a unique possibility to learn from each other, to exchange experiences and ask questions. In TCS Retail we define competence as the collection, development and sharing of knowledge and experience.

TCS Retail's model for competence development

All managers are responsible for planning and controlling organizational and individual competence needs derived from business goals. Each individual must have a personal development plan. The basic steps for this are shown in figure 5.2. The process entails defining the competence demands for the various professional roles, and then estimating the proficiency levels required for the various competencies. Individuals' current competencies are assessed and a gap analysis is conducted by comparing required with current competence. Activity plans are based on a matching between individual needs and ambitions and the organizational requirements for business goal fulfillment.

The basic competence model comprises professional, business, and social skills. Each professional group has developed its own competence profile in the form of a wheel or compass (see figure 5.3). This process has been rather difficult, but as in the Merchant Bank (chapter 3), management felt that those actually conducting the job should play the key role in its analysis, partly to utilize their practical experience, partly to give the profile legitimacy and acceptance. Similarly, the required proficiency estimates will differ in offices in different parts of the country depending on the local business and labor markets. The profiles are discussed in the teams. When profiles have been established, the discussions continue as to how the gaps may be closed. The

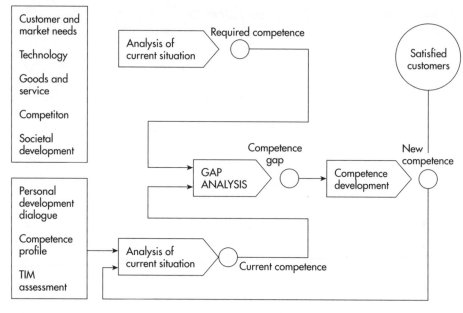

Figure 5.2 TCS's competence model

discussions utilize the advantages of being *a team.* It is the teams and not individuals who are to "close the gap" by utilizing individuals' strengths and particular interests, and by eliminating weaknesses. The exercises are summarized in terms of individual development plans.

If someone checks the competence profile on the intranet, the spokes on the wheel give guidelines to further development. By following the scale on the spoke (from 1 to 5: little, basic, good, extensive, and exceptional), information is provided on what training is available, including the e-learning courses that are prioritized in TCS Retail. Information is also provided on experts who are prepared to answer questions and discuss problems. These experts may be more competent colleagues or people from TCS's partners or suppliers. The intranet is referred to as the "Interactive Academy," indicating the extent to which it has replaced traditional education. The range of courses available is very wide. It covers practically every professional area, ICT, and topics such as rhetoric and mental training.

Competence development in TCS Net

TCS Net is responsible for selling TCS's products and services to private customers and small enterprises. It has approximately 4,000 employees and is represented over the entire country, which is divided up into 38 business units,

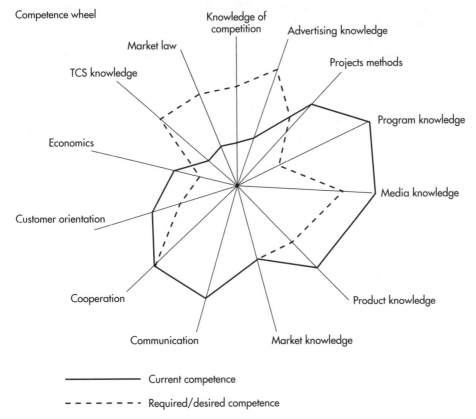

Figure 5.3 Current and required/desired competence profile for a salesperson in TCS Retail

each unit having a management function and 6–8 teams of 10–15 members, 280 teams in all over the country. The teams are cross-functional, including shop assistants, service technicians, and customer service for line and mobile telephony. Initially it was difficult to identify natural opportunities for these different personnel categories to cooperate. People continued to "do their own thing." Similarly, many order clerks were faced with the job of being a salesperson. A positive development has been to name the teams "learning teams," switching the focus from joint production to joint learning through the exchange of experience at monthly meetings of 2–4 hours. This is leading to a clearer understanding of the team's task and the customer's total situation.

TCS Net uses the same wheel or compass technique to establish competence profiles. However, TCS Net uses different practical work situations as the spokes of the wheel instead of different competencies. The logic is that competence entails being able to deal with such practical situations proficiently. This solution emerged from discussions between competence managers and experienced workers and managers. Competence is defined as the ability to execute tasks. The competence planning tool is a questionnaire that is completed by all the units. Questions are of the type "How do you judge your ability to inform customers about our products by: describing the usefulness of our products and services; meeting comparisons of the competitors' offers; seeking/getting additional information via support systems?". The individuals' answers are summarized. Then the team makes a joint assessment of the required competence. The third step is for the team to determine a joint goal for competence needs, requiring the identification of competence needs, target groups, and suitable actions. A checklist of questions is provided for discussion of the areas with the major gaps, for example: Is this a key area for improved competence? Is competence here low generally or with respect to a specific task? Why is it low? Who requires improvements (target groups)? What can be done? By when must it be done?

A clear result of TCS Net's approach is that there is a high demand for competence development in the division. The approach outlined above has been used by groups of managers to develop a management tool of the same type for themselves. The focus for managers has been towards coaching and this type of support is in high demand so that a special tutor training has been developed and 80 people have been trained to support the activities "learn where you are" and "learn as you are." In the latter activity each individual is encouraged to explore his/her own learning style by using the Myers–Briggs test with the aid of a tutor. The results are used to form the individual development plans. Experiments have been made with "learning rooms." Such a room is made available for an individual team as a studio where they can seek information, listen to experts, test or experiment with their personal learning styles, as a team, learn who is good at what in the team. Now a group of "competence advisors" have been given the task of establishing "learning rooms" in their areas.

The organization is built on creating high-performing teams with strong personal responsibility for their own learning. There are a number of fundamental ideas behind this organizational idea:

- Learning programs are based on the ability to deal with situations.
- There is a focus on learning in groups – permanent or temporary.
- Creating a demand for coaches, trainers, training camps.
- Creating conditions for on-the-job-learning – learn-where-you-are.
- Creating networks for the exchange of experience and learning.
- Starting from individual learning styles – learn as you are.
- Manager (leader) development in the direction of the coach role.
- Investment in special competence advisors.
- Investment in tutor-led education, training.
- Creating special learning rooms.
- Creating common goals for competence development.

Discussion

This transformation case had the character of an organization facing radical changes in its environment: the national and "worldwide" deregulation of monopolies, launching of new technology generations, entailing the integration of computing and communications technology, as well as radical changes in the organization's relation to its customers, competitors, and societal institutions. Its initial reactions had "painted it into a corner." Viable solutions had to be new solutions.

Management and unions: From adversaries to partners

Perhaps the first and most distinctive development in this case is the abandonment of a traditional adversarial industrial relations strategy in favor of a social partnership. The main union on the TUC side was the state-employed Workers' Union. This organized workers in the national public utilities, such as railways, post and telephone, and electricity production and distribution. It was clear that all these were to be deregulated and the union had already changed its structure and mission to become the "Service and Communication Workers Union." The telecom branch of the union had developed a change strategy for the telecom industry that was a value-added strategy and fitted "hand-in-glove" with the new management's thinking. Developments in the company have, by and large, lived up to both parties' expectations as outlined in their strategy documents. That both parties have been so proactive has undoubtedly facilitated the speed of change.

Though there has been a willingness to cooperate in achieving a positive partnership, the parties have heeded their more well-established behavior of getting things "on paper." This led to two local joint agreements. The first concerned the formation of the Personnel Development Division, which re-skilled and outplaced 6,400 people in a three-year period. During this period, 2,000 new people were recruited to the company. The agreement ratified the personnel's employment security in terms of "employability" and "competence-switching." This created a positive "readiness for change" in the company and management could concern itself the radical change efforts to be conducted in the company, to realize their integration of "business and competence development." The union could also give their attention to this in the safe knowledge that the PDD division was taking care of redundant members.

The second agreement covered such issues as participation, negotiations, and work environment. The shift from a public utility to a limited company gave the opportunity to alter the character of the relations between management and unions at the local level. At point 1 in figure 5.4, it is the experts

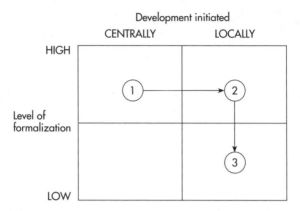

Figure 5.4 Development in the character of union–management cooperation

from both sides who draw up the main rules of the game at the local level; matters came to be delegated at point 3 where the "practitioners" on both sides deal with the issues from positions of interest and trust. This "local-based" way of working was ratified in 1995. Current discussions indicate that the union's responsibility and authority may be delegated to work teams, changing the whole concepts of participation and relations between the social partners. In the current agreement, management states that the union is an important resource in company development and the union states its understanding of the company's need for change.

Thus the major goals of individual security and company flexibility have been reconciled and ensured in binding agreements.

Management strategy

The turnaround started with several new members in the top management team, including a new CEO and a senior vice president for business and competence development. The latter was responsible for the learning organization development and was to ensure the integration of business and competence. Personnel administration was changed to human resource management and under the parole of "total leadership," line managers received responsibility for handling their staff. The CEO made the statements on personal security through employability and the new joint agreements with the union. A new Balanced Score Card-type management system was introduced, in which human capital was one of the specific areas, covering recruitment, development, and severance. About 30–40 percent of a manager's bonus was tied to how well competence development was handled. The TIM management system provides further data in this context. Management's aim was to create a "win–win–win" situation for the individual, the investor, and society, generating goodwill externally and contributing to a positive company culture.

HRD and divisional pluralism

TCS has a system approach to HRD. Management and control have been outlined above. The "participation" contracts created positive conditions for continual development and the application of a "boxing and dancing" strategy between the social partners (Huzzard and Nilsson, 2002). The company has developed centrally guidelines, methods, tools, and routines for a comprehensive program of competence development. The examples given show how the individual divisions can adapt these to their own conditions. It has created an infrastructure, coupled to the competence advisors, to provide for the exchange of experiences between the different divisions. It has striven to create a "total learning environment" with pilot projects regarding the physical, spatial milieu for the everyday workplaces, "learning rooms," and learning centers. It has a well-developed intranet for information and advice and for e-learning with advanced ICT applications.

Learning is being conducted on several levels. All individuals have personal development plans. Team learning is being actively facilitated in many areas. The competence networks and the systematic follow-up of the Human Capital dimension of the Balanced Score Card address the organizational level. Traditional trading and courses have to a great extent been replaced by on-the-job learning and on-the-job training. Most formal learning is conducted at or adjacent to the learner's workplace. The work organization is designed to allow many cross-functional contacts and teams have a development responsibility for their work and their business.

The change from being a public utility to being a limited company has been accompanied by a switch from being production-oriented to being customer-oriented. TCS's process perspective is oriented to value chains with high customer loyalty in the creation of value for customers. From having a self-sufficient attitude towards others, alliances and joint ventures are valued, not least from a learning perspective, as in bench-learning (Karlöf et al., 2000).

The transformation has demanded new roles for everyone. Management has less order-giving and more coaching and responsibility for competence development. Union representatives have gone from being solely negotiators to even being change agents with management, while delegating a number of their union duties to their members and supporting them in this.

Learning Requirements, Design Dimensions, and Mechanisms

Table 5.1 shows the learning requirements, design dimensions, and mechanisms for TCS. Regarding requirements, these are formulated at a higher level

Table 5.1 Learning requirements, design dimensions, and learning mechanisms at the TeleCom Services Company, TCS

Transformation learning requirements	Learning design dimensions	Learning mechanisms
Corporate philosophy regarding learning	Value base	Employability contract Individual development for all Management–union dialogue
	Social dialogue–partnership	Corporate joint agreements
Corporate learning strategy	Individual, team, organizational elements, recruitment, development, outplacement elements	Corporate learning language Common tools, methods, routines (profiles, scales) Focus on on-the-job and at-the-job learning Learning centers Explicit freedom for local innovations in policy application, e.g., learning styles Learning infrastructures (experience exchange network) Corporate/Co. competence Intranet Re-skilling and outplacement function Alliances, cooperation with other organizations (bench-learning)
Management strategy for learning	Management involvement/ responsibility	Balanced Score Card incl. HRD Management reward system with HRD Managers' roles in LO
Total learning environment	Plans, methods, roles, technical support, resources	The above plus the design of the physical environment

of abstraction than in, for example, the bank case (chapter 3). The aim here is to identify requirements for the creation of the learning organization. Thus the requirements consist of the management philosophy and values around learning, its corporate strategy, management systems, and the total learning environment. TCS has taken active decisions and actions on all these points which have reached through the organization and left their "mark."

The design dimensions concerned the social dialogue (management–unions), work organization and roles, and the various aspects of the planning, conduct, and follow-up of the learning processes. These, in turn, were supported by the specific mechanisms described above. Again, there are specific mechanisms for the separate processes at the different levels in the organization. Again, the focus has been on "critical design specifications," i.e., giving the structure that ensures understanding, acceptance, and enthusiasm, while allowing discretion for adjustment to the specific conditions prevailing in different parts of the organization.

Useem and Kochan (1992) note that establishing a learning organization to engage a systemic change will promote sustainability. TCS made a concerted effort to do this. Its initial efforts have been focused on learning in production or first-order learning. The next two cases illustrate clearly learning associated with development processes in the organization, concerning Total Quality Management processes in the paper mill (chapter 6) and Knowledge Management in the software company (chapter 7).

References

Arvedson, L. (1998). *Downsizing: När företag bantar* (Downsizing: When companies slim). Stockholm: Trygghetsrådet.

Cressey, P. (1998). *Innovations in Companies with Union–Management Co-operation in Learning and Human Resource Development: Experiences from a Leonardo da Vinci Project.* Unpublished working paper. Bath: University of Bath, Dept of Sociology.

Dunphy, D. and Stace, D. (1990). *Under New Management: Australian Organizations in Transition.* Sydney: McGraw-Hill.

Hansson, R. (1999). *Personalförsörjningsmodellen – Ett projekt i tiden: Övertalighetshantering* (Personnel flow model – a timely project. Redundancy management). Stockholm: Svenska Strukturforskningsinstitutet HB.

Huzzard, T. and Nilsson, T. (2002). *Boxing and Dancing: New Relations between the Social Partners.* Paper to 20th Labour Process Conference, Glasgow: University of Strathclyde, April 2–4.

Karlöf, B., Lundgren, K., and Edenfelt Froment, M. (2000). *Bench Learning: Förebilder som Hävstång för Utveckling* (Bench learning: Star cases as levers for learning). Stockholm: Ekelids Förlag.

Kochan, T. and Useem, M. (1992). Achieving systemic organizational change. In T. Kochan and M. Unseem (eds), *Transforming Organizations.* New York: Oxford University Press, pp. 3–14.

Morris, J. R., Cascio, W. F. and Young, C. E. (1999). Downsizing after all these years: Questions and answers about who did it, how many did it, and who benefited from it. *Organizational Dynamics,* Winter, 78–87.

Pfeffer, J. (1998). *Human Equation: Making Profits by Putting People First.* Boston, MA: Harvard Business School Press.

Useem, M. and Kochan, T. (1992). Creating the learning organization. In T. Kochan and M. Useem (eds,) *Transforming Organizations.* New York: Oxford University Press, pp. 391–406.

6

Development Processes, Learning and Competitiveness[1]

■ What is the role of learning in improving key development processes for sustainability and competitiveness?

■ Why is it critical for business strategists to identify key development processes and integrate business strategy with organizational learning?

■ What are some of the learning mechanisms that can support development processes?

The design and redesign of developmental processes in organizations can be viewed as a fundamental learning process. Furthermore, developmental processes are viewed as key components of the firm's strategic capability. As we have seen in chapter 2, integrating a resource-based view of the firm with an organization design perspective sets the stage for the exploration of learning around the development of key processes. Thus, while chapter 3 focused on individual competencies and learning, chapter 4 on team learning, and chapter 5 on learning in business transformation, this chapter focuses on learning in and around developmental processes. The chapter emphasizes the learning aspects of a few developmental processes and illustrates how their

[1] This chapter is a result of a ten-year study that was conducted by Professors Yoram Mitki and A. B. (Rami) Shani. The first draft of the manuscript was contributed by Yoram. The chapter was developed in collaboration with him. We are grateful to Professor Mitki for his insights and contribution.

design and the support configurations that were created around them contributed to sustaining learning and firms' competitiveness.

Core capabilities of the firm are developed in organizations through a complex transformation process by which standard resources, within and outside the organization boundaries, are used and combined with organizational routines to produce capabilities (Mitki, Shani, and Meiri, 1997). Organizational routines are viewed as particular ways of doing, developed and learned over time, that have become almost automatic, a "natural" reflection of its "way of being" (Andreu and Ciborra, 1996; Argyris and Schön, 1978). Thus, capabilities involve the organization's human capital developing, carrying, and exchanging information (Ingelgård et al., 2002).

Improving the firm's capabilities, increasing its competitiveness and the long-term viability of the firm were the goals established by the management of the Paper Mills Corporation (PMC). The strategic decision was to focus on improving the capabilities of key development processes that were viewed as crucial for the long-term survival and success of the firm. The management team decided to develop learning mechanisms around the development processes of quality, continuous improvement, workers' involvement, and teamwork. The structural organizational learning mechanism that has evolved to lead and facilitate the effort – since the late 80s – continuously transformed itself to allow the organization to optimize and develop the most appropriate processes. Furthermore, the learning focus facilitated the continuous regeneration of resources and thus fostered system sustainability.

Quality as a Development Process

The concept of quality is increasingly becoming a primary concept of organizational strategy and policy. Mounting demands of customers and the need to meet severe standards in order to obtain proper permits for the production and marketing of commodities and services require the continuous development and adoption of a quality policy and the development of effective tools for its implementation. Some of the characteristics of the development that centered on quality are the shift from quality control to quality assurance, the move from end-control of commodities or services to systematical ongoing control of production and service processes, the introduction of methodical data collection and analysis, corrective actions and continuous improvement of performance, and enhancing the connection between producers and customers.

The central development process at PMC in the area of quality focused both on the transfer of total responsibility for quality to all the organizational members and the development of shared philosophy that continuous improvement of quality must become the standard for behavior and action. The structural learning mechanism, as will be described, provided the platform for the development processes, mapping of alternative processes, and development of procedures, methods, and tools to address these issues.

► Continuous Improvement as a Development Process

The notion that continuous improvement is an integral part of the business competitive strategy emerged in the early 1960s and has become one of the central issues of organization design in the 1990s (Imai, 1986; Lillrank et al., 1998; Lillrank, Shani and Lindberg, 2001). Continuous improvement is a part of a broader paradigm shift: a movement from resource allocation strategies focusing only on profit maximization to resource-building strategies adding to profit maximization with a view toward the development of organizational capabilities that provide more value to customers. As such, continuous improvement is viewed as an organizational process crucial to the long-term success of the firm. Continuous improvement is a developmental process that involves everyone, employees and managers alike. It is a process that involves the ongoing rearranging and redesigning of elements of the organization; it requires the continuous rethinking of the patterns that connect and relate different elements of the organization and connect them with the environment; it is a process that bundles together data collection, interpretation, research, experimentation, and diffusion; and it involves the individual, the team, and the total organization. As such, continuous improvement with a developmental focus seeks to create new cognitive frameworks, mental models, interpretive schemes, and actions on ongoing bases.

The core process of continuous improvement at PMC was essential in enabling the company to become streamlined, to reduce costs, and to become attractive and competitive in open market conditions. The concept of continuous improvement as a critical developmental process, as perceived by the management and later on assimilated in the organization, included two major components. The first assumed that everything that was performed, whether in production or services, could be done better. The second emphasized the insight that what is done today will not necessarily be done tomorrow. As we will see later in this chapter, an organizational learning mechanism was designed so as to achieve these goals by means of varied structures, processes, and activities.

► Workers' Involvement and Teamwork as Development Processes

The importance of developing workers' involvement and teamwork as an integral part of work design can be found in the pioneering work of sociotechnical systems (STS) in the early 50s. Cherns (1976), for example, emphasized the fact that in order to achieve optimal utilization of production means (machines and people), a number of principles must be adopted. One principle is Minimal Critical Specification, the essence of which is to define the "what" rather than the "how." That is to say that the managers set the goals, whereas the workers are involved in determining how to perform. A second principle, Variance Control, stresses the fact that irregularities and deviations in the work process should be treated where and when they occur. This means that the responsibility for discovering and dealing with the deviations lies on the workers. They are involved in diagnosis and in decision-making about how to address malfunctions. This principle later became one of the milestones of TQM. A third principle is Information Flow, which means that all the information required by the workers so that they can control their work process and not be dependent on external factors, should flow. By receiving the information, the workers can become involved in the organizing of their work and in real-time decision-making in a valid and significant manner. The Multifunctional Principle, developed by STS experts, is also important, as it emphasizes the fact that there is more than one way and more than one means to achieve goals. It is furthermore based on the assumption that the worker is free to choose the most suitable way. These principles are the infrastructure of the concept of autonomous work groups, which are a cornerstone of the STS approach. We refer to work groups that function as independent production or service units, and which have a great deal of autonomy in all internal operation and management issues. A later development of the concept is what is today called Profit and Cost Centers. Other approaches that deal with continuous improvement, mainly the Total Quality Management (TQM) approach, also emphasize worker involvement and teamwork.

The PMC management considered worker involvement a critical process that needed to be developed, and made clear design choices around initiating and enhancing the process. Historically, the company's managerial style, since its establishment, had been centralized and had not encouraged worker involvement. Moreover, the firm's economic crisis in the mid-80s and the wave of staff reductions that followed did not induce an atmosphere of cooperation and teamwork – neither for the managers nor for the workers. The learning mechanisms that were created for the purpose of enhancing the development of key processes facilitated the transformation of the culture – into more of a participative and involved workplace.

The Paper Mills Corporation

The Corporation and its targets

The Paper Mills Corporation (PMC) was founded in 1952 as a joint venture of Israeli and American investors. Commencing operation in 1952 with one paper machine producing 10,000 tons, the company grew over the years and produces about 250,000 tons annually on six paper and board machines. PMC manufactures approximately 40 percent of the paper consumed in Israel. Most of its products are for the local market. In 2000 its sales amounted to $530 million, and its operating profit was $40.9 million. The number of employees is 2,160. The plants are dispersed around ten sites in Israel, but the main activity takes place in a medium-sized city located in the center of the country.

The Corporation's policy is based on several targets and principles: attaining a profit for the firm's continued existence and as a base for achieving its other targets; securing the existing market share and increasing the scope of sales to the local market; providing products and/or services which will meet the requirements of customers and their expectations; increasing productivity and improving product quality; decentralization of authority to the plants by delegating business, managerial, and operational responsibility; adopting advanced managerial systems; fostering environmental quality and quality of work life; contributing to immigrant absorption and to the community.

The central reason that motivated management to design a learning mechanism to enhance the development of key processes was the need to reduce manufacturing costs and to improve the quality of the products. Increasing profitability and overseas competition were viewed as issues that will influence PMC survival and success for the long term. For almost 40 years, the Israeli paper industry had enjoyed a monopoly of paper supply and price setting, and all of its products had a guaranteed market in Israel. The government's decision to remove protective customs barriers and open up the Israeli market to products from overseas served as a catalyst in exploring ways to improve key processes. These circumstances also led to the decision to investigate potential markets overseas. Adopting innovative management systems and attaining the ISO-9002 certification were established as the paths to growth and success. The process that was chosen by the corporation entailed a gradual process with two sequential phases: first, develop a Quality Circle (QC) Program within each of its four divisions; second, implement a Total Quality Management Program. Furthermore, in the first phase, the Paper and Board Division was the only division chosen to carry out the experiment.

The Paper and Board Division

Background

The Paper and Board Manufacturing Division includes three plants for manufacturing paper (white paper, brown paper, and household paper) and three support and service units (engineering, projects, and administrative). The number of employees in the Division is 800, and it is the largest among the Corporation's units.

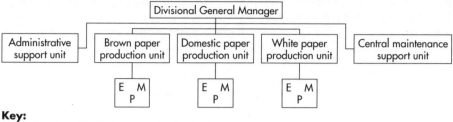

Key:
E = Engineering, M = Maintenance, P = Production

Figure 6.1 The Paper Mill and Carton Division: the new structure

Strategic reasoning

The Paper and Board Division's business strategy is derived from the targets set by the Corporation's management, and stresses several elements: the centrality of the customer in organizational perception, which mean viewing product quality as the highest value; introducing an approach and habits for continuous improvement; involving workers in the developing of advanced processes and innovative technologies; widespread implementation of team-work; creating channels of communication at all levels and in all directions; and the management commitment to achieve these aims, and to adopt and lead the required changes.

The initiative for entering the program was led by the Divisional General Manager. The first task was to create a divisional structure that would be more conducive to learning and continuous improvements. Following a study of altern-ative design configurations, a design that is based on three semi-autonomous business units, each based on three different production processes, was adopted and implemented. Among many advantages, this design was based on the pro-duction processes; provided clearer focus on processes, products, and services; and allowed for better integration between the support and staff departments and the production plants – see figure 6.1.

Business idea and the learning strategy

Following the division's redesign, the General Manager wanted to implement the basic principles he had set as part of the company policy. He chose to rely on an approach that would facilitate the development of quality improvement, achieve continuous improvement, and generate worker involvement as indi-viduals and as teams. Starting with the development of a QC program was perceived as a safe first step that would be likely to yield the targets set by Corporate and set in motion a developmental orientation. In particular, changes can be brought about in organizational culture, fostering teamwork and the provision of tools for managers and workers, with whose assistance the quality level of products would be improved. The risk of introducing QC is relatively lower and the required investments for its implementation are also low. A Quality Circle Structural Configuration was established to house and guide the change effort. By the end of 1988, nine Quality Circles operated in the Paper & Board Division, and by the end of 1995 the program encompassed 51 Quality Circles, involving 665 workers who were approximately 88 percent of all workers in the Paper Mills. The success of the QC program earned the Division the first prize in 1991 as an organization excelling in the implementation of Quality Circles in Israel. The Quality Circles provided the infrastructure for the TQM effort that follows.

A system-wide TQM program was launched during 1992. The program was set to accomplish the following objectives: supply products and services which would answer customer demands and expectations; every worker must accept and receive full responsibility for his or her part in executing the work process; everyone is responsible for quality; the company will choose suppliers who meet and conform to the quality policy and requirements; the management and the workers, as one, lead the company to work quality improvement and to fulfilling the aims and targets set in its policy; the Quality Assurance Procedure is prepared according to the ISO-9002 principles and the Corporation's quality policy.

The vision of the quality program is that of a long-term program that results in cumulative and continuous improvements. Accordingly, the program's implementation is gradual and its stages are constructed layer on layer. Successful existing activities and mechanisms that have already been implemented aid in widening and deepening the program. Table 6.1 summarizes the process of introducing the quality program, and indicates the stages of its development.

The realization of learning

The integration of quality in the Division's business strategy, coupled with management commitment to a continuous quality program, resulted in the creation of a Parallel Learning Structure Mechanism (Mitki, Shani, and Meiri, 1997; Shani and Mitki, 2000). This mechanism was chartered with the responsibility for developing and implementing the continuous improvement program. Its main functions were to translate the strategic quality targets into operative programs and to lead and guide its implementation. The Parallel Learning Structure Mechanism was in charge of determining the tools, methods, systems, and the rate of the program's implementation. This body was also responsible for the development of the essential learning processes, evaluation, and feedback. The Parallel Learning Structural Mechanism included a central steering committee, a central quality steering committee, and seven clusters of different learning teams. The Central Steering Committee was headed by the Divisional General Manager, and its participants were all the unit managers in

Table 6.1 An overview of the organization learning process

I. Context	
A. Business Situation	Dynamic business environment; Increased competition; Cancellation of protective customs on imports.
B. Business Strategy	Maintaining market share; Achieving the European standard in quality and price (attaining ISO-9002); Identify market niches for export in the European market.
II. The Nature of the Quality Program	
A. Vision	Improvement of effectiveness. Developing a quality system while modifying the organizational culture in order to maintain competitiveness.
B. Orientation	System-wide Continuous Improvement Program; QC. Team-based organization.
C. Key Events and Activities	
1987	Managerial decision to enter the quality program; QC as first stage. Workshops on Quality Circles for managers and setting up steering committees. Building Quality Circle structural support configuration. Implementing two experimental Quality Circles.
1988	First course in organization for Quality Circle leaders/facilitator. Implementing 9 Quality Circles.
1989	Increasing number of Circles to 14. Organizational survey for evaluating results of quality program.
1990	Publishing a Manual for Quality Circle leaders/facilitator. Crystallization of strategy, structural support configuration, & quality policy.
1991	Activating quality leaders/facilitator forum. Number of quality circles increased to 30. Fifth course for QC leaders/facilitator. Plant management decides to implement Total Quality Management Program.
1992	Establishing mechanism for implementing the TQM program. Plant gains Quality Award of Israel Quality Association. Two Process Improvement Teams begin their activity.
1993	Seven Process Improvement Teams active in plant. Forty-two Quality Circles involving 600 participants employees (80% of all employees). Eighth course for Quality Circle leaders.
1994	Five Process Improvement Teams active in plant. Forty-five Quality Circles involving 620 participants. Completion of 10th course for QC leaders/facilitator. Six pilot "Internal Customer–Client Improvement Teams" were formed. Eight "Lost Time Analysis Teams" were formed. Twelve "Cost Cutting Teams" were formed. Attaining the ISO 9002 Certification.
1995	Process Improvement Teams, Internal Customer-Client Improvement Teams, Lost Time Analysis Teams and Cost Cuttings Teams continued their activities. Fifty-one Quality Circles are at work. System-wide diffusion of new methods, skills, and work behavior that were gained through the different team-based structure learning. Increased teams' autonomy in the identification of tasks, problem-solving, and implementation of changes.

Table 6.1   continued

1996	Reduction of the number of Quality Circles due to the feeling that they had been exhausted. The General Manager introduces the concept of autonomic work groups to the board, with the aim of increasing worker cooperation in the production units.
1997	All learning process groups are turned into improvement groups. No more Quality Circles, but their theoretical basis is well instilled and is expressed in current performance. Further implementation of manager development and worker promotion programs.
1998	External strategic partners join Paper Mills, and as a result: structural change in the paper division. The paper division is split into seven independent units, which act as profit centers. As a result of the organizational change, the central structural mechanism of organizational learning disintegrates. The responsibility for organizational learning is passed on to heads of the independent divisions The central program of manager development is terminated.
1999	Each division establishes a mechanism of organizational learning, which is based on preservation of the value of quality and process improvement. The divisions rewrite quality procedures, as required by their areas of performance and customers' demands.
2000	Some divisions establish improvement teams, and there are internal training programs.
III. The Learning Mechanisms A. Goals	To translate the strategic quality targets to an operative program. To provide the structural support and the linking spines between the different continuous improvement initiatives. To set the broad continuous improvement policies and to determine devices, systems, and rate for executing the program. To develop evaluation, feedback and learning mechanisms.
B. The Structural Configuration 1. Key Elements:	The supplemental structure responsible for continuous improvement organizational learning includes: Central Steering Committee; Central Quality Steering Committee; Process Improvement Teams; Quality Circles; Statistical Process Control Teams; Internal Customer–Client Improvement Teams; Lost Time Analysis Teams; Communication Improvement Teams; Cost Cutting Teams.
2. Key Characteristics:	Formalization High Centralization Moderate Flexibility Moderate Integration High
C. Involvement of Customers and Suppliers	High involvement of internal organizational customers and suppliers. Low involvement of external organizational customers and suppliers.
D. Training E. Rewards	Multi-level learning programs. No direct monetary rewards for participation. Certificates of Merit, managerial.

the Division and five members of the TQM Authority. The committee convened once every two or three weeks in order to refine vision and general strategy, establish broad procedures, and review progress. The committee did not interfere in internal departmental topics chosen for handling by Quality Teams. It decided, at this stage, on inter-departmental or overall divisional processes needing improvement, appointed Process Improvement Teams, and discussed and reviewed recommendations presented by the teams.

The Central Quality Steering Committee was responsible for the ongoing daily operation of the quality program both on the logistic and professional side. This body was composed of the Administrative Unit Head and four members, each of whom is in charge of one of the operative fields of the quality program: QA (Quality Assurance), TQM, training, and finances. The central quality steering committee convened at least once a week. The learning mechanism also included seven clusters of different learning teams that reported to the central quality steering committee: the Quality Circles (QCs), the Process Improvement Teams (PITs), the Internal Customer–Client Improvement Teams (ICCITs), Communication Improvement Teams (CITs), Lost Time Analysis Teams (LTAs), Statistical Process Control teams (SPCs), and Cost Cutting Teams (CCTs). The Process Improvement Teams were composed of 4–7 members, from different units in the Division, and they functioned as an ad hoc team to address a specific topic.

The structural mechanism and its dynamics with the formal organizational system influenced its ability to achieve its aims in an effective manner. Knowing the structural characteristics of the quality program permits understanding of the internal dynamics of its operation, and also permits making a comparison between it and other programs (see, for example, Shani and Rogberg, 1994). One characteristic is the degree of formalization of the program, which is expressed in the extent to which processes and procedures upon which the activity is performed in the organization is carried out (Damanpour, 1991). The level of program formalization in the Paper Mills is high (see table 6.1.) The procedures and courses of action are clear and fixed, use of tools and methods is defined, the framework for convening is given in advance, and the communication and information sharing mechanisms (including summaries of discussions and post-performance follow-up) are permanent and predictable.

A secondary characteristic, the degree of program centralization, refers to the measure of authority and autonomy for making decisions given to the various units (Thompson, 1967). The level of centrality in the Paper Mills is moderate. The Quality Teams are given autonomy in everything related to process improvement and work efficiency proposals in the organic departments. Ninety-five percent of the decisions taken in QC are also implemented. But in inter-departmental or plant-wide processes, the decisions are taken by the Central Steering Committee. Process Improvement Teams and the Central Quality Steering Committee's power in these areas are relatively limited.

A third characteristic is the degree of program flexibility, which allows the program to adapt itself to new needs arising from internal and/or external changes. The flexibility level in the Paper Mills is moderate. The training setup in the organization is based on a perennial, annual, and monthly program and almost all the programs are planned, scheduled, and budgeted. The various units in the organization are planned in advance in order to release managers and/or workers for training. Organizational activity of this type reduces the scope for flexibility. At the same time, there is great flexibility for Quality Circles and Steering Committees to choose topics needing improvement. The selected processes can be adapted to varying states of reality.

The fourth characteristic is the program's degree of program integration. This dimension measures the coordination and mutual nourishment performed between all the factors participating in it (Lawrence and Lorsh, 1967). There is a high degree of integration in operating the program in the Paper Mills. The program is an integral part of the business strategy; it is clearly articulated; control and reporting mechanisms are in place; and the Steering Committee, which oversees this program, includes all the unit managers. Furthermore, the program is coordinated by the Central Quality Steering Committee (CQSC) and meets regularly to coordinate and review working processes. Members of the CQSC are also a part of the Central Steering Committee. Another factor that contributes to integration is the permanent updating received by workers of all levels via periodic meetings with managers, and via ongoing information sharing about every phase of the program.

Some reported outcomes

The twelve-year follow-up study at the Paper Mill indicates the impressive results that were achieved, both in performance measures, in developing processes, and in attitudinal-based measures.

Performance measures

Work hours required for producing a ton of paper were reduced over recent years by more than 60 percent, from 16 hours in 1988 to 8.2 work hours per ton in 1999. Furthermore, the average output of the four major paper production machines was raised between the years 1991 and 1999 by 14.9 percent. Figure 6.2 illustrates the reduction of work hours and the increase of output in machine no. 4, which is the main production machine at the site.

The **water consumption** for manufacturing a ton of paper went down by 47.3 percent without damaging the production process or the paper quality. Water conservation is a national target in Israel.

Electrical consumption in the manufacturing process is supplied from two sources: transmission line electricity and self-produced electricity. The self-produced electricity is cheaper by more than two-thirds than the linear form (linear electricity costing 1.5 kW/h). As a result of the improvements initiated

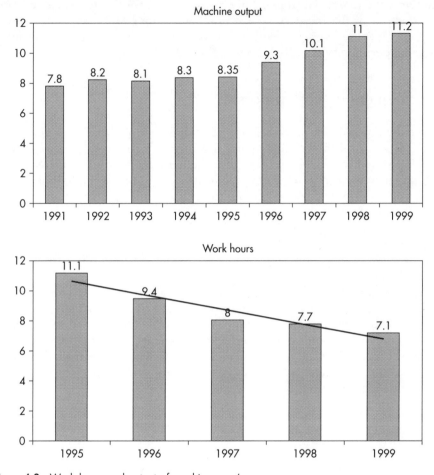

Figure 6.2 Work hours and output of machine no. 4

by the quality improvement efforts, a decrease occurred at a rate of 9.9 percent of linear electricity and there was an increase of 34 percent in self-produced electricity. The savings gained by the Corporation as a result of the above are $830,000 per annum.

The raw material for paper manufacturing is based on fibers arriving from two sources: cellulose imported from overseas, and waste collected in Israel. The Corporation's objective was to reduce the use of cellulose as much as possible, and to increase the use of waste. The improvements suggested by the Process Improvement Teams resulted in a decrease of 9 percent from 1991 to 1998 of the percentage use of cellulose fibers for paper manufacture, and the percentage use of recycled fiber consumption rose by almost 6 percent.

In the paper production industry, quality of products is measured by **defect ratio** per 10,000 sheets of paper. For example, the defect ratios in machine number 4 were reduced from 6.2 in 1991 to 2.2 in 1999. **Customer satisfaction** is measured in the industry by the number of complaints per month. From 1991 to 1998 the average number of complaints was reduced significantly; from 8.8 per month in 1991 to 2.6 in 1995 and 1.7 in 1998.

Improvement in work processes

Improvement in work processes is a key ingredient of a quality program. At PMC, as a part of the continuous improvement effort, several processes were developed and improved, in order to make work more efficient, increase saving, and increase profits. One example is developing the de-inking (ink extraction) process. This process of treating paper waste and recycling it permits the exploitation of many elements of waste cleaning for paper manufacture. Waste can be used in this manner instead of cellulose, a way that saves the Division and the state the expense of foreign currency. Similarly, inherent in this is a contribution to environmental quality by preventing pollution from refuse which is not recycled.

A second example is developing an entire setup of water recycling that includes instrumentation for cleaning water and fiber extraction (which are reused), and extracting dirt and various pollutants. The recycled water serves for the operation of some of the production machines, mainly those that manufacture boards. Water recycling lowers the cost of water consumed, minimizes the Division's dependence on fresh water supply, and reduces the amount of water flowing out into industrial waste.

Improvement in work behavior

One of the measures for testing the implications of the change program is absenteeism. Even though presence at work can be explained by many factors, the assumption of the learning mechanism designers at the Paper Mills was that the core processes would influence worker satisfaction and attendance. The average rate of **absenteeism** by workers in 1988 was 18 percent, 15 percent in 1992, 10.2 percent in 1995, and in 1998 it had decreased to 8.9 percent. The cumulative rate of **lost workdays** stemming from absenteeism, work accidents, and illnesses went down by 50 percent between 1988 and 1998. Finally, in 1990 there were 83 **work-related accidents**. Following a gradual drop, 37 accidents were reported in 1999, as can be seen in table 6.2.

▶ Reflections and Lessons

Organizational learning centered on the development of key processes, as implemented at the PMC, is one strategy that can serve management when

Table 6.2 Number of accidents with absenteeism of at least one day in the years 1990–9

Year	Number of accidents with absenteeism of at least one day	Total days of absenteeism
1990	83	1442
1991	76	1215
1992	66	976
1993	70	1232
1994	73	1243
1995	64	1245
1996	58	1209
1997	48	934
1998	43	595
1999	37	798

it wishes to achieve business sustainability, learning, and competitiveness in an increasingly competitive market. The design of an organizational learning system around the development of key processes raises a number of challenges. In the discussion that follows we address the relationship between business strategy and organizational learning around development processes such as quality continuous improvement and employee involvement, the dynamic interplay between sustainable learning mechanisms, development processes, and organization design, the relationship between organizational learning mechanisms, and the facilitation of organizational performance and business sustainability.

Business strategy, learning, and development of key processes

The PMC case illustrated a high degree of compatibility between the Corporation, the Division, and the single plant's strategic goals and learning goals. The focus on the development of key processes of quality, continuous improvement, and workers' involvement as an integral component of the corporate strategy was developed and articulated in the specific learning strategy document. This shared authorship of documents at different levels of the firm fosters the shared vision and priorities throughout the organization and its multiple units (Garvin, 2000). The congruency between the business strategy documents and the three developmental processes' emphasis within them both sets the stage and provides the legitimacy for managerial and organizational activities that focus on the creation of learning mechanisms for the purpose of enhancing the development of the key business processes. This legitimacy allowed for exploration and experimentation with the design of alternative learning mechanisms.

At the foundation of the effort was the willingness to map out the basic organizational routines around the processes that emerged over time and the systematic and critical examination of them. The systematic reflective activities and actions that were taken led to the increase of organizational capability to improve practices. The continuous search for design alternatives (design dimensions) and making specific choices of the most appropriate learning and action vehicles facilitated organizational learning and helped in the continuous refinement of congruency between the business strategy, competitiveness, and sustainability.

The learning mechanisms around development key processes and organization design

The PMC created unique learning mechanisms around the development of three key processes – quality, continuous improvement, and workers' involvement and teamwork – which are connected and influenced by one another. The mechanisms served as an impetus for continuous improvement. Structures and processes were established to facilitate knowledge and concepts acquisition, competency and skill development, and tools attainment. Processes that link the different learning teams were established to foster system-wide learning synergy.

The change process that was established during the Quality Circle Improvement Project – of stepwise and gradual experimentation, careful review and learning from each step, appropriate modification – follows the basic experiential learning model. Continuous improvement – at the most basic level – is anchored in the experiential learning model (i.e., Kolb, 1984). An organization can improve continuously to the extent that it establishes the mechanisms that guide the process of learning through the spiral of active experimentation, reflections, generalizations, and corrective action.

One of the distinct characteristics of learning systems is the uniqueness of each learning mechanism. The learning mechanisms that evolved in the PMC developed distinct features. The organizational context coupled with the organizational culture and structural configuration sets the stage for the dynamics of most improvement efforts – and as such are likely to shape the nature of learning systems (Ledford, Lawler and Mohrman, 1988; Schein, 1993, 2002). At the PMC, the learning mechanism emerged as a result of the learning requirements that have set the stage for specific learning design dimensions and the specific choices that were made about which one to implement in order to facilitate the accomplishment of the specific business objectives. Table 6.3 provides a synopsis and an illustration of some of the learning design requirements, learning design dimensions, and learning mechanisms that were developed at the PMC.

Our study points towards some common features that seem to foster learning by design. First, certain degrees of learning mechanisms' structuration

Table 6.3 Improving key development processes at the Paper Mill Corporation: a synopsis and a few illustrations

Improving key development processes' learning requirements	Learning design dimensions (different possible ways to respond to the learning requirements)	Learning mechanisms
Commitment to the development and utilization of human capital and the continuous improvement of individuals and work processes as an integral part of ordinary work	* Mapping individual skills and knowledge * On-the-job training * Multiskilling * Union–management cooperative agreement and joint activities	* Formal and informal ongoing dialogue between managers and employees about development and improvement processes * Formalized developmental goal setting and progress review processes * Involving large portion of employees in business development activities
A legitimate forum for the exchange of ideas must be created	* Representation of all functions and business areas * Clarity of purpose * Flexibility around emerging projects * Shared views on the relationships between the formal organization and the emerging exchange forum and on the procedures of work	* Creating parallel learning structure with steering committees and many study/project teams organized to focus on the improvement of the key business processes * Periodic review of progress both within the parallel learning structure and the formal organization top management
The design and development of improvement processes must fit the totality of the organization (not just parts) and the business strategic directions and goals	* Shared vision * Partnership with union * Experimentation climate and willingness to take risks	Dual management role in the formal management hierarchy and parallel learning structure (linking pins)

seem to exist. As can be seen in table 6.1, the learning mechanisms at the Paper Mill Company can be characterized by a high degree of formalization, a moderate degree of centralization, a moderate degree of flexibility, and a high degree of integration. Second, the dynamic interplay between the four dimensions of learning mechanisms' structuration seems to vary from company to company and might play a crucial role in the success of the development of continuous improvement effort (Lillrank and Kano, 1989). Generally speaking, some distinct company features and culture – such as size, technology, management philosophy, maturity, experience, structure, strategy, norms – are likely to set the stage for the specific learning design requirements that are likely to influence the startup and evolution of the effort.

Third, the structural inertia of the company does not always welcome the introduction of a development process around quality, continuous improvement, and worker participation efforts (Cole, Bacdayan, and White, 1993). Some reports indicate that one of the major roadblocks in continuous improvement implementation is the existing organizational structure (Krishnan et al., 1993). Furthermore, CEOs report that finding a way to bypass the current structure (structural inertia) may be one of the biggest challenges they face (Easton, 1993). As we have seen in the PMC case, the creation of the learning mechanisms around the development of key processes provided the structural mechanism that overcame these potential roadblocks.

Fourth, the basic philosophy of the learning process that seems to guide most of the learning mechanisms encompasses a framework, concepts, and tools that are interrelated. In addition, the learning process is composed of clear goals, a set of phases and activities, and a never-ending learning process. Multiple levels of learning – individual, team, inter-unit, and organizational – take place simultaneously and learning is anchored in solving business-related problems both at the micro and macro levels. The organization provides the tools, time, and space for learning to occur, and at the same time an integral part of the learning process is continuous evaluation and feedback.

Organizational learning mechanism, performance and sustainability

The recent literature in organizational sciences advocates the relationships between organizational learning and organizational performance and productivity (i.e., Garvin, 2000; Ingelgård et al., 2002; Lipshitz, Popper, and Oz, 1996; Marquardt, 1996). Yet, the actual development and design of organizational learning mechanisms, structures, and processes seem to be a major challenge. While some organizations have managed to foster organizational learning by using existing processes and structures, others have created supplementary structural mechanisms and processes (Shani and Stjernberg, 1995; Friedman, Lipshitz, and Overmeer, 2001). Regardless of the mechanisms, the cause-and-effect relationship between organizational learning and organizational results is documented in the literature mostly in an anecdotal fashion. As we can see in the PMC case, the learning in and around the development of key processes significantly improved the business results and changed human behavior at work.

Furthermore, the PMC case illustrated a clear set of design choices that were made by management, namely, building upon a structure and processes that were developed for the purpose of the Quality Improvement Program and expanding it towards a new structure and processes that would serve as the foundation and engine for the development of other key processes. The transition from the one set of learning mechanisms to others was smooth and easily accepted. The positive experience with the mechanism that was developed for the QIP helped set in motion positive expectations. This design choice was possible first and foremost because the learning was designed a priori around a core process that did not change with time. The choice of these processes was successful for two reasons. First, the processes that had been chosen aimed to serve a clear business objective. Second, there was a natural connection between the development of key processes: quality, continuous improvement, and workers' involvement.

The very nature of organizational learning is a reflective process of inquiry in which organizational members develop shared meaning and generate action based on past experience and knowledge. At the core of sustainable work systems one can find the capability to continuously generate and develop resources, improving the quality of working life and competitive performance, and achieving the critical balance between competing stakeholders (Docherty, Forslin, and Shani, 2002). In the PMC case the systematic nature of the reflective inquiry process that occurred throughout the learning mechanisms activities, coupled with the organizational learning mechanisms that were developed, seems to enhance the company's sustainability and overall competitive performance.

Implications and Conclusion

The increasing levels of environmental and business complexity seem to dictate new business strategies, whose implementations require innovative organiza tional structures and management systems. One way to deal with the challenges derived from complex, dynamic, and uncertain environments is to design for business sustainability. The PMC case is an example of how an organization that decided to focus its learning efforts around the development of three intertwined central processes, quality, continuous improvement, and worker involvement, managed to transform itself and create a sustainable and competitive organization. Table 6.4 provides a snapshot reflective summary for managerial action.

The creation of learning mechanisms with specific features, structures, and processes was the result of design choices among few alternatives. The learning

Table 6.4 Sustainability and competitiveness of improving key development processes: managerial implications

- Learning around the improvement and development of key processes must be an integral part of overall business strategy.
- Designing the organizational learning mechanisms around development of key processes is likely to enhance sustainability and competitiveness.
- The design of the organizational learning mechanisms must complement the design of the organization.
- The design of the organizational learning mechanisms needs to follow a reflective exploration of different design options in terms of structure, processes, and procedural arrangements that will allow the organization to accomplish its long-term objectives.
- Reflective inquiry – an integral component of learning – around development of key processes is likely to enhance organizational capabilities and sustainability.

mechanism has housed, led, and provided the focal point for the effort since 1987. In the area of quality, the learning mechanism created a context in which there was internalization of the value of quality and understanding of its importance to customers, workers, and the company as a whole. A new culture was created, part of which is that all members of the organization understood that, before prices and delivery dates, the element of quality existed. The customer expects to receive a quality product, and his or her claims or expectations are legitimate. As a result, the barriers between producer and client are removed, which is manifested by constant contact between the production floor and the customers, problems are dealt with on site, and processes and products improve. Production teams learn from their own and others' mistakes, and there is no fear to admit to failure. The workers submit truthful reports, and the customers feel that the products they receive are as good as those manufactured in other European countries.

In the area of continuous improvement, the learning mechanisms instilled in the organization members the awareness that continuous improvement is not just a symbol or slogan, but an essential ingredient of the company's continued existence. The workers identified the connection between improvement as a way of life and their remaining with the organization for an extensive period. Continuous improvement and development of performance are perceived as an incentive to economic success and occupational security.

In the area of worker involvement, the learning mechanisms generated widespread cooperation of workers on all levels and promoted teamwork (see Edmonson, Bohmer, and Pisano, 2001, 2002). The Quality Circles, which were active for almost ten years, significantly changed the work environment. The workers determined work procedures and methods, changed the internal departmental organization, and also influenced their way of life and health. The quality teams improved work and production processes and influenced contacts with the internal and external environment. Workers' involvement, which started with work teams, widened and increased to multidisciplinary or inter-departmental teams. The former teams determined the area of improvement for themselves, collected data, examined alternatives, reached decisions about solutions, and executed them. The latter teams were appointed by management or by the Quality Council, who also determined the issues for them. Their job was to examine the issue and suggest alternative solutions, but they were not directly responsible for its implementation. Improvement teams made it possible to deal with issues that had a bearing on the total organization or at least considerable parts of it.

Learning mechanisms that focus on the development of key processes seem to help organizations achieve internal changes that result in timely responses to changing external environments. Furthermore, they seem to foster an organization's continuous improvement culture. Our study of the Paper Mill Company illustrated that the learning mechanisms created the time and space and provided the tools to develop alternative patterns of work behavior, fostered the development of new structures and processes to address and resolve quality issues, and significantly altered the company's culture and performance.

The increasing pressure for quality, continuous improvement, and teamwork is seen by some as key components of business survival in this decade. While many frameworks, concepts, tools, change processes, and gurus can be found, what seems to be lacking is the actual mechanisms that have the potential to make the mentioned concepts an integral part of organizational life. This chapter illustrates that learning mechanisms might be the vital engine needed for the development, sustainability, and competitive performance of the firm. Chapter 7 explores the crucial processes of knowledge management and the learning mechanisms that can enhance and maintain such processes.

References

Andreu, R. and Ciborra, C. (1996). Core capabilities and information technology: An organizational learning approach. In B. Moingeon and A. Edmonson (eds), *Organizational Learning and Competitive Advantage*. Thousand Oaks, CA: Sage Publications, pp. 121–38.

Argyris, C. and Schön, D. A. (1978). *Organizational Learning: A Theory of Action Perspective*. Reading, MA: Addison-Wesley.

Cherns, A. B. (1976). The principles of sociotechnical design. *Human Relations*, 29, 783–92.

Cole, R. E., Bacdayan, P., and White, B. J. (1993). Quality, participation, and competitiveness. *California Management Review*, 35(3), 68–81.

Damanpour, F. (1991). Organizational innovation: A meta analysis of effects of determinants and moderators. *Academy of Management Journal*, 34(3), 555–90.

Docherty, P., Forslin, J., and Shani, A. B. (Rami) (eds) (2002). *Creating Sustainable Work Systems: Emerging Perspectives and Practice*. London: Routledge.

Easton, G. S. (1993). A Baldrige examiner's view of U.S. Total Quality Management. *California Management Review*, 35(3), 32–54.

Edmonson, A., Bohmer, R., and Pisano, G. (2001). Speeding up team learning. *Harvard Business Review*, 79(9), 125–33.

Edmonson, A., Bohmer, R., and Pisano, G. (2002). Disrupting routines: Team learning and new technology implementation in hospitals. *Administrative Science Quarterly*, 46(4), pp. 685–718.

Friedman, V., Lipshitz, R., and Overmeer, W. (2001). Creating conditions for organizational learning. In A. B. Antal, M. Dierkes, J. Child, and I. Nonaka (eds), *Handbook of Organizational Learning and Knowledge*. New York: Oxford University Press, pp. 757–74.

Garvin, D. A. (2000). *Learning in Action*. Boston, MA: Harvard Business School Press.

Imai, M. (1986). *Kaizan*. New York: Random House.

Ingelgård, A., Roth, J., Shani, A. B. (Rami), and Styhre, A. (2002). Dynamic learning capability and actionable knowledge creation: Clinical R&D in a pharmaceutical company. *The Learning Organization*, 9(2), 65–77.

Kolb, D. A. (1984). *Experiential Learning*. Englewood Cliffs, NJ: Prentice-Hall.

Krishnan, R., Shani, A. B. (Rami), Grant, R., and Baer, R. (1993). The search for quality improvements: Problems of design and implementation. *Academy of Management Executive*, 7(4), 7–20.

Lawrence, P. R. and Lorsch, J. W. (1967). *Organization & Environment*. Boston, MA: Harvard Press.

Ledford, G. E., Lawler, E. E., and Mohrman, S. A. (1988). The quality circle and its variations. In J. P. Campbell and R. J. Campbell (eds), *Productivity in Organizations: New Perspectives from Industrial and Organizational Psychology*. San Francisco: Jossey-Bass, pp. 255–94.

Lillrank, P. and Kano, N. (1989). *Continuous Improvement*. Ann Arbor, MI: The University of Michigan Press.

Lillrank, P., Shani, A. B. (Rami), Kolodny, H., Stymne, B., Figuera, J. R., and Liu, M. (1998). Learning from the success of continuous improvement change programs: An international comparative study. In W. Pasmore and R. Woodman (eds), *Research in Organizational Change and development*. JAI Press Inc., pp. 47–71.

Lillrank, P., Shani, A. B. (Rami), and Lindberg, P. (2001). Continuous improvement: Exploring alternative organizational designs. *Total Quality Management*, 12(1), 41–55.

Lipshitz, R., Popper, M., and Oz, S. (1996). Building learning organization: The design and implementation of organizational learning mechanisms. *Journal of Applied Behavioral Science*, 32(3), 292–305.

Marquardt, M. (1996). *Building the Learning Organization*. New York: McGraw-Hill.

Mitki, Y., Shani, A. B. (Rami), and Meiri, Z. (1997). Organizational learning mechanisms and continuous improvement: A longitudinal study. *Journal of Organizational Change Management*, 10(5), 426–46.

Schein, E. H. (1993). On dialogue, culture, and organizational learning. *Organizational Dynamics*, 22(2), 40–51.

Schein, E. H. (2002). The anxiety of learning. *Harvard Business Review*, 80(3), 100–6.

Shani, A. B. and Mitki, Y. (2000). Creating the learning organization: Beyond mechanisms. In R. T. Golembiewski (ed.), *Handbook of Organizational Consultation*. Marcel Dekker, Inc., Ch. 117, pp. 911–20.

Shani, A. B. (Rami) and Rogberg, M. (1994). Quality, strategy, and structural configuration. *Journal of Organizational Change Management*, 7(2), 15–30.

Shani, A. B. (Rami) and Stjernberg, T. (1995). The integration of change in organizations: Alternative learning and transformation mechanisms. In W. A. Pasmore and R. W. Woodman (eds), *Research in Organizational Change and Development*, vol. 8. Greenwich, CT: JAI Press, pp. 77–121.

Thompson, J. D. (1967). *Organization in Action*. New York: McGraw-Hill.

Knowledge Management Processes and Learning[1]

- What are some of the characteristics of learning in the knowledge-based work environment?

- What is the role that learning mechanisms play in the firm's ability to continuously improve the ways it creates, transfers, exploits, and manages knowledge?

- What learning mechanisms are necessary to sustain learning and competitiveness in knowledge-based organizations?

The topics of knowledge management, organizational knowledge, and organizational learning have received much attention from different disciplines during the past decade. The increased level of interest in these topic areas reflects the transition from the industrial era to the knowledge era (Sanchez and Heene, 2000). This new focus, also referred to as the "knowledge revolution," is characterized by the realization that knowledge is the principal asset of the corporation that needs to be developed, created, nurtured, protected, managed, and exploited as a competitive advantage of the firm (i.e., Nonaka, Toyama, and Byosière, 2001; Quinn, 1992).

Furthermore, some argue that knowledge has become the only meaningful resource in business (Drucker, 1993). Managing organizational knowledge

[1] The first draft of this case was contributed by Professor James Sena. The chapter was developed in collaboration with Jim. We are grateful to Professor Sena for his contribution.

creation is a critical organizational competency (Grant, 1999). Despite all the growing interest and attention given to organizational knowledge, our understanding of how organizations create knowledge, how knowledge is being managed, and what are some of the most critical elements of knowledge management processes is limited (Liebowitz, 1999; Sena and Shani, 1999). Recently the argument that knowledge gets created, accumulated, and managed through organizational learning processes was advanced (Grant, 1999; Shani and Sena, 2002). Thus, this chapter focuses on knowledge management processes and supplements the previous chapter (chapter 6) which focused on development processes in the firm. In the two sections that follow we explore the possible relationships between knowledge management processes, organizational learning processes, and organizational learning mechanisms.

▶ Knowledge Management Processes and Organizational Learning

Notions about the dynamic nature of the relationship between knowledge management processes and organizational learning have a relatively short tradition in organizational sciences (Ingelgård et al., 2002; Schulz, 2001). The emerging challenge to organizations and management is the understanding of the nature of knowledge management processes. Specifically, what are the processes that facilitate knowledge creation, knowledge production, and knowledge transfer within and between teams and sub-units. Before we proceed any further, we need first to define knowledge management and then to examine and map out the current body of knowledge about knowledge management processes in organizations.

Recently, in a survey of the literature on knowledge management, Beckman (1999) conceptualized the published studies into six clusters: conceptual, process, technology, organizational, management, and implementation. This chapter focuses on knowledge management processes. Thus, for the purpose of this chapter we define knowledge management as an emergent process in which bits and pieces of information are integrated, within and outside the organizational boundaries, to produce new knowledge that is simultaneously usable and generalizable. The purpose of knowledge management processes is to enhance the firm's performance by explicitly designing and implementing tools, processes, systems, structures, and culture to improve the creation, acquisition, application, and exploitation of knowledge essential for present and future competitive success. Thus, in order to transform knowledge into a valuable organizational asset, knowledge, experience, and expertise need to be formalized, distributed, shared, and applied (Reinhardt et al., 2001).

Few guiding models for the knowledge management process can be found in the literature. All the models seem to be based on a few phases or steps and activities that are often concurrent and are not always in a linear process. For example, Marquardt (1996) identified four steps: acquisition, creation, transfer and utilization, and storage. Holsapple and Joshi's (1997) model consisted of six steps: acquiring knowledge, selecting knowledge, internalizing knowledge, using knowledge, generating knowledge, and externalizing knowledge. Ruggels (1997) suggested a three-step model: generation (creation, acquisition, synthesis, fusion, and adaptation), codification, and transfer.

Beckman (1997) proposed an eight-stage process for knowledge management: identify – determine core competencies, sourcing strategy, and knowledge domains; capture – formalize existing knowledge; select – assess knowledge relevance, value, and accuracy; store – represent corporate memory in knowledge repository with various knowledge schema; share – distribute knowledge automatically to users based on interest and work; apply – retrieve and use knowledge in making decisions, solving problems, automating or supporting work, job aids, and training; create – discover new knowledge through research, experimenting, and creative thinking; and develop, market, and sell new knowledge-based products and services.

Finally, Dixon (2000), focusing on the knowledge transfer process, identified a nine-step model: select a unit that has an interest in knowledge-sharing, establish a steering committee, conduct a knowledge assessment, establish the framework for knowledge transfer, identify the organizational goal and corresponding knowledge component, identify the appropriate transfer process for each type of knowledge, locate current informal systems that can be enhanced, identify resources, and develop an integrated system for knowledge transfer.

At the very foundation of all the knowledge management process models, conceptualizations, and implementation practices briefly described above is an organizational learning cycle and process orientation. Yet, careful review of the different models reveals that only a few of the authors seem to acknowledge this fact or focus on organizational learning processes that facilitate knowledge management processes (Antal et al., 2001; Matthews and Candy, 1999; Sena and Shani, 1999). In the context of the knowledge management process, organizational learning refers to the ability of the system as a whole to continuously improve the way it creates, manages, transfers, and exploits the organization's knowledge. Thus, focusing on the organization as a unit for learning, we argue that while individuals are important agents of learning, organizational structures and processes, rules, and standard operating procedures influence the organizational ability to manage learning and thus influence the knowledge management process.

Organizational Learning Mechanisms and Knowledge Management Processes

Information technology is critical to knowledge management processes because they deal with the conceptualization, review, consolidation, and action phases of creating, securing, combining, coordinating, and retrieving knowledge (Liebowitz, 1999). Furthermore, in the context of knowledge management processes, organizational learning theories within the information technology environment provide focus on a few aspects: what are some of the learning mechanisms that facilitate knowledge creation, the acquisition and sharing of knowledge, knowledge transfer within and between units, and the exploitation of knowledge.

In chapter 2 we defined organizational learning mechanisms as a formal configuration – structures, processes, procedures, rules, tools, methods, and physical configurations – created within the firm for the purpose of developing, enhancing, and sustaining performance and learning. Thus, in the context of the knowledge management process, organizational learning mechanisms refer to the formal configuration created within the firm for the purpose of continuously improving the way an organization creates, transfers, exploits, and manages knowledge. As will be seen in the case to follow, in the context of the intense information technology workplace, different learning mechanisms were developed within a software development firm (JRSD) around knowledge management processes.

▶ The Software Development Firm (JRSD)

In the late 1990s the limited computer-assistance capabilities reflective of decision support-based software [DSS] were being replaced by integrated, multi-agent, cooperative systems. These signaled the emergence of a new generation of DSS software in which the contributions of several components were coordinated through an inter-process communication facility. The components, commonly referred to as agents, are separate modules depicting one or more processes. They are rule-based expert systems, procedural programs, neural networks, or even sensing devices. They reflect learning on the part of the individual, the team, or the organization. Increasingly, these agents have the ability to explain their actions and proposals, as they interact spontaneously with each other either directly or through coordination facilities.

▶ Setting the Context

Software development is by its nature an intensive work situation due to cyclical development, pressure to reduce development time, a competitive global market, keeping abreast of ongoing technological innovations, and increasing personnel turnover rates. At the micro level there are pressures to get a product to market that may not be complete or that does not meet all of the specifications. Reusable code, modules, and agents are all assisting mechanisms.

Work intensity is viewed as a socially constructed phenomenon that is embedded in the increasing rate of change in the nature of software development. In this context, changes in the software development industry seem to occur at many levels: increasing rate of technological hardware development and new software products are being introduced into the marketplace; individuals are required to make a continuous effort to acquire new knowledge and skills; expectations and pressure to reduce development cycle times are increasing; individuals are pressured to integrate variety of knowledge bases into the process; and last, organizational members are pressured to integrate customers (and at times suppliers) into the process. Two major causes of work intensity are scope creep (unplanned changes to the scope of work as the product development progresses) and the actual delivery of the finished product to the customer (time-to-market). Another negative consequence of the increasing work intensity seems to center on the difficulty in retaining talented software development engineers and management information system specialists. As turnover increases, it is accompanied by a loss of knowledge and understanding of core processes. At the same time, as information technology becomes a critical success factor, especially within firms whose product is the actual development of a software product, loss of key personnel has a major impact.

Based on these characteristics, the development of software products can be categorized as an information-intensive activity that depends for its success largely on the availability of information resources and, in particular, the experience and reasoning skills of the managers and the staff's learning environment. It follows that the quality of the solutions will vary significantly as a function of the problem-solving skills, wisdom, knowledge, and development solution process. This clearly presents an opportunity for the useful employment of learning mechanisms in which the capabilities of the human decision maker are complemented with knowledge bases, expert agents, and self-activating conflict identification and monitoring capabilities.

Agent technologies, with respect to the software industry, are self-contained, intelligent, adaptive software modules that are used as building blocks to construct complex software products. Through the use of collaborating expert agents, product development provides the flexibility and range needed for product design sustainability. Heterogeneous, semi-autonomous knowledge-based software components are integrated into coordinated applications. Through the use of interoperability standards and methods, information can flow seamlessly through an application across heterogeneous machines, computing platforms, programming languages, and data and process representations (Lander, 1997).

In the broadest sense, an agent may be described as a computer-based program or module of a program that has communication capabilities to external entities and can perform some useful tasks in at least a semi-autonomous fashion. These aspects exhibit learned behavior. According to this definition, agent software can range from simple, stand-alone, predetermined applications to the most intelligent, integrated, multi-agent decision-support system that advanced technology can produce today.

The multi-agent software requires a high-level internal representation of the real-world objects and their relationships that are central to the problem situation. This is a prerequisite for the reasoning capabilities of the agents and also for the interaction of the user(s) with the system. The objective of multi-agent software is not to automate the decision-making activity, but to create an effective partnership between the human decision maker and the computer-based agents. In this partnership the human agent must be able to communicate with the computer-based agents in terms of the same real-world objects that are used so effectively in all human reasoning endeavors. In their role as active collaborators, the computer-based agents will have information needs that cannot be totally predetermined. Therefore, similar to the human agent, they require the capability to dynamically generate database queries and initiate user interactions. At least some of the information sources accessed by the agents will be prototypical in nature (i.e., standard practices, case studies, and other typical knowledge pertaining to the problem situation), consistent with the notion of knowledge-based systems.

This chapter discusses systems wherein software developers and computer-based agents assist each other in the exploration, analysis, and creation of software products in which there are many variables with complex relationships and dynamic information changes. The software firm under study, which we term JRSD, has developed a framework for generating computer-supported decision aids consisting of an overall architecture, an object model, an agent engine, and an object browser interface. Most of the applications developed were military-related.

The organization

JRSD is in the business of building, implementing, and supporting agent-based "cooperative decision-making" tools for distributed problem-solving. Application areas include facilities management, transportation planning, military logistics and control, and engineering design. JRSD began as a university-based research facility and evolved into a private R&D organization. JRSD's differentiating factor has been the development of an agent-based methodology to deal with spatial problems for organizing engineering design with respect to space management, space constraints, and storage priorities from an architectural perspective. Their approach used a series of agents to assist human decision-making.

Resource capabilities: expertise and longevity

JRSD describes their resources very succinctly – the expertise of their employees and longevity. They combine this expertise with a set of reusable code, software agents, a process called "extreme programming," and a small managerial set. With respect to longevity, most of the core team members have been together somewhere between four and seven years.

JRSD has created a generic set of agents designed to respond to changes in the problem state spontaneously, through their ability to monitor information changes and respond opportunistically. Information may be passed to them in some chronological order based on time-stamped events or predefined priorities. The various agents are able to generate queries dynamically and access databases automatically whenever the need arises. In other words, these service-agents have similar data search initiation capabilities as the user and are not dependent solely on the user for access to external information sources.

The foundation of a knowledge-based organization may be characterized in terms of three kinds of capital, namely, human capital, organizational capital, and relational capital. Within the continuous interactions among these spheres the human capital constitutes the source of knowledge that is responsible for generating the capabilities of the organization. The organizational capital generalizes these capabilities through a distributed framework of leadership that communicates the organization's collective intent to all parts of the organizational web network. The relational capital leverages the capabilities of the organization to generate products.

Human capital plays a vital role in knowledge-based organizations and is receiving considerable attention in both government and corporate organizations. Since knowledge management involves the effective acquisition, development, and utilization of the human capital in an organization, as in the case of JRSD, it is in the best interest of the organization to maximize the contributions of the individual for the collective benefit of the organization. At JRSD knowledge management is viewed as a facilitating vehicle – with the object of enabling (via agent technologies) the human and organizational capabilities.

In JRSD's application designs a distributed framework of leadership and communication is assumed. Here the framework utilizes the organizational capital and knowledge management capabilities of the client to execute their enabling role in several ways. First, JRSD recognizes that every member of the client organization is a contributor and a potential decision maker. They provide methods via a knowledge-about-knowledge approach to emphasize the encouragement, cultivation, and motivation of the individual. Second, JRSD recognizes that knowledge management relies on local autonomy and concurrent activities. Their principal tools of leadership are the continuous analysis of feedback, the meticulous explanation and justification of intent and direction, and the maintenance of effective self-development opportunities. Third, JRSD believes that knowledge management must foster the formation of internal and external relationships, because the relationship capital of the organization becomes one of the most important catalysts for increasing productivity.

Learning mechanisms

Any useful representation of information in the computer must be capable of capturing the relationships among the entities (i.e., objects) in the problem system. While some of these associations are fairly static, many of the associations are governed by current conditions and are therefore highly dynamic. They depend on a wide range of factors that relate to both environmental and personal circumstances and dispositions. These factors can be only partially accounted for through embedded knowledge and rules, and therefore become largely the purview of the human members of the collaborative human–computer partnership. They must be learned.

JRSD adopted a modular approach to their product development, aligning their structure, processes, and product architecture. This work design is characterized as a "platform architecture." At the most basic level, platforms provide a basic core that is altered and enhanced to produce product variants with different features (Zhang and Doll, 2001). A product platform may be defined as the set of parts, subsystems, interfaces, manufacturing and operational processes that are shared among a set of products and that facilitate the development of derivative products with cost and time savings (Ebrahimpur and Jacob, 2001; Krishnan and Gupta, 2001; Muffatto, 1999). Sharing common software architecture across a product line brings a core set of knowledge and assets to the development process. Complexity and the development and maintenance costs are reduced and the production of documentation, training materials, and product literature is streamlined. This approach means that the firm would need to undertake certain knowledge-based activities, including identification of core competencies, and might even consider such alternatives as outsourcing some of its tasks.

JRSD made significant use of agent technologies to extend the platform architecture. Through the use of these collaborating expert agents, product development provides the flexibility and range needed for product design sustainability. These heterogeneous, semi-autonomous knowledge-based software components are integrated into coordinated applications. Through the use of interoperability standards and methods, information flows seamlessly through an application across heterogeneous machines, computing platforms, programming languages, and data and process representations (Lander, 1997).

Foremost though, JRSD prides itself on "learning from each other." There is very little outside training. Where the need exists, such as new employees needing orientation, they create in-house training, "the school house" where experts give lectures and relate software concepts and programming styles for their product suite. At the team level "extreme programming" was adopted – very short iterative cycles. They did not "read a book and implement" but instead "learned from their mistakes." The overriding ability of a developer is "eagerness to learn." Responsibility is based on eagerness to work and the amount of work that a developer is willing to do. JRSD realized that "most problems are human, not technological."

Within the team everyone has to be aware of the domain (realm of the project). Everyone has to know how to use every piece of software ("although managers only know about half of what the developers are doing"). Learning takes place starting with technical expertise in a broad field – everyone looks at the actual data – sharing information with support groups. Most of the developers learn in a narrow architecture – they teach themselves to become experts.

Conceptually, JRSD employs a common project across the company. Building on their original successes they have created a Tool Kit. The Tool Kit has been used in all of their projects, and in turn, each project has contributed to the Tool Kit and the Knowledge Data Management. The tools consist of components that support each other. These components are sets of routines, procedures, and methods for combining words, codes, and rules which together allow work to be completed quickly. Every project is cohesive yet restrictive in that the product is proprietary. In any event, cross-learning takes place from one product development to another. One key to their success is that the Tool Kit belongs to JRSD and is furnished to the clients at no charge. The code belongs to the client but the ten percent ingredient resident in the basic tools is not transferred.

The procedure for handling and adopting new hardware and software products is a team decision. Generally a demo version with full capabilities and limited time usage is obtained. A team member "plays with it," but the decision to actually adopt is a multi-team decision influenced by the primary group. Most of the staff on projects are "so young that they have the drive to want to look at something new – what's really cool and neat!"

Strategy and Design

The organization of JRSD, on the surface, does not appear to be untypical for a software development firm. However, the various departmental units function with a minimum of supervision, behaving in a manner that resembles an internal form of outsourcing. A good infrastructure of networks and electronic communications, and a well-thought-through layout of workspace facilitate the firm's operation. There is a dual overlapping organizational mapping of departments and project teams – the firm is not unlike many product-based organizations. Much of the product work is conducted by cooperative supporting groups existing within the department structure. It has a flat organizational hierarchy divided along product and support entities. The leadership of each product team is divided between a product leader and a technical leader. The dual leadership is intended to address these problems by assigning external and internal direction and as a check-and-balance control mechanism.

Within the product structure, responsibility and direction of the support groups are divided and/or shared between these two leaders and the various departments (e.g., testing, customer support and training). Disputes or differences have to be resolved through discussion or are brought to senior management for resolution. This has not been a significant problem because the work content and work constituency are relatively homogeneous. New products evolve from existing products and involve technology transfer and adherence to grounded technologies that utilize JRSD's spatial agent approach.

The approach used by JRSD for achieving their application development objective is to represent information in the computer as objects with behavioral characteristics and relationships to other objects (Myers et al., 1993). JRSD's approach allows real-world objects (buildings, products, networks) to be represented symbolically so that computer software modules can reason about them. It is important to note that the relationships among these objects are often far more important than the characteristics that describe the individual behavior of each object. The main idea is to design software components – to make them "generic – plug-and-play." As the team becomes more mature, more components are being developed and enhanced – thus reducing the time-to-market for a product.

Most of the teams have worked together for three to seven years. They termed what they were doing as they evolved "extreme programming." The software development process is very open. Control is readily shared by all team members – roles and parts are only partially planned. The teams are divided into layers, all of which are software architecture related, such as the model, façade, graphical user interface, database, and agent groups. Experts in each area perform research and dialogue/share the results with the team. This design split enables team members to work on several projects simultaneously – enabling reuse and fostering enhancements.

JRSD categorizes their agents as intelligent, multi-domain service agents. Examples of such service-agent systems can be found in the literature (Durfee, 1988; Lesser, 1995). In JRSD's approach is a networked environment wherein the service-agents pertaining to a single multi-agent system are distributed over several computers, as well as the coordination facilities (i.e., planning, negotiation, conflict detection, etc.). JRSD also provides for several single multi-agent systems to be able to be connected. In this case each multi-agent system functions as an agent in a higher-level multi-agent system. They envision such systems to be suited for planning functions in which resources and viewpoints from several organizational entities can be coordinated. Of particular interest is the agentification of the information objects that are intrinsic to the nature of each application. These are the information objects that human decision makers reason about, and that constitute the building blocks of the real-world representation of the problem situation.

At JRSD these agents are programmed to serve different purposes. Mentor agents, special computer programs, have been designed to serve as guardian angels to look after the welfare and represent the interests of particular objects within the application system. For example, in a typical JRSD application a mentor agent would be designed to simply monitor the fuel consumption of a car or perform more complex tasks such as helping a tourist driver to find a particular hotel in an unfamiliar city. Service agents may perform expert advisory tasks at the request of human users or other agents. At the same time, planning agents can utilize the results of tasks performed by service and mentor agents to devise alternative courses of action or project the likely outcome of particular strategies. Facilitator agents can monitor the information exchanged among agents and detect apparent conflicts. Such facilitator agents could detect a potential non-convergence condition involving two or more agents, and apply one of several procedures for promoting consensus or merely notify the user of the conflict situation.

The need for high-level representation is fundamental to all computer-based decisions, and forms the basis of any meaningful communication between user and computer. Without a high-level representation facility the abilities of the computer to assist human decision makers are confined to the performance of menial tasks, such as the automatic retrieval and storage of data or the computation of mathematically defined quantities. While even those tasks may be highly productive they cannot support a partnership in which human users and computer-based systems collaborate in a meaningful and intelligent manner in the solution of complex problems.

JRSD looks upon knowledge management and decision-support systems as partnerships between users and computers. The ability of the computer-based components to interact with the user overcomes many of the difficulties, such as the representation and validation of knowledge, that continue to plague the field of machine learning (Thornton, 1992; Johnson-Laird, 1993). Human and computer capabilities are in many respects complementary. Human capabilities are particularly strong in areas such as communication, symbolic reasoning, conceptualization, learning, and intuition.

All of this aside, work on new projects starts with a very small management team; more dollars are put in up front – there is an in-depth report analysis, data gathering, and ontology building. This process could take six months without forming a development team. A very large project may need only one or two people to do the design. All during this time there is very close coordination with the customer. The data collection is thoroughly documented and analyzed. Key to the project is an ontology relating data, people, and processes, and a clear, precise definition of the user interface.

Looking at the case, the following are a few of the design requirements that seem to have been utilized: legitimate formal and informal arenas for exchange of ideas were created; the continuity of support and improvement efforts for the products was maintained over a long period of time; the composition of the team reflected the totality of the business functional areas of expertise; goals, scope, and purpose for the teams were defined and refined on an ongoing basis; and there were effective processes for implementing continuous improvements during the software development process. At the team level, coordination is not necessarily the role of the project manager. In many aspects the team is shielded – they are not aware of cost issues – but they are deadline driven.

The design dimensions represent different possible ways to respond to the design requirements. Design dimensions can be conceived on a continuum.

The following are a few examples: the team members from one-to-several functional areas; the team members from same-to-different levels in the firm; and goal setting made centrally at one extreme to in the team at the other. Along each design dimension there would be a range of choices that the organization designer needs to make. This is especially true in the configuration of the specific platform for product launching. The potential cause-and-effect relationships among the design requirements, design dimensions, platform architecture, and sustainability are an area that requires significant research efforts in the future.

Performance: sustainability

Platform-based work design provided the foundation for sustainability at both the team and organizational levels. JRSD's modular-based design allowed for simultaneous autonomy and scope boundary for work at different levels and phases. The iterative cycles and extreme programming enhanced ongoing knowledge acquisition, the flow of information, and continuous improvement of the software development process. Scope creep was reduced by adhering to the modules and boundaries defined in the platform architecture. The time-to-market for the product was insured through the use of the agent structure.

One of the key findings from the case is that JRSD established some type of legitimate forum for the exchange of ideas and actions. From an organization design perspective, the forum is seen as a mechanism with a structural configuration and processes that are devoted to improvements and learning. The iterative cycles approach, coupled with the deliberation mechanisms for information-sharing and the view typified by the product architecture, provides an ongoing opportunity to improve and sustain business results and a way to foster learning at all levels and across all levels of the firm (Shani and Sena, 2002). Our case suggests that not only is a learning mechanism (such as mentoring and face-to-face dialogues) an integral part of sustainability but that the type of learning mechanism is a clear managerial choice that has a significant influence on the organization's ability to develop and nurture sustainability. The very way that the firm chooses to lay out the work environment and the support patterns facilitates and establishes the ongoing learning environment.

Learning mechanisms seem to have played a critical part in sustainability at JRSD. As we have seen, the establishment of mechanisms for information-sharing and deliberations at JRSD provided an ongoing opportunity to improve and sustain business results and a way to foster learning. Managers at JRSD made choices about the design and deployment of specific learning mechanisms. The platform-based architecture for software development work seems to provide a context that has the potential to foster a work environment that can increase the organization's ability to develop and nurture sustainability.

One of the foremost elements is the focus on the team. The team process mandates that "everyone has to work with everyone else." Any new hire or layoff consideration is discussed openly with the team. All interviews for new employees are conducted at the team level and hires are based on team consensus. One interesting observation is that 100 percent of the software developers and staff all came from the same university. Many of the present employees started out as part-time workers – in support functions such as testing, quality assurance, hardware configuring, etc.

Performance: competitiveness

JRSD attributes their success to several reasons. As an R&D organization they sold an "intellectual concept" that required a long period of time to analyze. Their goal was not to make money but instead to make change. Management felt that if they had to make money they would have to sell to the most common demands. Instead they chose to sell only what they wanted to sell. They have been in business for fifteen years without having to be "successful" – money was never a factor. JRSD has no debt, has always operated at a profit, and has a sustained growth in business and staff. Their tactics were to start slowly and only grow once a client gave them a contract. Their success was centered not only as a niche player but also because they maintained a lower pricing structure than the large R&D concerns. Their core competency was the ability to develop a "rapid" prototype that "is bullet-proof, has intelligence, and has a completely scalable architecture." In effect, their products are not really prototypes but something that the client can build from.

They chose to stay within a narrow domain, a niche with limited competition. This was purposeful – "to survive as a small business you go with a knowledge area – an umbrella which you can control – stay within your area of expertise." They realized that for most software R&D firms it was inevitable that they most likely would be taken over by a large company. However, with no debt, no ambitions to "grow," and a steady clientele it was difficult to be bought out. The production software business was of no real interest to JRSD. However, unlike most R&D organizations employed by the military, they always provided a tangible product. In most cases this product was a working prototype software system – a proof of concept. JRSD's Tool Kit, inherent in each product, provides the nucleus that insures that no other contractor can take over their work. The client must agree to data rights protecting JRSD's object schema, library of code, information searches, agent engine, and the user interface components.

Discussion and Reflections

The JRSD case involves a company that attempts to create, transfer, and exploit its knowledge in a very competitive market. The organizational learning mechanisms that were implemented at JRSD were an integral part of the strategy to achieve success. The intentional design of organizational learning mechanisms around knowledge management processes, while using advanced information technology infrastructure, raises a number of challenges. In the discussion that follows we address: the characteristics of learning mechanisms in a knowledge-based work environment; the causal relationship between organizational learning mechanisms and the firm's ability to continuously improve the way the organization creates, transfers, exploits, and manages knowledge; and the relationship between organizational learning mechanisms, knowledge management processes, and sustainability.

The characteristics of learning mechanisms in a knowledge-based work environment

Software development organizations are viewed as workplaces that are characterized as knowledge intensive – their major emphasis is on knowledge. As we have seen, knowledge work is a complex process requiring multidisciplinary expertise in order to achieve a complex synthesis of highly specialized state-of-the-art technologies and knowledge domains. In knowledge-intensive work environments competitive advantage and product success are a result of collaborative, ongoing learning (Sena and Shani, 1999).

At JRSD, learning mechanisms centered on teams and the enhancement of knowledge management processes. The different teams and units, regardless of whether they are the software developers, quality control, user interface specialists, network engineers, or other specialized computer technologists, all must keep abreast of technologies within their specific areas of specialization. The advanced information technology infrastructure provided an opportunity to facilitate knowledge creation, knowledge-sharing, and knowledge transfer within and between units.

However, this quest for knowledge is not restricted to specializations but moreover to understanding the needs and interests of the other team members and other teams. At JRSD, learning was encouraged and fostered by self-study and sharing of "best practices." (Similar findings were reported in chapters 3 and 4.) As we have seen in the case (and as captured in table 7.1), the creation of the platform-based work design, code modules, and generic agent technologies provided the learning mechanisms and building blocks wherein the developers built on existing knowledge and practices to create a "better, improved agent" and contributed to an ever-expanding repertory of program code.

As we saw in chapter 2 of this book, a critical element of learning is the need for a space in which learning occurs. The importance of "space" for knowledge creation was advanced by Nonaka and Konno (1998), based on the concept of *ba* proposed by Kitaro Nishida, a Japanese philosopher. The flexible architecture design of the workplace – another distinct learning mechanism that was created at JRSD – facilitated human interaction for the purpose of

Table 7.1 Learning by design at the software development firm (JRSD)

Software developers' learning requirements	Learning design dimensions	Learning mechanisms
Continuous improvement and enhancement of software development skills	* Support for self-learning * Explicit path for progression of task and skill development * Explicit assessment and reward process for skill development	* Recruitment process for highly skilled and newly trained individuals * Formal and informal dialogues among team members and between teams about continuous enhancement of skill development * "School house" – on-the-job training for new employees
A work environment that fostered and facilitated software development and learning	* Cluster-based workplace design * Open workplace architecture design	* Flexible architecture design that facilitates human interaction for the purpose of learning, knowledge creation and knowledge transfer among and between teams * Platform-based work design * Clear mapping and direct linkages to individual experts and expertise
Access to knowledge bases and best practice software modules	* Information technology infrastructure * Access to external knowledge bases * Re-usable software component library	* Formal and informal dialogue mechanisms * Search and discovery process IT routines – portals * Agent technology assistance

learning, knowledge creation, and knowledge transfer among individuals, teams, and units. This finding supports Caramelo, Aouad, and Ormerod's (2001) argument that the architectural design of a workplace that takes into account the importance of social interactions is likely to foster learning and knowledge creation.

Organizational learning mechanisms and the firm's ability to continuously improve the way the organization creates, transfers, exploits and manages knowledge

The JRSD company case described above identified a few formal organizational learning mechanisms that were designed and implemented by the company for the purpose of continuously improving how the firm was creating, transferring, and exploiting knowledge (see table 7.1). More specifically, the flexible architecture design of the workspace created the space and facilitated human interaction for the purpose of learning and knowledge creation; the continuous mapping of expert and expertise via the multi-agent mechanism and the direct linkages to them allowed for knowledge transfer; and the platform-based work arrangement allowed for knowledge transfer and exploitation between the different new product development projects.

At JRSD, management was there when they were needed but provided the project teams with leeway to make mistakes, learn from each other, and build on what others had done. The survival of the organization hinged on the reputation of their work. New business was generated based on the quality of prior projects. As was described earlier, there were both formal and informal dialogue mechanisms at the organizational level. The physical work environment that was created encouraged the exchange of ideas to a point where one individual stated the following: "one wonders how anything can get done given the way we are all clustered together, but surprisingly things get done even though it appears to be chaotic at times." The network and software development infrastructure provided a template for new and developing staff to learn by merely using the system mechanisms. Finally, all team members had a common development interface and access to the complete library of software and all past and existing project work – "the design of the developers' pod is intended to facilitate the development of the product."

Organizational learning mechanisms, knowledge management processes and sustainability

A sustainable workplace takes into account the economic, human resources (what some call social), and ecological consequences of its operations (Caramelo et al., 2001). Creating the conditions that will stimulate innovation and facilitate sustainable growth was identified as one of the most critical managerial challenges for the twenty-first century (Docherty, Forslin, and Shani, 2002a). At the most basic level, instead of depleting the resources it needs to operate, sustainable work systems develop and reproduce human resources in the process of deploying them (Docherty, Forslin, and Shani, 2002b).

As can be seen in the case described earlier, JRSD developed learning mechanisms that facilitate the sustainable growth and knowledge management of the firm. Being a knowledge-intensive firm, the development of the information technology infrastructure, the multi-agent system, the platform-based work design mechanisms, the iterative cycles of product development process, and the formal and informal dialogue mechanisms all fostered sustainable growth. The result was a workplace that contributed to the well-being and development of employees while the system promoted creativity, motivation, commitment, interpersonal skills, learning, resources for long-term coping, knowledge creation, and knowledge exploitation.

With each project or new product development JRSD believed that they were continuously improving on their work. They were building, not only a knowledge repository, but also a better mousetrap. Their Tool Kit with restrictive code content affords them protection from competitors "stealing" their code modules. The unique knowledge of the principals affords the organization the luxury of true specialists from the top down. Foremost though, the main performance indicator is the desire to excel in their work without the goal of just making money but instead to create a product that "they are proud of creating." In the next chapter – chapter 8 – we present a case in which there is a key element of the knowledge management process. As we will see, managing the knowledge management process in a networked organization presents a new set of challenges.

References

Antal, A. B., Dierkes, M., Child, J., and Nonaka, I. (2001). Introduction. In A. B. Antal, M. Dierkes, J. Child, and I. Nonaka (eds), *Handbook of Organizational Learning and Knowledge*. New York: Oxford University Press, pp. 1–10.

Beckman, T. J. (1997). *A Methodology for Knowledge Management*. Banff, Canada: IASTED.

Beckman, T. J. (1999). The current state of knowledge management. In J. Liebowitz (ed.), *Handbook of Knowledge Management*. New York: CRC Press, pp. 1-1–1-22.

Caramelo, C., Aouad, G., and Ormerod, M. (2001). The sustainable workplace and workplace design. In P. Jackson and R. Suomi (eds), *Business and Workplace Redesign*. London: Routledge, pp. 39–59.

Dixon, N. M. (2000). *Common Knowledge*. Boston, MA: Harvard Business School Press.

Docherty, P., Forslin, J., and Shani, A. B. (Rami) (2002a). Emerging work systems: From intensity to sustainable. In P. Docherty, J. Forslin, and A. B. (Rami) Shani (eds), *Creating Sustainable Work Systems: Emerging Perspective and Practice*. London: Routledge, pp. 3–14.

Docherty, P., Forslin, J., and Shani, A. B. (Rami) (2002b). Sustainable work systems: Lessons and challenges. In P. Docherty, J. Forslin, and A. B. (Rami) Shani (eds), *Creating Sustainable Work Systems: Emerging Perspective and Practice*. London: Routledge, pp. 213–25.

Drucker, P. (1993). *Post-capitalist Society*. Boston, MA: Butterworth-Heinemann.

Durfee, E. (1988). *Coordination of Distributed Problem Solvers*. Boston, MA: Kluwer Academic Press.

Ebrahimpur, G. and Jacob, M. (2001). Restructuring for agility at Volvo Car Technical Services. *European Journal of Innovation Management*, 4(2), 64–72.

Grant, R. (1999). *Contemporary Strategy Analysis*. Malden, MA: Blackwell Publishers Inc.

Holsapple, C. and Joshi, K. (1997). Knowledge management: A threefold framework. Kentucky Initiative for Knowledge Management Paper No. 104. July.

Ingelgård, A., Roth J., Shani, A. B. (Rami), and Styhre, A. (2002). Dynamic learning capability and actionable knowledge creation: Clinical R&D in a pharmaceutical company. *The Learning Organization*, 9(2), 65–77.

Johnson-Laird, P. (1993). *Human and Machine Thinking*. Hillsdale, NJ: Erlbaum.

Krishnan, V. and Gupta, S. (2001). Appropriateness and impact of platform-based product development. *Management Science*, 47(1), 52–68.

Lander, S. (1997). Issues in multi-agent design systems. *IEEE Expert*, March/April.

Lesser, V. (ed.) (1995). *Proceeding of the First International Conference on Multi-Agent Systems*. ICMAS 95. Cambridge, MA: AAAI Press/MIT Press.

Liebowitz, J. (ed.) (1999). *Handbook of Knowledge Management*. New York: CRC Press.

Marquardt, M. (1996). *Building the Learning Organization*. New York: McGraw-Hill.

Matthews, J. H. and Candy, P. C. (1999). New dimensions in the dynamics of learning and knowledge. In D. Boud and J. Garrick (eds), *Understanding Learning at Work*. London: Routledge, pp. 47–64.

Myers, L. J., Pohl, J., Cotton, J., Snyder, K., Pohl, S., Chien, S., and Rodriguez, T. (1993). *Object Representation and the ICADS-Kernel Design*. San Luis Obispo, CA: CAD Center technical report (CADRU-08-93).

Muffatto, M. (1999). Introducing a platform strategy in product development. *International Journal of Production Economics*, 60/61, 145–63.

Nonaka, I., Toyama, R., and Byosière, P. (2001). A theory of organizational knowledge creation: Understanding the dynamic process of creating knowledge. In A. B. Antal, M. Dierkes, J. Child, and I. Nonaka (eds), *Handbook of Organizational Learning and Knowledge*. New York: Oxford University Press, pp. 491–517.

Quinn, J. B. (1992). *Intelligent Enterprise*. New York: Free Press.

Reinhardt, R., Bornermann, M., Pawlowsky, P., and Schneider, U. (2001). Intellectual capital and knowledge management: Perspectives on measuring knowledge. In A. B. Antal, M. Dierkes, J. Child, and I. Nonaka (eds), *Handbook of Organizational Learning and Knowledge*. New York: Oxford University Press, pp. 794–820.

Ruggels, R. (1997). Tools for knowledge management: An introduction. In R. Ruggles (ed.), *Knowledge Management Tools*. Boston, MA: Butterworth-Heinemann.

Sanchez, R. and Heene, A. (2000). A competence perspective on strategic learning and knowledge management. In R. L. Cross and S. B. Israelit (eds), *Strategic Learning in a Knowledge Economy: Individual, Collective and Organizational Learning Process*. Boston, MAs: Butterworth-Heinemann, pp. 23–35.

Schulz, M. (2001). The uncertain relevance of newness: Organizational learning and knowledge flow. *Academy of Management Journal*, 44(4), 661–81.

Sena, J. and Shani, A. B. (Rami) (1999). Intellectual capital and knowledge creation: Towards and alternative framework. In J. Liebowitz (ed.), *Handbook of Knowledge Management*. New York: CRC Press, pp. 8-1–8-16.

Shani, A. B. (Rami) and Sena, J. (2002). Integrating product and personal development. In P. Docherty, J. Forslin, and A. B. (Rami) Shani (eds), *Creating Sustainable Work Systems: Emerging Perspective and Practice*. London: Routledge, pp. 89–100.

Thornton, C. (1992). *Techniques in Computational Learning*. London: Chapman and Hall.

Zhang, Q. and Doll, W. (2001). The fuzzy front end and success of new product development: A causal model. *European Journal of Innovation Management*, 4(2), 95–112.

8

Learning in a Networked Organization[1]

- What learning mechanisms are necessary for maintaining learning, competitiveness, and sustainability in a networked organization?

- What are the relationships between the networked organization and learning mechanisms' characteristics?

- What is the role of top management in the networked organization in the facilitation of learning?

Organizations characterized by large size, extensive division of labor, and deep-rooted culture are often difficult to change. This is particularly evident where the organization has reached maturity but is not faring well in the marketplace and has not adjusted well to the external environment. This chapter deals with such an organization – a Medical Service Provider (MSP) – and its attempt to orchestrate a major turnaround through assertive top leadership, unique structural learning mechanisms, and redesign of its core business processes. While all were vital to change program success at MSP, this chapter will mainly focus on the networked organization and network learning rather than the redesign of the core business processes or transformational leadership.

[1] The first draft of this manuscript was contributed by Professor Michael Stebbins. The chapter was developed in collaboration with Mike. We are grateful to Professor Stebbins for his contribution.

This last case in the book was chosen to illustrate a number of important elements about learning by design that were not found in chapters 3 through 7, due to its focus and the networked organization level of analysis. Specifically learning in a networked organization is dependent on the specific structure and processes that are created for the purpose of enhancing learning across organizations in the network. The structure for learning is viewed as dynamic and as such it changes as the learning processes mature over time. We begin with a brief review of the network literature and a synopsis of what we know about learning mechanisms. The MSP case is then introduced, followed by reflections and implications for both theory development and practice.

▶ Networks and Networked Organization

Network-based organizations are described in a vast body of literature in social, anthropological, behavioral, political, and economic science disciplines. The term itself has many connotations. In some cases, network implies a set of external relationships (i.e., a global web of alliances and joint ventures). In other cases, network means informal ties among managers where there are teams that work across functions and maneuver through bureaucracy. Some authors define networks as new ways for executives to share information using management information systems, group decision support aids, and related processes. One common theme in the literature is the focus on sets of relations among two or more participants – individuals, teams, and organizations (Chisholm, 1998; Lane, 2001). At the very basic level, a network is a set of autonomous units that come together to reach goals that none of them can reach independently. Furthermore, network organizations are recorded under a variety of labels: networks, social networks, social exchange networks, industrial networks, communication networks, strategic networks, hybrid organizations, internal networks, local vs. regional vs. global networks, internal vs. stable vs. dynamic networks, static vs. dynamic networks, spherical vs. cellular networks, and multi-stakeholder networks (Cravens, Shipp, and Cravens, 1994; Miles and Snow, 1995; Snow, Miles, and Coleman, 1992; Tsui-Auch, 2001).

The networked organization – the focus of this chapter – has certain attributes that are unusual and noteworthy (Hakansson and Johanson, 1992; Cravens et al., 1996). For example, in a networked organization, independent units and individuals perform certain core and support business functions. The network is a relatively "flat" organization, relying on close interaction of network partners rather than the conventional hierarchy. Operations, technology, and service-based partnership as well as product distribution in the conventional sense are often involved. Snow, Miles, and Coleman (1992) describe three types of networks: the *internal network* that allows an organization to share its diverse resources internally with limited outsourcing, the *stable network* where outsourcing is used to inject flexibility into the overall value chain, and the *dynamic network* where the form is pushed to the limit in that the lead firm identifies and assembles assets owned largely by other companies. The dynamic network can be extended even further as a *spherical* or *cellular* network of small firms which form an alliance to take on major projects involving big customers and external alliance companies (Miles et al., 1997; Miles and Snow, 1995). Different companies can be loosely matched to one of the three basic forms. For example, in the automobile industry, BMW is said to be a stable network as it relies to a considerable extent on outsourcing and partnering, in contrast to GM which is almost entirely an internal network. Our case company in this chapter, MSP, would be classified as between a dynamic network and a stable network in that it relies on *hospital* and *other healthcare companies* to provide direct services and acts as a broker to market different health plans and to arrange reimbursement claims submitted to MSP. The company is not very large, but has revenues in the billions of US dollars due to its reimbursement activities.

In this chapter we focus on a networked organization *as a strategic response to environmental pressures that provide incentives to devolve and disaggregate business functions to specialist partners* (Cravens et al., 1996). In the case to follow, the networked organization had a long history of outsourcing important functions such as information and communication technology infrastructure. This level of outsourcing was not at all trivial, as it involved mission-critical functions tied to the generation of revenues. Moreover, while MSP is in the healthcare industry, it does not actually provide many healthcare services directly to its members. This means that the service operations component is left to organizations better equipped to be providers. The "operations work" done by MSP relates to the design and marketing of health plans, medical review, and claims processing. MSP acts as a broker, and is comfortable looking outside its boundaries to create new organizational capabilities. For example, it is easy for MSP to make a decision to hire consultants, such as the organization development consultants who helped MSP create a comprehensive change program. Other specialist consultants were also hired on a temporary basis to introduce capabilities that the company did not have, such as the creation of reward systems to reinforce new work designs. Thus MSP is a prime example of a multi-stakeholder network organization, and as will be described below, the structural learning mechanisms that it developed during the change program were designed to fit with its complex environment and multi-stakeholder structure.

Learning Mechanisms

As was argued in chapter 2, learning mechanisms are key to the facilitation and sustainability of learning in most forms of organization. Learning mechanisms also can be used to orchestrate and conduct change programs and to provide a context for organizational learning (Marsick and Watkins, 1999;

Shani and Stjernberg, 1995). Some authors believe that to a great extent, learning mechanisms can determine change program success (Kettinger et al., 1997; Mitki, Shani, and Meiri, 1997; Pasmore 1997). According to Shani and Mitki (2000), learning mechanisms are diverse and, as the literature indicates, can be arranged on a continuum from parallel learning mechanisms to highly integrated learning mechanisms.

The *parallel learning mechanism* is a set of small teams that are created as a microcosm of the formal organization for the purpose of addressing organizational issues and operates parallel to the formal structure (Bushe and Shani, 1991). In this instance, the formal organization relies on existing knowledge to create efficiencies while the parallel mechanism is engaged in knowledge acquisition and action – a learning entity (Schein, 1993). Members of the parallel learning organization spend most of their time performing their regular work and only a portion of their time dealing with learning tasks.

On the other end of the continuum, an *integrated learning mechanism* is created as a separate division of the organization. Structurally, this division can resemble any other division of the company in terms of roles, hierarchy, role relationships, and work routines. But more likely, since the mission of the new division is change, the psychological climate in the unit and ways of working are quite different. Members of the division are more likely to regard each other as peers and change agents. Between the two extremes of parallel and fully integrated mechanisms are a wide variety of structural learning mechanisms that can help manage change. As will be seen in the case to follow, different mechanisms can be used at different stages of the change program.

▶ The Medical Service Provider (MSP)

Background

The case occurred during the 1995–7 time period and was part of an overall turnaround program for a company that at the beginning had great difficulty competing within the California healthcare services market. The turnaround program was simply known as the "Change Initiative" and will be referred to as CI throughout the case description. The Change Initiative was a multi-pronged effort to address market image, internal operations, structure, organizational culture, and management support system issues within a rather traditional and conservative organization. By all accounts, the redesign of the key processes (Hammer and Champy, 1993; Hammer and Stanton, 1995; Stebbins et al., 1998) was the most important part of the change initiative and much of it involved conversion of eleven remote service centers into three large operations service centers. The redesign of the core business processes component involved sales and marketing, installation of new customer groups, a new approach to claims processing, and other customer-oriented projects. While this was clearly the dominant component of the overall program, other change initiatives included vision and values, market assessment and business strategy, organization restructuring, company-wide human resources support, and communications initiatives. According to the CEO, the best way to change the company was to "unfreeze" everything at once, and therefore the overall change program was sweeping in breadth.

The Context and Players

In September 1993, a new President and CEO was appointed at MSP. Prior to his appointment, the new president was a president and chief operating officer of another MSP within one of the largest health maintenance organizations (HMO) in the USA. The MSP board of directors chose him to orchestrate a turnaround effort in an internal environment of flat membership and revenues, outdated business systems, high administrative cost ratios, and a traditional command and control work climate. His experience in the expanding HMO sector of the US healthcare market, record of leadership in national healthcare administration societies, and knowledge of the fiercely competitive US western region market were all instrumental in the board's hire decision.

Initial Assessment

As noted in figure 8.1, the president began the change initiative program with an assessment phase. Five teams were established to study the situation, to rethink and redesign, and to suggest changes. The five teams included market assessment, process reengineering, human resources, communications, and management/organization structure. Culture transformation was considered the foundation of the overall change program, and it was initiated top-down through a vision and values program. Separately, a modified version of GE Workout was conducted in the first year to achieve immediate change and to signal a shift to a new culture. The GE Workout is a renewal program developed at General Electric. The central idea of the Workout process was to create a forum where a cross-section of employees in each business could speak their mind about how the business was managed, without fear of retribution. The intent was to identify problems and develop solutions in small groups and town hall meetings with a timeline for a follow-up on actions taken. In brief, the MSP version of GE Workout involved open fora where employees could vent frustrations, identify problems, and offer ideas for change. It focused on short-term remedies rather than systemic change. Use of GE Workout at MSP was a deliberate attempt to foster an atmosphere of urgency and widespread change. Other events contributed to the sense of crisis normally associated with a turnaround. Changes in top executive personnel, middle manager and

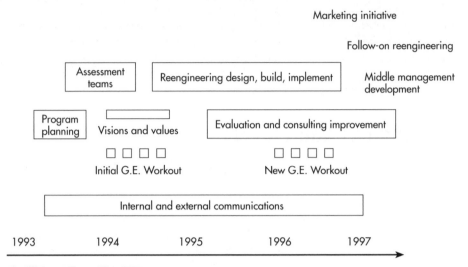

Figure 8.1 The change program: an overview

staff involvement in the assessment teams, and GE Workout changes were widely communicated within MSP.

▶ The Parallel Learning Mechanism – Structure, Processes, Tools

The CEO wished to involve middle managers and staff in the assessment phase of the work. The parallel learning structure that the CEO created was composed of several levels of management plus consultants (see figure 8.2) but did not include rank and file employees. The teams developed separate approaches to dealing with the five areas of focus, and met periodically to share progress and discuss obstacles to change. The CEO met separately with all teams and led the structure team (restricted to top management). In parallel learning organization meetings, the entire group focused on identification of high-leverage core processes for the reengineering effort, but time was also devoted to other CI components. For example, with support from external organization development (OD) consultants and communications experts, assessment team members conducted focus groups at all organizational levels. Focus groups were designed to identify sources of information used by employees, levels of trust, degree of candid communications, and the like. Based on the data from focus meetings, vision and values statements were then drafted by top managers and their immediate teams and then repeated in all areas of the company in a downward cascading fashion. The new values stressed high performance, risk-taking, and accountability.

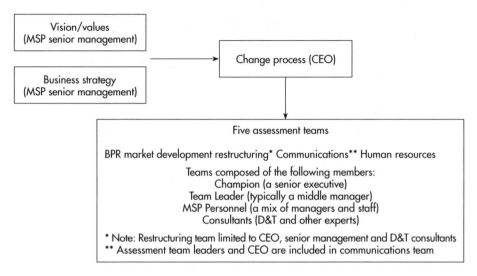

Figure 8.2 The change program structural configuration

Follow-up Activities

At the end of the assessment phase, entirely new teams were created to follow up on the findings. The second phase called for greater involvement of existing MSP stakeholders as well as expansion of the multi-stakeholder network. Notably, Electronic Data Services (EDS) became involved as well as Deloitte and Touche (D&T) for operations consulting support. To drive and coordinate the overall effort, a second structural learning mechanism was created (see figure 8.3). The CEO did not wish to be as involved in the second learning organization. A sales director who led one of the original assessment teams was appointed Vice President of Change Management and became the overall change initiative leader. A second middle manager within the operations part of the business became Vice President of Human Resources with the task of providing training and other support to the CI program. A third assessment team member later became Vice President responsible for all operations centers.

An important part of follow-up was the recruitment and assimilation of outside consultants. In all, the CI program involved fifteen D&T on-site consultants (reengineering), ten EDS consultants (information technology support), two consultants for strategic planning support, one consultant for compensation/rewards support, and one external organization development consultant. In all, fifty internal and external people worked full-time on the project for sixteen months, and a much larger number of MSP people worked on a part-time basis. The consultants and staff were organized into a design and

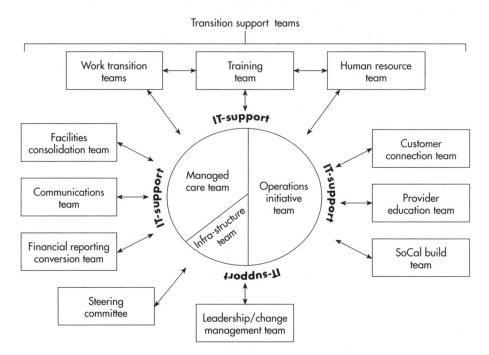

Figure 8.3 Design and implementation structure

implementation structure (figure 8.3). This new structure marked a significant shift toward integrated learning mechanisms.

▶ The Integrated Learning Mechanism

The second structural learning mechanism (figure 8.3) was more complex than the parallel learning mechanism, involving a steering committee composed of heads of CI support and project teams. Otherwise, the mechanism had very little hierarchy. The membership changed often; personnel were added and then returned to their home organizations as required. The core of the effort was reengineering work within newly created service centers. The reengineering projects required significant information and communication technology (ICT) hardware, software, and consulting support, provided by D&T and EDS (represented by the circle in figure 8.3). Additionally, there were major BPR projects within the marketing and medical review parts of the MSP network. This new learning mechanism provided opportunities for goal-setting and sound project management. The steering committee wanted to create projects that were close-ended within the context of a larger change effort. Accordingly, all projects had goals, statements of scope and approach, milestones, budgeted costs, and expected results.

Staffing the projects

Typically, the project teams worked off-line in a separate environment creating new systems and "model offices." Much later, they were linked to managers and staff performing the existing work functions. From the outset, the project groups all had process owners, consultants, team leaders, and full-time staff. For example, the claim and encounter processing team's goal was to strengthen the accuracy and timeliness of claims processing while substantially reducing costs. Reengineering of claims involved new transaction processing systems and the creation of new ICT workstations within model offices. As the project teams completed their work they began to work on conversion of the eleven independent service centers into three new facilities. Reengineering and the model office approach resulted in reduced staffing, fewer managers, and the use of self-managing work teams in place of traditional bureaucratic work units.

Coordination, communication, learning

This second phase of CI required significant coordination and communication across teams. The Vice President (VP) of Change Management wished to make it clear that MSP was in control, not the consultants. Accordingly, she established ground rules for program direction and teamwork, and scheduled periodic team meetings for team leaders and other key personnel. Meetings included a kickoff event for all project team leaders and consultants, a change management conference for all full- and part-time players, and eventually meetings for over 60 consultants and MSP personnel that focused on implementation planning. The goal of the series of meetings was to build the overall CI vision and to bring all team efforts into synchronization.

Figure 8.3 provides a glimpse of the learning mechanism's complexity. Notice that both the managed care team and the operations initiative team (including all the project teams) relied heavily on over ten transition support teams. The VP of Change Management and her steering committee concentrated on linking IT and other support groups including facilities consolidation, communications, financial accounting and reporting, training, and other resources needed for overall success.

During the late stages of implementation, the integrated learning mechanism (figure 8.3) was modified somewhat to facilitate the transition to operations managers. The Vice President of Change Management and the managing D&T consultant became co-directors for the transition. "Summit meetings" involving team leaders were held every other week for project planning and control. Additionally, weekly "huddle meetings" were hosted on a rotating basis by one of the three service centers. The huddle meetings featured conference calls across all twenty CI teams. In the conference calls, each team had 3–5 minutes to raise issues and identify team interdependencies. For example, the facilities team leader would list specific telecommunications tasks that had to be completed before MSP employees could be moved to work stations at a new center. And facilities team members at the site could report on unique aspects of the site that had to be dealt with during installation.

To complete reengineering milestones, operations teams were especially dependent on ICT, training, and human resources support. Figure 8.3 depicts ICT as closely connected to core reengineering groups. New hardware and software were critical to project success, and over time staff/company identities were lost in the pursuit of teamwork and project accomplishment. The VP of Change Management felt that this was one measure of the quality of the emergent partnership among consultants and employees during transition work.

Dynamics within redesign teams

MSP top leaders were convinced that after the CI projects had been launched, decision-making should occur at the team level. But MSP was highly dependent on consultants to help lay out the reengineering process, to train team members in statistical analysis and other required techniques, and to develop the model office pilots. The overall plan dictated that new processes would reside in reconfigured facilities and the new organization design was to be less hierarchical and more team-centered. While the CEO and other top executives had been involved in the early assessment and design stages, they were not personally involved in the model office pilots and implementation. Instead, the project teams took charge of implementation with support arranged through huddle meetings, the VP of Change Management, and the newly appointed VP of Operations.

Learning

Implementation at the large service centers was sequential. This allowed the teams to learn from successes and mistakes at the first facility and adjust at the next. For example, employee training in new processes/technology had to be continuously retooled to reflect learning at the last facility and process enhancements occurring in real time. The operations and support teams initiated the changes and kept the leadership groups informed of progress. Team member burnout was a real factor, as both consultants and employees often rotated back to their respective organizations earlier than anticipated.

The strategy both inside and outside the centers was to move new processes to local managers as soon as possible to stimulate additional testing and to foster creativity by employees who had to live with redesigned work. Members of the steering committee attempted to facilitate this transition, but it was not easy and the change management team observed that the project groups and consultants had a hard time giving up control to permanent managers. The CEO decided to force the issue and support from reengineering consultants ended in April 1996 with the official close of the program.

Downsizing and structure changes

Downsizing was clearly part of the redesign activity that resulted in the new service centers, but it also occurred in upper and middle management and staff units as well. Recall that CI involved drastic change. Between 1994 and 1996, employment at MSP fell by 1,000 (full-time equivalent) or 25 percent of the workforce. Most employees at the small service centers did not want to leave their home communities and relocate near centralized facilities, often over 100 miles away. Nearly 70 percent of these employees were women and relocations were disruptive to families. MSP lost experienced supervisors and operations workers and as a result faced significant hiring and training issues at the new centers.

MSP had operated the small service centers for many years, and there were obvious human and community costs associated with the business decision to centralize claims and other functions. The CEO and other executives personally called service center managers the day before public announcements were made of center closures. They then met with employees in day-long meetings to present the business rationale for closure, and to deal with frustrations over the decisions. The CEO reasoned that since management had initiated the changes, management ought to be there to deal with the issues and provide a measure of support. Additional support provided later included relocation and training assistance, severance pay, and expressions of gratitude on the last day of work.

Communicating about change

The "change everything at once" philosophy meant that as the large service centers were built, MSP faced new pressures to communicate with health plan members and healthcare providers about service changes. In a somewhat unrelated move, the CEO decided to change the marketing part of the organization. New regional offices were created in the western US region to address the needs of target markets. A communications team followed these developments as well as the context for change. The team created publications that provided an overview of the CI program, videoconferences to explain the rationale for executive decisions, CI hot lines, "back to you" flyers that answered specific questions about CI, CEO newsletters, and other mechanisms to promote dialogue about the changes in process. The intensive communications along with the integrated learning mechanism were considered necessary due to the scope and complexity of the CI program.

▶ Strategy and Marketing Changes

Less publicized changes in marketing began to occur in 1995. Based on the original assessment work, marketing initiatives focused on sales, new distribution channels, and reducing costs for each sale closed. Additional marketing initiatives during CI focused on the creation of HMO products. MSP was able to lower prices for both new products and more traditional products as a direct result of the combined reengineering efforts. For the short term, reduced costs and lower prices enhanced MSP's competitive position in the marketplace.

▶ Other Results

There were significant results beyond the workforce reduction and marketing gains reported above. Due to the program, the company achieved a 15 percent reduction in administrative costs ($54 million), managed care savings of $31 million (lower payments to medical providers), a 50 percent reduction in floor space, a 43 percent reduction in types of employment positions, a 77 percent reduction in time to install new customer groups, and an increase of 60 percent in data entry productivity.

On the downside, customer service indicators fell more than 25 percent during and after the transition to the service centers and remained low for one year despite use of rescue teams and other back-up tactics. It is evident that the CI program had negative consequences for many MSP customers. However, by 1999 customer service indicators returned to prior levels, and MSP was ranked "number one for service" nationally among 63 health plans serving Federal government employees.

Dollar results for the overall CI program are hard to decipher given the many forces impacting MSP during the 1994–6 period. Operating income fell to a negative $23.8 million in 1994 due to reengineering, human resources, and other downsizing costs. By 1995, MSP was again in the black and this positive trend continued throughout the 1996–2000 period. In 1999, MSP posted record revenues of $3.0 billion and operating income of $22.0 million. Significantly, administrative costs as a percent of revenue declined from 23.1 percent in 1995 to 17.5 percent in 1999. In annual reports, management attributed the cost savings to new technology and changed processes throughout the organization. In 1999, MSP was awarded the only "A" rating for HMOs in the USA by the Weiss Safety Rating organization. This rating reflects overall financial health for a five-year period and considers risk-adjusted capital, five-year profitability, liquidity, and stability.

MSP is a nonprofit organization. Cost savings from specific projects have been reinvested in products, marketing, and customer service areas. In 1996,

MSP became the first health plan in the region to offer online benefits and enrollment information. Also, in a strategic move, MSP became the first health plan to offer members direct access to medical specialists within their physician's medical group (without primary care physician approval). In 1998, MSP launched a website to improve member access to MSP information and resources. This was followed in 1999 by numerous initiatives to improve e-business, including an alliance with another provider to provide prescriptions and drugstore products online. More recent innovations include secure online messaging between doctors and patients, and online medical monitoring for members with chronic diseases.

Discussion and Reflections

The MSP case involves a company turnaround program that was system-wide with multiple change initiatives. The initiatives were integrated through two different structural learning mechanisms and through use of external and internal change agents. This concluding section will explore lessons concerning the learning mechanisms along with implications for their use within network organizations.

The creation of structural learning mechanisms is critical in order for learning to occur within network organizations

MSP created structural learning mechanisms that nurtured the change initiative and proved to be valuable in integrating and guiding the separate initiatives that were taking place simultaneously (see figures 8.1, 8.2, 8.3, and table 8.1). The structural learning mechanisms facilitated knowledge and concept development and enabled people to acquire new skills and managerial tools. Based on past experience, the CEO and his staff felt that different structural learning mechanisms were needed at various stages. In the case, we see a gradual progression from a parallel structural learning mechanism (which was limited to managerial personnel) toward integrated structural learning mechanisms in the middle and end of the change initiative.

The rather management-dominated flavor of all the structural learning mechanisms is likely due to both internal and external factors. The company was ailing when the CEO assumed control, and he was brand new to the internal situation. He felt that a cross-section of managers was needed to conduct the initial assessment, but selection of people for the assessment teams was problematic. This may well explain the lack of representation from people at rank and file levels. Team members reported surprise that they had been selected to join the groups and further surprise when people were selected from the assessment teams to staff the transition organization.

Beckhard and Harris (1987) provide a familiar change model that states that in between the current and future states of an organization, the transition must be actively managed. It is noteworthy that the second structural mechanism was complex and evolving in importance as the project teams readied their reengineered processes for implementation. The structural learning mechanism changed to facilitate the transition between laboratory and pilot models to reconfigured operations at the service centers.

Networked organizations such as MSP rely tremendously on outside organizations and individuals. In this case, EDS and D&T consultants and staff brought new technology and processes to the model offices, and eventually to the service centers. While the reengineering teams did have "process owners" (managers in the affected departments) and some MSP assigned staff, they were not truly linked together until the changeovers at the new centers. Members of the integrated learning mechanism were challenged to capture the gains of the model offices and to encourage further testing and modification within the new centers. Ultimately all of the consultants that were part of the integrated learning mechanism left MSP, except EDS which continued to be the firm's ICT provider. Table 8.1 provides an example of a few of the learning requirements faced by MPS, the learning design dimensions, and the specific learning mechanisms that were chosen and implemented.

Table 8.1 Learning by design in a networked organization: a few examples from MSP

Networked organization learning requirements	Learning design dimensions	Learning mechanisms
Shared mental model of the network's purpose, the nature of the strategic partnership, and its learning requirements	* Continuous scanning and exchange of information related to environmental scanning * Goal setting (compatible goals between network partners) * Contractual agreements	* Infrastructure that fosters centres of exchange within and between partner units using learning structure and ICT tools * The utilization of both internal and external consultants with specific needed expertise
Communication arenas for dialogues and decision-making	Initiating multiple modes, methods, and procedures for dialogue between and within entities	* The creation of a parallel learning mechanism, as microcosm of the network for the sharing and creation of knowledge * Continuous exchange of human capital within the network based on entities' needs
The design of the network processes must fit the totality of the network as well as the operational nature of each partner organization	* Control processes (i.e., shared standards) * Benchmarking and bench-learning * Partnership with unions	* Multiple management role in the different levels of the network * Transfer of learning between projects and between partner entities via periodic meetings of key actors

The structural learning mechanism must provide new change processes, tools, and communications that facilitate learning

The transition from "model office" to real operations and from one service delivery model to another requires special attention to change processes, managerial skills, and communications. Opening new centers was a pressured time for the parties, particularly in enrollment and claims processing services where small community-based facilities were being phased out in favor of large service centers. The leaders of the integrated learning mechanism provided scheduled meetings and changeover deadlines that helped create a sense of urgency and commitment. The huddle meetings in particular provided warning of unanticipated problems, advances and breakdowns in employee training, facility issues, and communications glitches. The huddle meetings brought people from remote sites together by telephone, as a substitute for teleconferencing and other more expensive groupware options. The VP of Change Management played a critical role in facilitating the meetings and conferences and providing needed support. The integrated mechanism provided built-in support since training, ICT, D&T, and other vital resource groups reported to the VP. In the latter stages of phase two, the VP and lead D&T consultant acted as co-directors in planning and running meetings and in expediting the delivery of support services. This support was critical as model offices were tried, modified, and eventually modified again in the path from one new service center to another. Training in the new systems had to be altered continuously as both hardware and software were improved along the way.

One of the overall program goals was to reduce the levels of management and to foster more self-managing teams. While this phenomenon is well understood in the management and change literature, it is inevitably a surprise when introduced in a new setting (Pasmore, 1988; Stebbins, Shani, and Sena, 1995; Vansina and Taillieu, 1996). Since MSP was rather conservative and hierarchical, many managers were unprepared for new roles of coaching and supporting self-managing teams. Moreover, it is doubtful that the redesign consultants were in a position to bring self-management to MSP through the model office approach (which was heavily technology- and process-focused). Problems persisted, and some of the post-CI follow-up work addressed training for managers on these issues.

The internal communications aspects of the MSP change process were covered in an in-depth way. The CEO was aware of the value of a separate communications and publicity effort, and his management team members were personally involved in documenting improvements, and communicating progress through multiple media.

The quality of the emergent partnership among stakeholders is critical to learning within a networked organization

In the MSP case, the change structure that was created served as an integrated learning mechanism for the purpose of driving and coordinating significant changes in the operations. While more stakeholders were directly involved in the second phase of the change program, important players were not included. For example, members of the eleven outlying centers were on the sidelines for much of phase two, and there were serious issues connected with staffing the new centers as the old centers closed. MSP's customers (employers in the communities) who had been used to dealing with local service representatives now found that they had to work through regional call centers with changed personnel and processes. Clinic and hospital partners also experienced changes in service due to the creation of new HMO products and the new medical review and claims review processes. This may account for at least some of the drop in customer satisfaction during and shortly after the change program. Further, the management team viewed its task as MSP-internal rather than one that would intensively involve outside organizations in the network. The involvement of EDS, D&T, and other consulting firms is impressive but it is noteworthy that healthcare providers and the consuming public were to a great extent left out. MSP's strategic purpose is to create HMO and other products that appeal to employers as customers, to price services so that they break even or provide a return, and to hold internal administrative costs in check. This inevitably brings in the health providers (clinics, hospitals, other providers) who serve MSP members and the employers that offer MSP health plans. Relationships between MSP and these important stakeholders are contractual. While it is not evident how they might have been directly involved in the change program, stronger communications outward were warranted. Again, MSP saw the need for a quality communications effort to support the change program internally, but involvement and communications with other stakeholders were limited.

The potential application of learning mechanisms to other networked organizations

An extension of learning from the MSP case to other networked organizations may be limited outside the healthcare industry context. MSP is not particularly unique as a networked organization – similar organizations exist throughout the USA, so applications to other healthcare organizations are possible. It could be applicable to situations where comprehensive action is needed to bring about new capabilities, values, and widespread learning. The integrated learning mechanism was structurally elaborate and it employed innovative processes and tools to carry out its purpose.

As organizations face increasingly competitive markets, they will increasingly be drawn toward outsourcing and alliances to conduct business. A shift, for example, from a stable network toward a dynamic network (Snow et al., 1992) means that the organization is increasingly dependent on a variety of resources it does not own or control. This type of transition may well call for unique partnerships among the players, coordinated through customized and innovative learning mechanisms that truly consider the needs of different stakeholders. While there are a few cases on dynamic network organizations, much more work must be done on the startup and evolution of these important organizational forms.

This chapter provided an illustration of learning mechanisms in a networked organization. The complexity of networked organizations seems to drive the need to create specific structures in order to focus, enhance, and maintain learning. As we have seen in this case, the structural learning mechanisms seem to change over time as the learning processes mature, and thus become more integrated with existing organizational structures and processes. The next chapter – chapter 9 – provides the integration across the cases and learning themes.

References

Beckhard, R. and Harris, R. (1987). *Organizational Transitions*, 2nd edn. Reading, MA: Addison-Wesley.

Bushe, G. R. and Shani, A. B. (Rami) (1991). *Parallel Learning Structures: Increasing Innovations in Bureaucracies*. Reading, MA: Addison-Wesley.

Chisholm, R. (1998). *Developing Network Organizations*. Reading, MA: Addison-Wesley.

Cravens, D. W., Shipp, S. H., and Cravens, K. S. (1994). Analysis of cooperative interorganizational relationships, strategic alliance formation, and strategic alliance effectiveness. *Journal of Strategic Marketing*, March, 55–70.

Cravens, D. W., Piercy, N. F., and Shipp, S. H. (1996). New organizational forms for competing in highly dynamic environments: The network paradigm. *British Journal of Management*, 7, 203–218.

Håkansson, H. and Johanson, J. (1992). A model of industrial networks. In B. Axelsson and G. Easton (eds), *Industrial Networks – A New View of Reality*. London: Routledge.

Hammer, M. and Champy, J. (1993). *Reengineering the Corporation: A Manifesto for Business Revolution*. London: N. Brealey Publications & Co.

Hammer, M. and Stanton, S. A. (1995). *The Reengineering Revolution*. New York: HarperCollins.

Kettinger, W. J., Teng, J. T. C., and Guha, S. (1997). Business process change: A study of methodologies, techniques, and tools. *MIS Quarterly*, March, 55–80.

Lane, C. (2001). Organizational learning in supplier networks. In A. B. Antal, M. Dierkes, J. Child, and I. Nonaka (eds), *Handbook of Organizational Learning and Knowledge*. New York: Oxford University Press, pp. 699–715.

Marsick, V. J. and Watkins, K. E. (1999). Envisioning new organizations for learning. In D. Boud and J. Garrick (eds), *Understanding Learning at Work*. London: Routledge, pp. 199–215.

Miles, R. E., Snow, C. C., Mathews, J. A., Miles, G., and Coleman, Jr., H. I. (1997). Organizing in the Knowledge Age: Anticipating the cellular form. *Academy of Management Executive*, 11(4), 7–24.

Miles, R. E. and Snow, C. C. (1995). The new network firm: A spherical structure built on a human investment philosophy. *Organizational Dynamics*, Spring, 5–18.

Mitki, Y., Shani, A. B. (Rami), and Meiri, Z. (1997). Organizational learning mechanisms and continuous improvement. *Journal of Organizational Change Management*, 10(5), 426–46.

Pasmore, W. A. (1988). *Designing Effective Organizations: The Sociotechnical Systems Perspective*. New York: Wiley.

Pasmore, W. A. (1997). The future of jobs and organization design: Required shifts in our thinking. Paper presented at the Academy of Management Annual Conference, August, Boston, Massachusetts.

Schein, E. (1993). On dialogue, culture and organizational learning. *Organizational Dynamics*, 22(2), 40–51.

Shani, A. B. and Mitki, Y. (2000). Creating the learning organization: Beyond mechanisms. In R. T. Golembiewski (ed.), *Handbook of Organizational Consultation*. New York: Marcel Dekker, Inc., pp. 911–20.

Shani, A. B. (Rami) and Stjernberg, T. (1995). The integration of change in organization: Alternative learning and transformation mechanisms. In W. A. Pasmore and R. W. Woodman (eds), *Research in Organizational Change and Development*, vol. 8. Greenwich, CT: JAI Press, pp. 77–121.

Snow, C. C., Miles, R. E., and Coleman, Jr., H. J. (1992). Managing 21st century network organizations. *Organizational Dynamics*, 20, 5–20.

Stebbins, M. and Shani, A. B. (Rami), Moon, W., and Bowles, D. (1998). Business process reengineering at Blue Shield of California: The integration of multiple change initiatives. *Journal of Organizational Change Management*, 11(3), 216–32.

Stebbins, M., Shani, A. B. (Rami), and Sena, J. (1995). Information technology and organization design. *Journal of Information Technology*, 10, 101–13.

Tsui-Auch, L. (2001). Learning in global and local networks: Experience of Chinese firms in Hong King, Singapore, and Taiwan. In A. B. Antal, M. Dierkes, J. Child, and I. Nonaka (eds), *Handbook of Organizational Learning and Knowledge*. New York: Oxford University Press, pp. 716–32.

Vansina, L. P. and Taillieu, T. (1996). Business process reengineering or sociotechnical system design in new clothes? In W. A. Pasmore and R. W. Woodman (eds), *Research in Organizational Change and Development*, vol. 9. Greenwich, CT: JAI Press, pp. 81–100.

9

Designing a Sustainable Learning Organization

■ What can we learn across the cases presented in chapters 3 to 8 regarding:

- the conditions, structures, and processes necessary for sustainable learning organizations (SLO)?
- the relationships between company context, strategy, learning, and performance?
- the relationships between learning requirements, learning dimensions, and learning mechanisms?
- the patterns of learning mechanisms used in relation to sustainability?

Introduction

Our point of departure has been that, though there have been clear improvements in the past decade, individuals' personal development at work has, for the majority of people, been a process that has been randomly steered through the unplanned stream of events in the workplace. Surely people have learned, but the weight, character, and relevance of that learning for the benefit of the individual or the company have basically been a matter of chance. As stated in chapter 2, planning makes learning more conscious, better focuses effort, and increases measures for accountability. Planning allows people to nurture learning strategically and to take advantage of learning strategies that might otherwise be overlooked.

In chapter 2 we presented an overall framework or model that related an organization's context, especially its relations to its various constituencies or stakeholders, to its strategy, design, and resources. These, in their turn, influence the organization's performance. In this context we are especially interested in the organization's sustainability and its competitiveness (see figure 2.1). The central processes of interest are learning at the individual, group, and organizational level. We pointed out that the context, business strategy, and resources place key requirements on learning which, in their turn, will determine the appropriate choice and content or learning dimensions and mechanisms (see figure 2.2). Thus, for example, management's formulation of its human resource development (HRD) strategy is simply a first step in a process that will affect every individual in the company through HRD policies, systems, and programs that may include personal development plans for everyone. These processes should be supported by guidelines, policies, routines, methods, tools, processes, and structures, which we refer to collectively as "learning mechanisms." Learning has come into focus because, to quote de Geus (1988), "people's knowledge and skills and the way they are organized are probably an organization's most viable means of competition."

In chapters 3 through 8 we have presented case studies that, though taken from different industries and countries, represent companies who have taken these words to heart and have worked seriously with learning issues. All these companies are well respected within their markets. The majority of them are well established. It is possible to identify a time, if not an exact date, when each company made an active decision to prioritize learning or the key conditions that have promoted the key role of HRD in the company's further development. This was usually associated with the need for radical changes in the organization, for example in the form of a turnaround, or following the appointment of a new CEO. In some cases this was decades ago, in others relatively recently. One example, the software company, is a relatively newly started company, typical of the "new economy." Though differing from the others in many ways, not least in its learning methods and mechanisms, it fits the framework presented here well. We have conducted these case studies often together with other professional colleagues. They are based on many interviews that lasted between one and four hours with representatives for management, unions, production and service personnel, together with the analysis of secondary material from the companies, describing strategies, policies, methods, and tools regarding HRD and learning mechanisms.

In this chapter we present a summary and analyses of these cases with respect to the learning requirements that were identified in these cases and the design dimensions they used to plan their HRD activities. We have also identified the learning mechanisms that these companies had devised and implemented. Our analysis will present the main practices emerging and how they are related. These companies have come a considerable way in their efforts and are clear examples of good practice. Learning investments have helped establish their sustainability and competitiveness.

The structure of this chapter is based on the framework presented in chapter 2. The first section summarizes the cases in terms of the general model presented in figure 2.1 relating the companies' contexts in terms of important market and societal trends and constituencies to the companies themselves, in terms of their strategies, resources, and performance. These form the basis for an analysis of current generic learning requirements. The second section examines the cases in light of the specific learning framework presented in chapter 2, namely in terms of learning requirements, learning design dimensions, and learning mechanisms. This results in a schema showing the generic learning requirements and the basic learning design dimensions. Several design dimensions may be relevant to any given learning requirement. The third section relates the design dimensions to the learning mechanisms, in terms of both their general utilization and the specific character of the mechanisms currently utilized. The final section presents some general reflections on the cases and the model, not least concerning dilemmas and limitations.

Learning across Companies

Relations between context, strategy, learning requirements, and sustainability

Our first overview of the cases is presented in table 9.1. In this table the assessments of learning capability and performance have been made by the authors on the basis of the material from the cases and their knowledge of the literature and current practice. The companies have been chosen on the basis of their work with learning. They are, however, reasonably spread over industrial and service sectors. They are mainly large companies and all are major players in their marketplaces. The medium-sized company, JR Software Development, was a niche leader in its sector. It should be pointed out initially that there is much about each individual case that is unique. We comment on the general trends in the cases and on specific features we have reason to regard as distinctive of an individual case.

Considering contextual factors, the companies have faced the same general factors that have characterized the past twenty years: the rapid development in globalization that has not only entailed the growing dominance of the capitalist market economy, but also the shift to an economy dominated by the financial and not the industrial sector. Since the early 1970s the turnover in the global financial market has increased by a factor of 42, with a daily turnover now in the order of trillions of US dollars (Wikman, 2001). A central problematic factor that has confronted several of our cases has been deregulation, which has strongly influenced the "rules of competition" in a sector. Examples are the deregulation of state monopolies, as in telecommunications, eased regulations for entering a national market, as in banking, and the introduction and

Table 9.1 Company context, strategy, learning, and performance

Focus / Model elements	Individual — Bank	Group — Car mfg	Org. transf. — Telecom service	Dev. proc. — Paper mill	Know. mgt. proc. — Software Devel.	Network — Medical service provider
Contextual factors	Deregulation ICT development Industrial relations climate	Global competition Industrial relations climate	Deregulation ICT development Industrial relations climate	Deregulation Global competition Industrial relations climate	Niche Competition ICT development	Deregulation Industrial relations climate
Strategy	SCA*** Extended market lead HRM/HRD	SCA Highly skilled production workers HRM/HRD	SCA Regional market lead HRM/HRD	SCA Greater export market share HRM/HRD	SCA Sustainable growth Low personnel turnover HRM/HRD	SCA Improved profitability Regional market domination
Org. design	Decentralized teams Development projects Managers as coaches	Autonomous teams Development projects Team coaches	Some teams Managers as coaches	Team based Development projects Team coaches	Multiple project teams Self-learning Team coach Extended use	Development projects Team facilitators
Learning* capability	High	High Basic education	Moderate Basic education	Moderate	Moderate	Moderate
Perform.** sustainable	High	Moderate	Moderate	High	High	Moderate
Perform. competitive	High	High	Moderate	High	High	Moderate

* Learning capability: Human, financial, technical and temporal resources for learning.
** Performance assessments are based on the last data from c. the past 15 years.
*** SCA: Sustainable competitive advantage.

removal of national trade barriers, as in the paper industry. New generations and applications of information and communication technologies have been streaming onto the market and have radically changed ways of doing business in many areas. The development of management models such as lean production, time-based management, business process engineering, outsourcing, and downsizing have resulted in markedly reducing organizational slack so that work has become more intensive and the interdependencies between different individuals stronger.

Learning requirements

General consequences of these changes have been rising complexity, speed, intensity, and rate of change in business and work. This has increased the demands on companies for flexibility and responsiveness, at all levels and in both the short term and the long term. These conditions require prompt decision-making adapted to the specific situation (or customer) and often a sensitive balancing, or even trade-off, between the needs and demands of different parties. These also require a close integration in many cases between (current) production and development (coming production). These impact on such aspects of work as decision-making, core competencies, balance between goals, and task integration.

One of the current paradoxes in working life is that there are two distinct trends observable that represent widely different ways of meeting today's challenges. These trends have different names, the "high road" and the "low road," "high trust" and "low trust" organizations, "learning organizations" and "neo-Tayloristic" organizations. The main difference between these two approaches is whether or not they give due consideration to the legitimate needs and aspirations of the majority of members of an organization, its employees. The high road, high trust solutions give such consideration to personnel, regarding them as an organizational stakeholder on a par with other stakeholders. This broaches a vital aspect of sustainability, namely the principle of involving, or at least taking due consideration for the legitimate needs and ambitions of, *all* the organization's constituencies or stakeholders (Docherty et al., 2002). Taking this into consideration, we may formulate *learning requirements* for the majority of personnel in current contexts:

- Personnel must be multiskilled, with a broad spectrum of skills covering cognitive, technical, business, and social skills. (This has been illustrated in the cases for personnel in process, manufacturing, and service industries at both professional and skilled worker levels.)

- Personnel must be capable of making decisions in dealing with production problems and in contacts with customers and suppliers within and outside their own company. Their contacts with such stakeholders need to be characterized by respect, understanding, and efficiency.

- Personnel must be able to participate in both production and development work, in terms of continuous improvement, local development projects, and central development projects.

- The work situation must promote the personnel's commitment to their work with a personal readiness to utilize their initiative, to take risks, to tolerate differences of opinion, to accept change, and to continually learn new things.

- The structure of most work situations and the focus on "learning" as distinct from "training" entail the integration of learning in work. Zuboff has an excellent formulation of this point:

> The (truly successful) organization is a learning institution, and one of its principal purposes is the expansion of knowledge that comes to reside at the core of what it means to be productive. Learning is no longer a separate activity that occurs either before one enters the workplace or in remote classroom settings. Nor is it an activity preserved for a managerial group. The behaviors that define learning and the activities that define being productive are one and the same. Learning is not something that requires time out from productive activity. To put it simply, learning is the new form of labor. (Zuboff, 1988, p. 395)

The main stabilizing and constructive factor reported in five of the cases was the positive relationships between the social partners at the company level, i.e., between management and unions. The sixth case, the software development company, was non-unionized, though it had a strong culture and HRD program. In an analysis of an EU study of HRD strategies, Cressey and Kelleher (2000) refer to the "fusion of learning and social dialogue for organizational transformation," that the social partners have strong mutual interests and often work closely together at the local level to promote competence development and employability. Field with Ford (1995) found labor leaders envisioning new roles for unions that emphasize partnership, collaboration, and consensus-building, and they see learning as central to their new focus. In an ongoing international project, Huzzard and Nilsson (2002) note a growing interest on the part of trade unions in moving from a purely adversarial role at the local level to a more nuanced, contingent stance in which joint ventures are regarded as both practical and desirable in fields such as learning. How such efforts can be rigged in practice has been documented earlier in the cases. Management has also shown strong interest and been an active partner in these situations. There have been a number of studies that indicate positive relationships between such nuanced relations between the social partners and developments in the companies' performance. The reasoning is that management's positive attitudes to the unions lead to positive attitudes to management on the part of union members. This, in its turn, influences their work positively which leads to improved company performance (Sako, 1995; Fernie and Metcalf, 1995; Guest and Peccei, 1999). This precondition for a wholehearted investment in learning for all members in the organization has been spelled out in some detail in chapters 3 through 6 where the union came to play active roles in the realization of the HRD efforts.

A common aim with strategy in all the participating companies was, not surprisingly, to create sustainable competitive advantage. Given the available data, the companies seemed to be living up to their multi-stakeholder ambition. Their business strategies aimed at further improvement of their already positive positions and aimed similarly at new goals regarding learning. Considering organizational design, the trends related to learning were the further decentralization of decision-making and responsibility, multiskilling, the introduction of (semi-autonomous) teams, the integration of production and development, and of business and learning processes. Managers' roles are changing through added responsibility for HRM and especially HRD. In several of the companies the managers' reward system is coupled to how well they deal with their HRD duties. In addition to planning and follow-up tasks and the integration of business and competence development, managers must often plan on-the-job learning and function as mentor, coach, and tutor to their staff. The primary learning mechanisms being used in these companies included strategy and policy documents, business and competence development plans, methods and tools for competence assessment, work design, management and reward systems, ICT applications, including intranet and e-learning, and workspace design. The performance and estimated sustainability of the firms are high or moderate in all cases.

Learning requirements and learning design dimensions

Our structuring of the learning activities in the companies has been around the main concepts presented in chapter 2, namely learning requirements, design dimensions, and learning mechanisms. An overview of the cases in these regards is shown in table 9.2.

The broad requirements are formulated on the basis of an analysis of the organization's context; the demands of the constituencies and management's vision and strategy for the business will depend heavily on management's values and view on static and dynamic effectiveness: is it to be a learning organization or a neo-Tayloristic organization? The business idea will strongly influence the core competencies required. Burton-Jones (1999) exemplifies a number of these types of issues in the case of the knowledge-based firms such as JR Software Development. Thus, for example, their decision to internalize transactions involving high levels of specialized and tacit knowledge leads to such consequences as the entry levels for employment are raised, cross-functional teamwork will increase, emphasis on learning will increase, performance-based incentives will increase, dependence on key knowledge workers will increase, and the development of knowledge management will increase. Similarly, the redefining of the links between

Table 9.2 Learning requirements, design dimensions, and learning mechanisms

Learning:	Individual Bank	Group Car mfg	Org. transf. Telecoms	Development processes Paper mill	Know. mgt proc. Software Devel.	Network Med. serv provider
Learning requirements	Job skills: Business Customer-orientation Social responsibility On-the-job learning	Skill range Competence overcapacity On-the-job learning	Management philosophy Mgt learning strategy Mgt of learn strategy Total learning environment	Management philosophy Integrating dev. & prod. Learning infrastructure Integrating business & learning org.	Continual learning 'as need arises' Work environ. for learning & development Access to databases and best code modules	Shared mental model for network members Arenas for learning & dec.:making Learn. process integrated in business operations
Learning design dimensions	Integration in business idea Integration in business plan. & cycle / Focus on 'own customer responsibility' Moral Competence On the job learning	Team required Skills * Min. required status per skill area Methods/work organization/skills.	Management value base Social dialogue Indiv./tech/ organization HRD: recruit, develop outplace Management responsibility Plans, methods, roles, technology assessments	Gap analysis Multiskilling Social partnership Design of arenas Design of relations between arenas & operat.organ. Climate for experiment.	Explicit development progression path, assessment, & reward Open workplace architecture IT infrastructure Internal/external databases Reusable code library	Org. of envir. scanning Goal-setting formalized Cooperation (contracts) Org. dialogues (modes, proc. methods) Control process Bench learning Union-partnership
Learning Mechanisms	Life-time employment Culture document Mgt/personnel dialogue thru' business plan process OCR E-learning on-the-job w. mgr as coach Experience exchange workshops	Employability Gap analysis system Competence Reward system Indiv. + team development program Tutors Learning centers Learning meetings e-learning Re-skilling & outplacement	Employability Mgt/union dialogue On-/at job. Learning centers Arena infrastructure Learn.Intranet Re-skilling outplcement Benchlearning alliances Design of physical environment	Mgt/personnel dialogue Gap analysis Goal setting for learning Dev.tasks for production Personnel. Parallel learning structure Weekly revision of dev work & operations Dev. reward system Mgt's dual role: dev. & production	Competence recruitment 'On-the-job school' Project group dialogues Platform-based work design Clear linkages to experts IT search and discovery routines Flexible architecture design	Dialogue & communicat infrastruct. Network's parallel learning structure for joint efforts HRD exchange program Multi-manager role in networks Systematic transfer of project results

* Required skills: cognitive, social, technical, business and teaching skills..

education, work, and learning will lead to increased opportunities for high-skilled workers and decreased opportunities for low-skilled workers, the universal adoption of learning technologies, the erosion of boundaries between academic and vocational training, and the convergence of academic and commercial interests.

The learning design dimensions are specific areas in which active choices must be made, the outcomes of which strongly influence the what, when, how, and who of learning, its efficiency and effectiveness, its ease and difficulty. The mechanisms are the concrete realization of the design decisions or parameters.

Learning design dimensions

Dodgson (1993) defined learning organizations as "firms that purposely adopt structures and strategies to encourage learning." Popper and Lipshitz (1998) used the term "learning mechanisms" to describe institutionalized structural and procedural arrangements to systematically promote learning.

It is meaningful to distinguish between two levels when speaking of the learning requirements, namely a value level and a cognitive level. The value level concerns the values held by top management in general and by the CEO in particular. How do they view other people, and their subordinates in particular? Early Swedish research showed that senior managers regarded themselves as X-people and their junior staff as Y-people in McGregor's terms (Magnusson, 1974). In general, many managers give priority to investors and customers at the expense of personnel. The orientation of top management to stock exchange analysts and the need to have good quarterly, or now monthly, figures is becoming the bane of many companies.

A key value that has been explicitly expressed in formal documents in many of the companies here is management's respect for and trust in personnel and their assurance of striving to preserve their security, if not in the firm, at least in the labor market, i.e., their employability. This value, which has a moral character, is part of the sustainability principle concerning constituencies (see above). It also strongly influences the range and character of learning measures taken by the companies.

Managements that have respect for and trust in their employees usually have little difficulty in getting on with their elected representatives, namely the unions. This was the second clear value-based precondition in the companies that have unions. Management has very good relations with the unions within the company. In several cases management was not interested in having anything to do with the unions at the national level. The social partners were well versed in the fine balancing act of working together in vital development projects in the company at the same time as pursuing hard negotiations on matters where distinctive interests were of primary concern – the so-called "boxing and dancing" relationship (Huzzard and Nilsson, 2002).

Table 9.3 Generic learning requirements and learning dimensions in the cases

Learning requirements	Learning dimensions
• "High road," "high trust" solutions – Multiskilled personnel – Decision makers: problem-solving, social competence – Personnel committed to performance and learning • Production and development integrated • "Learning where you are" and "as you are": experiential, 'on-the-job' learning	• Clear values and culture • Integrated business and HR strategies • Organizational design for learning • Management and reward system for learning • "Ba," Learning space, virtual and physical • Learning processes – Distinctive competences – Processes – Dialogues, communication infrastructure – ICT support

The more cognitive requirements coupled to this value base are management statements of ethics, social responsibility, values, business and HRD strategy, including directions of action, distinctive competencies, development processes, and dialogue issues, including infrastructure such as arenas.

The next area is the design dimensions. These may be grouped to relate to the learning requirements (see table 9.3). The value-based, cultural dimension is to ensure the clarity and legitimacy of the position of learning in the company; whom it concerns and what it entails for different groups of personnel. The integration of learning in the work situation has several dimensions: 1) the integration of the business and the learning processes, 2) the integration of the work and the learning processes, and 3) the integration of first- and second-order learning, or learning for production and learning for development (see chapter 2). The first of these is at a group or business unit level. The others concern individuals. These are dealt with partly in the strategies and partly in the organizational design. A second group of dimensions concerns the management processes regarding learning, namely the sophistication of the learning management system, for example the number and character of the steps in drawing up individual plans, their integration into team development plans and business plans, both for production and product and process development. It also concerns the tools and methods used, the character of feedback and evaluation procedures, the frequency with which follow-up sessions are held, the coupling of these processes to reward systems for the personnel and for managers, and the coupling to the business management cycle. The further group of dimensions concerns learning itself, including the assessment of the distinctive competencies, methods, tools, and routines. This also covers the scope of learning methods, such as on-the-job learning, e-learning, group learning, development projects, and continuous improvement. A further area concerns dialogues, the arenas, the groups participating, and their different character: planned/ad hoc, documented/undocumented. These reflect the scope of the companies' activities and the extent of their investments in learning.

In choosing a name for the final dimension here, we decided on the Japanese term "*ba*," which roughly means "place" (see chapter 2). The concept was originally proposed by the Japanese philosopher Nishida and defined by Nonaka et al. (2001) as a context in which knowledge is shared, created, and utilized. It does not necessarily mean a physical space. It can be a physical space, a virtual space, a mental space, or any combination of these kinds of spaces. The most important aspect of "*ba*" is interaction. *Ba* is a space where interactions take place. It is conceived as the framework in which knowledge is activated as a resource.

As stated before, when examining a number of companies to understand their learning processes, some companies will have features that reflect the specific character of the case. Two of the cases presented here have such characteristics. The software house employed highly qualified systems analysts and programmers. Their professional competence and interest entailed them using ICT knowledge retrieval and learning aids of greater variety, number, and sophistication than in any of the other cases for the simple reason that the majority of personnel in other organizations lacked the professional knowledge and skills to use such systems. ICT offers tremendous potential for knowledge management and "organizational memory," structuring the organization's experience and making it available to others in the organization. However, there are three important hindrances. Firstly, this requires considerable investments if the experience is to be recorded in a fashion that makes it desirable, relevant, comprehensible, and easily accessible to its target groups in the organization. Those commercial companies that have made significant developments in this field are the international management consultant companies (Docherty, 1996a; Werr et al., 1997). Secondly, it requires special routines and organization, if this is to lead to learning and not just information retrieval (Stymne, 2001). Thirdly, as in the case presented here, it may require considerable ICT competence on the part of the users.

The second such case concerned the medical service provider network. This case had more legal documentation than the other cases due to the participation of so many different legal entities which necessitated formal contracts between different parties in different matters. The mere fact that different companies, legal entities, were participating in the network offered opportunities for learning that were not available in the same way in the other companies. These included coordinated environmental scanning, bench-learning projects, inter-organizational dialogues, a personnel exchange scheme, and greater investment in the systematic inter-company exchange of experience from projects.

Learning design dimensions and learning mechanisms

The learning mechanisms are the formalized, institutionalized results of active decisions by management regarding the company's position on the learning dimensions (see chapter 2). Some mechanisms derive directly from the

Table 9.4 Learning design dimensions and their associated learning mechanisms

Learning design dimensions	Learning mechanisms
Values and culture	Management/company value statements
Strategies, contracts, policies	Strategy documents (business, HRD) Management/union agreements
	Intercompany contracts (network, bench learning)
Management and reward systems	Balanced Score Card
	HRD management system
	Organizational climate and customer surveys Follow-up procedures (nature and frequency) Reward systems
	Integration of business and learning
Organizational design	Teams
	Development structures: networks
	Continuous improvement
	Parallel learning structures
	Bench-learning structure
Learning dimensions: Distinctive competencies	Methods and tools for assessment
	Special tests, e.g., learning style
Learning dimensions: Learning process	Integration of work and learning
	First- and second-order learning (prod. & dev.)
	Experiential learning
	Action learning
	Support infrastructure
Learning dimensions: ICT support	E-learning applications
	Learning centers
	Knowledge management systems, intranet
LD: Communication infrastructure	Arenas
	Networks
LD: Ba, spatial design	Type (workplace, learning room, center)

requirements level, such as formal documents from top management defining strategies and policies. Others are derived from the design dimensions. It should be possible to construct dimensions and scales for the instrument sketched in figure 2.2. Table 9.4 shows the learning design dimensions and their associated learning mechanisms. Appropriate scales could be designed for these specific dimensions.

Utilization of learning mechanisms

Table 9.5 shows the utilization of the different learning mechanisms in the six cases. Firstly, the companies all use a wide range of mechanisms. The category that is used most sparingly is the design of the physical work/learning space. The commitment to learning permeates the companies: it is ratified and communicated at every turn. Our assessment is also that the investment in the

Table 9.5 The utilization of learning mechanisms in different cases

Utilization of learning Mechanisms (**H**igh, **M**edium and **L**ow degrees of utilization)	Indiv. Bank	Group Car mfg	Transf. Telecom service	Devpr Paper mill	Know. mgt Software devel.	Network Med serv. provider
Values and culture	H	H	H	M/H	H	M
Strategies, contracts and policies	H	H	H	H	M/H	H
Organizational design	H	H	M	H	H	H
Management and reward systems	H	H	H	M/H	M/H	M
Learning: Processes	H	H	H	H	H	H
Learning: Dialogues, communication infrastructure	H	M	M	H	L/H	M/H
Learning: ICT support.	M	H	M	M	H	M
Learning: Ba, spatial design	L	M	M/H	L	H	L
Overall range of learning mechanisms used (H+M/H)	6	6	5	6	7	4

various mechanisms is wholehearted. We interpret this condition as reflecting the management value base, strongly supported by unions, and often initiated by a newly appointed CEO.

Learning mechanisms

Formal documents: values and culture, strategies, contracts and policies.

The main formal documents in this context are: value statements, joint agreements between the social partners, and strategy documents. For an organization's approach to learning to weather the turbulence and radical day-to-day shifts in priorities, it must be well anchored in the organization's value system – especially the values of top management. In this context it is essential that management's values are clearly stated and made known to all members of the organization. Otherwise genuine concern for and commitment to learning within the top management group may well be neutralized by managers in the levels nearest top management (Dilschmann et al., 1994). Brytting and Trollestad (2000) found that more and more companies are endeavoring to create common values as a means of integrating, guiding, and managing businesses conducted in decentralized forms. Lapidoth (1996) found that value statements function as a key reference point in high growth companies, where practically everything else was continually changing. The Bank case in chapter 3 in this volume exemplifies how a clear statement of values from the CEO can function as a foundation for a steadily developing learning strategy for the whole organization. Staff receive their personal copy with their name on it and must be prepared to show it to their manager on request. The document, which is revised somewhat every fifth year, details the company's main values with respect to its investors, customers, and personnel. The role of learning is clear in this document. Other cases, while not having separate value documents, can refer to management statements, for example, in the annual reports.

The cases presented here indicate several values that are key preconditions for the design of conditions, structures, and processes for learning. Three value choices are illustrated in these cases:

- *"Learning is a key business process."* Learning is a key element of the performance area "internal dynamic effectiveness" featured in many management systems, including the Balanced Score Card system in the Telecom Service case. De Geus (1988) emphasized learning as an organization's most viable means of competition. It is essential to meet changes in the organization's environment and marketplace and to master the growing complexity and rate of change.

- *"Learning includes all members in the organizations."* This is an essential element in Pedler's (1991) basic definition of a learning organization. It complies with Bengtsson's (1985) description of "human resource intensive" strategies in the OECD. The Japanese industrial leader, Matsuchita, maintained that it was the Japanese management's commitment to utilizing the full capacity of their personnel, including their intellectual creativity and decision-making ability, that gave their companies a distinctive advantage in the marketplace. Hamrefors (1999) observed that companies that engaged all their personnel in "environmental scanning" (so-called knowledge absorption) performed much better in this respect than those who delegated this task to a special staff department. This value is also coupled to the previous one and the learning requirements, for example, regarding the need for development, for multiskilling, and for problem-solving ability.

- *"Working with learning entails true partnership between the social partners."* In Europe there is a growing tendency for unions to prioritize the skills development of their members to ensure their "employability," i.e., to reduce members' dependence on their current employer and increase their personal attractiveness on the labor market. This goal is pursued both within the union itself and, at the local and even regional levels, by collaboration with management and employers' organizations. This may lead to formal or informal agreement on the design of structures and processes for learning and on design principles for flexibility and demands on the individual. Such discussions can avoid competence problems that may arise through a routine decision to retire all personnel that have reached a given age without considering their competence or capacity (Isaksson and Johansson, 1997). The third case (chapter 5) presents an example in which the collaboration between the social partners led to the reschooling and outplacement of 6,400 people in a three-year period which was calculated to have been a very economically profitable investment (Hansson, 1999).

Learning is not, generally speaking, a controversial issue: the social partners do not seem to have difficulty in collaborating on this issue. Bengtsson (1985) indicated that the Anglo-Saxon cultures traditionally had a different view on the division of responsibilities between management and staff in this area. A broad European interpretation is that management has a responsibility to provide the conditions and opportunities for learning and personnel has a responsibility to utilize them. This trend seems to have been accelerated due to the shortage of skilled personnel. In a European Union study, Cressey et al. (1999) established that agreements on permanent employment were being revoked and that the newer concept of "employability" was mainly to be found in Sweden. In all our cases there have been very positive and constructive relations between management and staff on learning issues. Management and unions have worked together on HRM and HRD strategy and policy statements, and in two cases joint agreements have been signed.

The cases indicate a high level of integration between business plans and HRD, both at the planning and the follow-up stages. This integration is especially clear in the basic production units, for example, the branch offices in the banks and the integrated production teams in the car manufacturing plant.

The work organization

The business demands of complexity, flexibility, and readiness for change require highly skilled teams with a high degree of autonomy. Although a recent EU report maintained that the concept of teams was "useful, but not used" in Europe, with the exception of Sweden and possibly the Netherlands, there are probably sectors or industries which are "leading" in this respect, for example, the car manufacturing industry (Benders et al., 1999; Kuhlmann, 2002). The cases, however, are strongly oriented to such "high road," "high trust" teams, which almost function as small independent enterprises with respect to their range of tasks, knowledge and skills, and responsibilities for production, economic results, product/service quality, delivery times, customer care, and HRM concerning the team. Individuals' personal development is coordinated with the team's. Doing the work and discussing these activities and their outcome is an important part of the development of a community of practice. Members of the team function as teachers, tutors, coaches, and mentors to each other in different fields. Tasks and competencies, resources, and goals must be carefully designed and may be broken down in different ways, for example, in accordance with sociotechnical principles.

In chapter 4, figure 4.3 illustrates clearly the development from simple administrative groups to "learning teams," showing the increasing complexity of the team's tasks and the competence demands made on its members. This figure shows that such groups have responsibility for development and improvement of products (services) and production/service processes. These developments may vary in character, organization, and resources. Two basic types are:

- *continuous improvement meetings*: often a component in Total Quality Management programs, in which members of a normal work team participate in meetings at regular intervals to discuss incremental improvements in the work situation;

- *development projects*: these entail members of a team being assigned to a temporary group with the task of solving a specific problem or realizing a specific development. The problems can be defined by different functions at different levels in the company. Variations on this theme are:

  - *Parallel Learning Systems* (PLS), in which a key goal in conducting a project is that those participating in the project shall learn, acquire new competencies, regarding the topic or the processes or both (Bushe and Shani, 1991; Shani and Mitki, 2000). Thus, such project groups are not staffed in principle primarily by the company's experts in the area. Project groups have access to support experts and coaches. PLS is usually organized as a permanent learning/development structure through which there is a continuous stream of people handling a wide range of problems.

  - *Bench learning* may be called a further development of "benchmarking" (Lessem, 1994), which, as with PLS, makes learning on the part of the project group and the company a clear goal in the project. It entails cooperation between the project group's own company and another company in which the former group studies the practices of the company they are visiting – that company being regarded as being a leading company in the field under study, e.g., marketing or HRD.

  - *Action learning* entails several companies participating, each with its own project group, in a "metaproject" whereby they meet together at regular intervals to discuss their progress in their respective projects and each get feedback from the others regarding interpretations of the developments and suggestions on further action (Argyris, 1999).

  - *Learning forum*: for example, representatives of the social partners in the company discuss developments in a specific area.

  - *Network*: for learning or development between representatives from different companies who work with a specific issue or problem.

All these alternatives are reported in the cases presented earlier.

Management and reward systems

The most advanced example here is when the regular management system specifically includes a section on "HRD." This was the case in the telecommunications service company. This included recruitment, development, and severance. Forty percent of managers' bonus was coupled to performance in this area. In a major plastics concern in Europe, managers' bonus was coupled to the extent to which they managed to utilize their personnel's competencies

(Docherty, 1996b). In several cases the HRD plans were coupled to the business plans and were sent together to senior management. The feedback systems in these companies were coupled to team/office follow-up meetings at which managers and personnel could together evaluate and interpret the results. These meetings also provided the opportunity to follow up personnel development at regular intervals throughout the year, instead of being an annual event.

Performance feedback is provided from the economic, accounting, and production systems. The latter include such items as products produced, quality statistics, and scrap. Several of the cases presented also conduct annual or biannual climate surveys among their personnel. Climate surveys are usually focused on certain areas, e.g., factors affecting learning or creativity or feelings of empowerment. Among climate factors influencing learning are "openness," "risk-taking," "tolerance of conflict," "readiness for change," "social support," and "management support." The results of these surveys are fed back to the different groups for discussion and the possible formulation of development projects. Similarly, in service companies such as the bank, customer surveys are conducted. These are fed back to front-office personnel with similar purposes and procedures.

It is relatively unusual for management compensation systems to assess managers' HRD performance. It is more usual for workers' compensation systems to include competence bonuses. These usually have a ceiling, e.g., 10 percent of the basic wage. The competence bonus is regulated to the number and difficulty of the competencies mastered by the individual. To encourage people's interest in less popular skills and moderate interest in the more popular ones, general bonuses may be awarded when teams reach the required competence level for a team, e.g., 30 percent qualified to evaluate "quality."

Learning and competencies

It usually requires specific studies to identify a company's distinctive competencies. These are not always immediately obvious.[1] Having identified these, they have to be assessed. There are literally dozens of methods available on the market for this purpose. A very common approach is the "gap analysis" method, in which knowledge and skills levels required by the company are compared with current levels among the personnel. This model was illustrated clearly in chapter 5 with the telecommunications service company. In addition, complementary tests may be given regarding learning styles, such as the Kolb instrument or the Myers–Briggs test.

---

[1] For example, what is taxi drivers' distinctive competence? In London, at any rate, it is not that they have a driver's license, but that they have 'the Knowledge', i.e., they know their way around London. They complete a long and difficult training before they are examined by a special unit in the Metropolitan Police and receive their green badges to be worn clearly on their jacket lapel.

There is distinct interest in "on-the-job" or experiential learning, e.g., the bank managers prefer their branch office staff to work with their own customers when learning new tasks. Boud et al. (1993) identifies the assumptions behind experiential learning as: experience is the foundation of, and the stimulus for, learning; learners actively construct their own experience; learning is a holistic experience; learning is socially and culturally constructed; and learning is influenced by the socioemotional context in which it occurs. Boud maintains that the main conceptions of experiential learning share the central notion of autonomy. It places reflection as the "bridge between experience and learning."

Participation in both production and development gives the individual the opportunity of developing both single- and double-loop learning, and possibly even deutero-learning (see chapter 2). In single-loop learning, a person learns to do a given task better. New knowledge is integrated with the old, and the person becomes more skilled within the given limits. A carpenter makes better desks because he learns to use materials better: the parts fit together better, the finish is better. A surgeon is better at appendectomies. She worries less about the next step in the operation. She wastes less movement. The operation takes less time. The scar is smaller. Much of the knowledge developed in this process is tacit knowledge. People develop a special feel for their craft. When a layman watches a skilled craftsman he is impressed by how easy it looks, how little hesitation there is.

In double-loop learning, people reflect over and question things they used to take for granted. They think about the given conditions, and they learn to see other ways to perform their tasks. Established truths and ways of acting are reappraised. Both require creativity. In deutero learning, people learn to learn better. The quality of learning is improved. Faced with the unfamiliar, people learn to handle it faster and better each time. The process goes more smoothly; sidetracks and dead ends are more quickly recognized and abandoned.

As reflection is essential for experiential learning, "ba" space must be created for the interactions, discussions, and discourses associated with such reflection (see chapter 2). A key role is played by all the impromptu and informal discussions at the workplace. Dixon (1997) coined the term "hallways of learning" for the arenas, informally furnished with whiteboards, where such unplanned meetings could take place. Other formal arenas are also necessary, such as team meetings, project meetings, and infrastructure for the exchange of experiences (Stebbins and Shani, 2002). Examples in the cases are the "learning infrastructures" for the HRD support staff in different units in the car manufacturing company and the telecommunications service company. Such an infrastructure also functioned smoothly between the development projects in the various node companies in the Medical Service Provider network. Only TCS Retail and JR Software Development actually designed the ordinary workplace to facilitate learning between team members. Perhaps this was due to the fact that both are ICT-oriented, development-oriented and project-oriented.

Some Reflections

The model proposed in chapter 2 has proved to be useful and relevant to apply to the cases. It focuses on those aspects of learning that can be radically enhanced by active and systematic planning. Learning is a key dimension at both the individual and company levels. For the individual it is essential for health, well-being, and personal development as well as for employability (attaining and maintaining attractive competence in the labor market). For the company it is an important performance dimension regarding dynamic efficiency, meeting the turbulence, complexity, and changes in its environment.

Our basic model focuses on the relations between an organization's strategy and resources and the context and the constituencies with which it operates and its resulting performance. These factors influence the organisation's learning requirements which may be formulated in terms of learning design dimensions where the relevant learning may be facilitated by specific learning mechanisms. Six extensive case studies have been described and analyzed using the model. The cases are all well-established companies, and are successful in their markets. There are a number of similarities between the cases. The strategic goal of "being a learning organization" demands wholehearted dedication. It is definitely not an assignment that can be delegated to an HRM department. It requires an active and continuous commitment from the members of the organization, starting with the top management group and the union leadership, usually together, for learning is of mutual interest for the social partners. It concerns everybody and all personnel must actively commit themselves to taking responsibility for their own learning and the organizational learning. Management provides favorable conditions and opportunities for learning. Key actors in this context are managers, from the CEO all the way down to supervisors and foremen.

The design dimensions concern all the main structures and processes in an organization: culture and values, strategies and policies, organizational design, the design of management and reward systems, communications infrastructure, the utilization of ICT, and the creation of "space for learning." Then comes the learning processes where experiential on-the-job learning plays a central role in today's organizations.

As mentioned above, learning is a key factor for sustainability and competitiveness. Company sustainability requires that the company maintains a sensitive balance in meeting the needs and aspirations of its various constituencies or stakeholders (Docherty, Forslin, and Shani, 2002). Today, personnel is the constituency that most regularly draws the short straw. Simply focusing on learning does much to redress the balance so that personnel is no longer so disadvantaged. This balance is to the advantage of all in the long run. Apart from these cases, there are considerable results to show that investing in learning generates high performance and competitiveness.

There are dilemmas and challenges concerning learning processes. Developments have been very rapid in the past two decades, but problems remain. One simple issue is that there are so many factors that affect learning in the workplace that it is practically impossible to sort all of them out. As Garrick (1999, pp. 220–7) points out:

> (Many authors) argue forcefully that it is not so much the relationship of workplace learning to formal learning, or how learning can be enhanced, or how it is defined, that is most critical. Rather it is the social, cultural and discursive effects on people (including relationships between people at various levels of work) that warrant careful consideration. When work *is* learning, there is clearly a range of critical issues and tensions arising. With the growth of interest in and demand for learning at work, future directions appear to include the need for workplaces to be active in supporting workers/learners as well as deconstructing the limiting conceptual differences between "workers," "managers," "supervisors" and "educators."

An example of this is the new management roles of teacher and coach. There are complex relationships between workers/learners and their managers (or supervisors) who often double as learning advisors, coaches, and mentors and it is quite possible that the power dimension may disturb the learning process.

Dilemmas may require special attention in the design of the learning situation. Examples are combining learning for production and learning for development, or first- and second-order learning. (This has been dealt with successfully in several of the cases presented.) Another is combining individual and group or collective learning. This issue has been raised in some of the cases by the staff as distinct from management. The latter tend to regard competence very much as an individual quality or property. A dilemma is that a routine application of ICT may create a situation where ICT conserves old learning patterns rather than developing them. Knowledge management systems may stop at being informational retrieval systems rather than learning systems.

Planning has a tendency to focus on structures and the observable, the manageable. The standardization and formalization it brings with it may well be harmful to learning processes. This is easily noted in experiential learning in which personal reflection is a key element (Kolb, 1984). Many people are not consciously aware that they are reflecting. If forced by circumstances to focus on this, the reflection process may be disturbed, if not impeded. Many learning aspects are subtle and complex. Our current understanding does not allow more than arranging certain positive conditions for learning. This holds, for example, for the development of tacit knowledge and "communities of practice."

Studies of learning at work are also indicating that there are many important factors and outcomes that are not usually taken into consideration in planning learning, for example, that informal discussions and conversations are very important in workplace learning. In addition, it is not only what is being learned that is important, but also the learning capability that is being produced through the learning process: the immediate product of learning is the ability to learn more. The social setting in which cognitive activity takes place is integral to that activity and not just the surrounding context for it. Lave and Wenger (1991) termed this "situated learning" and offer a powerful contribution to the study of workplace-based learning.

The pleasure we feel in observing experts in action may well turn to unease and uncertainty when we ourselves endeavor to follow the same path. The companies presented have been addressing the issues of learning in organizations for years, if not decades. Their efforts have been, and are, conscientious and wholehearted. They have been learning and continuing to learn. In the following chapter we present a generic model for the application of the "Learning by Design" model in organizations. In addition, we take up a number of issues that require further research and development to ensure improved efficiency and effectiveness in realizing learning in organizations for sustainability and competitiveness.

References

Argyris, C. (1999). *On Organizational learning*. Oxford: Blackwell Publishers.

Bengtsson, J. (1985). *Human Resource Strategies in the OECD*. Presentation to the Swedish Work Environment Fund Workshop on New Technology, Management and Working Life, August, 1985.

Benders, J., Huijgen, Fr., Pekruhl, U., and O'Kelly, K. (1999). *Useful but Unused – Group Work in Europe*. Dublin: European Foundation for Living and Working Conditions.

Bushe, G. and Shani, A. B. (Rami) (1991). *Parallel Learning Structures: Increasing Innovations in Bureaucracies*. Reading, MA: Addison Wesley.

Boud, D., Cohen, R., and Walker, D. (1993). Understanding learning from experience. In D. Boud, R. Cohen, and D. Walker (eds), *Using Experience for Learning*. Buckingham: SRHE and the Open University Press, pp. 1–17.

Brytting, T and Trollestad, C. (2000). Managerial thinking on value-based management. *International Journal of Value-Based Management*, 13, 55–77.

Burton-Jones, A. (1999). *Knowledge-Capitalism: Business, Work and Learning in the New Economy*. Oxford: Oxford University Press.

Cressey, P., Della Rossa, G., Docherty, P., Kelleher, M., Kuhn, M., Reimann, D., and Ullstad, C. (1999). *Partnership and Investment in Europe: The Role of the Social Dialogue in Human Resource Development*. Consolidated report. Brussels: EC Leonardo project EUR/96/2/1071/EA/III.2.a/FPC.

Cressey, P. and Kelleher, M. (2000). *The active roles of learning and social dialogue for organizational change*. Paper to the EU Forum Workshop on "Vocational Education and Training and Culture" in Wageningen, 23–5 November.

Dilschmann, A., Docherty, P., and Stjernberg, T. (1994). *Kompetensstrategier: Bärande Lärdomar* (Competence Strategies: Key Lessons). Stockholm: Arbetsgivarverket.

Dixon, N. M. (1997). Hallways of learning. *Organizational Dynamics*, 25(4), 23–34.

Docherty, P. (1996a). *Läroriket: Vägar och vägskäl in den lärande organizationen.*(The world of learning: Ways and crossroads in the learning organization). Stockholm: Arbetslivsinstitutet.

Docherty, P. (1996b). Manducher: A capability-based strategy in the plastics industry. In P. Docherty and B. Nyhan (eds), *Human Competence and Business Development: Emerging Patterns in European companies*. London: Springer Verlag, pp. 96–108.

Docherty, P., Forslin, J., and Shani, A. B. (2002). Sustainable work systems: Lessons and challenges. In P. Docherty, J. Forslin, and A. B. Shani (eds), *Creating Sustainable Work Systems: Emerging perspectives and practice*. London: Routledge, pp. 213–25.

Dodgson, M. (1993). Organizational learning: A review of some literatures. *Organization Studies*, 14, 375–94.

Field, L. with Ford, W. B. (1995). *Managing Organizational Learning: From Rhetoric to Reality*. Melbourne: Longman.

Fernie, S. and Metcalf, D. (1995). Participation, contingent pay, representation and workplace performance: Evidence from Great Britain. *British Journal of Industrial Relations*, 33(3), 379–415.

Garrick, J. (1999). The dominant discourses of learning at work. In D. Boud and J. Garrick (eds), *Understanding Learning at Work*. London: Routledge, pp. 216–31.

Geus, A. de (1988). Planning as learning. *Harvard Business Review*, 66, March–April, 70–4.

Guest, D. and Peccei, R. (1999). *The Partnership Company: Benchmarks for the Future*. London: IPA.

Hamrefors, S. (1999). *Spontaneous Environmental Scanning: Putting "Putting into Perspective" into Perspective*. Stockholm: Stockholm School of Economics.

Hansson, R. (1999). *Personalförsörjningsmodellen – Ett projekt i tiden: Övertalighetshantering* (Personnel flow model – a timely project: Redundancy management). Stockholm: Svenska Strukturforskningsinstitutet HB.

Huzzard, T. and Nilsson, T. (2002). *The New Trade Union: Boxing and Dancing*. Paper to the 20th International Labour Process Conference at University of Strathclyde, Glasgow, April 2–4.

Isaksson, K. and Johansson, G. (1997). *Avalspension på vinst och förlust*: (Swedish: *Earlier retirement pension – win or lose*). Stockholm: Folksam and the Swedish Council for Work Life Research.

Kolb, D. (1984). *Experiential Learning: Experience as a Source of Learning and Development*. Englefield Cliffs, NJ: Prentice-Hall.

Kuhlmann, M. (2002). Group work and democracy. In P. Docherty, J. Forslin, and A. B. Shani (eds), *Creating Sustainable Work Systems: Emerging Perspectives and Practice*, London: Routledge

Lapidoth, J., Jr. (1996). Organisatoriskt lärande i ett tillväxtföretag – SkandiaLink Lifeinsurance Co. Ltd (Organizational learning in a high growth company). Stockholm: Arbetslivsinstitutet.

Lave, J. and Wenger, E. (1991). *Situated Learning – Legitimate Peripheral Participation*. Cambridge: Cambridge University Press.

Lessem, R. (1994). *Total Quality Learning: Building a Learning Organization*. Oxford: Blackwell Publishers.

Magnusson, Å. (1974). *Participation and the Company's Information and Decision Systems*. Stockholm: Economic Research Institute working paper 6022.

Nonaka, I., Toyama, R., and Byosière, P. (2001). A theory of knowledge creation: Understanding the dynamic process of creating knowledge. In M. Dierkes, A. Berthoin Antal, J. Child, and I. Nonaka (eds), *Handbook of Organizational Learning and Knowledge*. Oxford: Oxford University Press, pp. 491–517.

Pedler, M. (1991). The need for self-learning organizations as part of an overall business/management strategy. In B. Nyhan (ed.) *Developing People's Ability to Learn*. Brussels: European Interuniversity Press, pp. 128–40.

Popper, M. and Lipshitz, R. (1998). Organizational learning mechanisms: A structural and cultural approach to organizational learning. *Journal of Applied Behavioral Science*, 34(2), 161–79.

Sako, M. (1995). The nature and impact of employees' voice in the European car components industry. *Human Resource Management Journal*, 8(2), 5–13.

Shani, A. B. (Rami) and Mitki, Y. (2000). Creating learning organizations: Beyond mechanisms. In R. Golembiewski (ed.), *Handbook of Organizational Consultations*. New York: Marcel Dekker, pp. 911–19.

Stebbins, M. and Shani, A. B. (Rami) (2002). Eclectic design for change. In P. Docherty, J. Forslin, and A. B. Shani (eds), *Creating Sustainable Work Systems: Emerging Perspectives and Practice*. London: Routledge, pp. 201–12.

Stymne, B. (2001). Kunskapsåtervinning eller lärande? (Knowledge retrieval or learning?) In T. Backlund, H. Hansson, and C. Thunborg (eds), *Lärdilemman i arbetslivet*. Lund: Studentlitteratur, pp. 195–214.

Werr, A., Stjernberg, T., and Docherty, P. (1997). The functions of methods of change in management consulting. *Journal of Organizational Change Management*, 10(4), 288–307.

Wikman, A. (2001). *Internationalisering, flexibilitet, och förändrade företagsformer. En statistisk analys av arbetsställernas utveckling under 90-talet* (Internationalization, flexibility and changes in the organization of business). Stockholm: National Institute for Working Life, report series: Work Life in Transition 2001.

Zuboff, S. (1988). *In the Age of the Smart Machine: The Future of Work and Power*. Oxford: Heinemann.

10

Learning by Design: Change and Future

- What are the implications for organizations and management interested in designing organizations for sustainable learning and competitiveness?

- What might be a possible roadmap or generic intervention model for a planned change strategy?

- What are some of the unanswered questions that require further study?

As we have seen in chapter 9, one of the major conclusions that can be drawn from the companies described in this book is that the learning by design approach emerged out of practice and not out of theory. Managers and organizations, in dealing with the ongoing challenges and problems, developed a variety of learning mechanisms as a way to sustain business. In his most recent book, Ackoff identifies four different ways of dealing with problems (labeled messes) in organizations (Ackoff, 1999).

In Russell Ackoff's words: "ignore the problem or mess and hope that it will take care of itself and go away of its own accord" or "do something that yields an outcome that's good enough, that 'satisfices'" or "do something that yields or comes close as possible to the best possible outcomes, something that optimizes" or "redesign either the entity that has the problem or mess, or its environment, in such a way as to eliminate the problem or mess and enable the system involved to do better in the future than the best it can do today, in a word, to idealize."

In the context of organizations, management, change, learning, and this book, our conviction is to follow the fourth strategy proposed by Ackoff. As we have seen in chapters 3 through 8, all six companies and their management took a proactive approach to fostering learning by design. The learning requirements created by their contextual environment (the mess) led them to explore a variety of design dimensions. Those served as the basis for the design and redesign of learning mechanisms (see figure 2.1). The learning mechanisms that were created (and continuously redesigned) served as system enablers for continuous improvements, enhancement of performance and sustainability, and building in an improved (and better) capacity for learning in the future.

Learning by Design: Towards a Change Process Model

The cases described in this book did not follow a specific change strategy. The firms have developed learning mechanisms, as they saw fit, based on their changing environmental context and firm dynamics. As we reflected on the cases it became evident that learning mechanisms are used and can be used for very different purposes. Furthermore, the learning design requirements seem to have been triggered by the business context, or what Ackoff calls "the mess." In turn, managers shoulder the responsibility of identifying the possible different design dimensions and explore the possible variations along each design dimension. The specific choices of which variation on each of the design dimension to adopt results in the specific configuration of the learning mechanism.

This section of the chapter presents a generic process model for facilitating learning by design in the firm. As such, we will identify some of the basic phases in implementing learning by design as well as the key processes that need to be managed in the process. Before we proceed with a discussion of the generic intervention model, it is evident to us that four developments in the field of organizational change and development have enormous impact on a possible learning-by-design intervention strategy, namely, sociotechnical systems design, reflexive design, action research, and appreciative inquiry.

At the basic level, the learning-by-design change intervention is not likely to follow a single theoretical change perspective. As we have seen in the cases, while some common phases are likely to be used by most organizations, the specific change process will emerge separately and uniquely depending on the nature of each company and its context. Yet at a generic level, the intervention change process is likely to be an eclectic process that integrates a variety of components from appreciative inquiry, action research, sociotechnical systems design, and reflexive design. While an account of the development and the comprehensive nature of each of the four schools of thought is beyond the scope of this chapter, the following is a brief overview of their essence.

Appreciative inquiry

Learning by design is anchored in a systematic collaborative inquiry process into the firm's learning experience and practice. During the past fifteen years, appreciative inquiry (AI) has been advanced beyond an ideological and philosophical orientation, to a theory and method for a system's learning and development. In its broadest focus, "appreciative inquiry involves a systematic discovery of what gives life to a living system when it is most alive, most effective, and most constructively capable in economics, ecological, and human terms" (Cooperrider and Whitney, 2001). Thus, "appreciative inquiry involves the art and practice of asking questions that strengthen a system's capacity to apprehend, anticipate, and heighten positive potential" (Cooperrider and Srivastva, 1987). AI is viewed as a cyclical spiral composed of four basic elements: *discovery* (what gives life), or the best of what is – appreciating; *dream* (what might be), or what the world is calling for – envisioning results; *design* (what should be – the ideal) – co-constructing; and *destiny* (how to empower, learn, and adjust/improvise) – sustaining. Thus, in the context of learning by design, AI fundamentally seeks to build a constructive ongoing dialogue between people in an organization about past and present learning capacities, processes, outcomes, achievements, strengths, innovations, opportunities, unexplored potentials, strategic competencies, visions of values and possible future. Taking all of these together, AI in a deliberate fashion seeks to facilitate a positive change orientation that will unleash untapped system learning capability.

Action research

Changing behavior and learning were some of the concerns that led Kurt Lewin in the development of action research (Lewin, 1951; Pasmore, 2001). Lewin's attempt to solve social problems using systematic data collection, feedback, reflection, and action were pioneering and are at the foundation of learning by design. During the past fifty years, action research has developed as a major field of research composed of a variety of activities and streams that integrates research and action in living systems (Reason and Bradbury, 2001). Action research is viewed as an emergent inquiry process, embedded in partnership between researchers and organizational members, for the purpose of addressing an organizational issue (or a problem) and simultaneously generating scientific knowledge (Susman and Evered, 1978; Shani and Pasmore, 1985). Moreover, action research seeks to improve the organization's ability to understand itself and develop self-help competencies – learning by design (Friedlander and Brown, 1974; Chisholm and Elden, 1993; Coghlan and Brannick, 2001; Stebbins and Shani, 2002).

Sociotechnical system design

Eric Trist of the Tavistock Institute coined the term "sociotechnical" (STS) to describe the interrelatedness of environmental, social, and technical systems of organizations (Emery and Trist, 1969). The principle of joint optimization is the backbone of the theory. An organization will function best if the social and technological systems are designed to fit the demands of each other and of the environment (Adler and Docherty, 1998; van Eijnatten, 1994; Pasmore et al., 1982; Taylor and Felten, 1993). As such, a specific set of organizational design principles were advanced as a guide for organization design (Cherns, 1987; Herbst, 1974; Pasmore, 1988).

STS provides a comprehensive planned change process with analytical tools and methods that were developed to facilitate the transformation of an organization towards a more STS-based design entity. The design processes, methods, and tools are elaborate and multilevel in nature. They utilize an action research orientation and provide linkages among business-environment analysis, vision and strategy statements, system analysis and diagnosis, exploration of new alternatives for joint optimization, experimental implementation, and system-wide diffusion. Parallel learning structures, composed of steering, study and action groups, plan and carry out the learning and redesign process (Bushe and Shani, 1991; Kolodny and Stjernberg, 1986; Pasmore, 1994).

Reflexive design

Reflexivity, reflexive action, reflection-in-action, and reflexive design evolved as key terms in a school of thought that has its origin in a variety of disciplines: anthropology, education, sociology, political science, family therapy, personal psychology, organization and management sciences. Reflection is widely recognized as a critical dimension in the learning process of individuals. The term reflection is generally used as a synonym for higher-order mental processes (Mezirow, 1990). Dewey emphasized the importance of reflective thought and set the stage for a major research agenda for many scholars on adult learning (Rigano and Edwards, 1998).

Refection-in-action (Schön, 1987) involves looking back on personal experiences to evaluate practical reasoning and build personal theories of action. As we have seen in chapter 2, Schön's work with Argyris on improving practices of professionals resulted in the development of single- and double-loop learning concepts. As can be seen in our cases, the companies seem to have harnessed reflection as a deliberate practice in the workplace in a variety of ways and at different levels. At the most basic level, learning by design is likely to have in each of its phases and activities, elements that can be viewed as reflective – a type of enlightened, self-critical, and systematic process of reflection.

▶ Learning-By-Design Intervention Model: An Overview

In the spirit of learning, we propose a generic learning-by-design intervention model that has some familiar program phases, but minimal constraints. As depicted in table 10.1, the learning-by-design intervention model is based on eight phases that are viewed as guidelines to support reflection, discovery, envisioning, design, and experimentation at each phase of the endeavor. The learning-by-design process is viewed as a spiral and never-ending system endeavor. The analytical tools and methods advanced by sociotechnical system design can be used at different phases of the process, as needed. In keeping with the learning-by-design orientation, phases can be recycled to earlier phases at any time in the process. In line with action research and appreciative inquiry, the process is an emergent inquiry process of appreciative inquiry partnership. True partnership is viewed as critical to learning. In the context of learning by design, some of the most relevant partnerships are between the organizational members at different levels of the hierarchy, between the social partners (management and unions), between the different members of the organizational supply chain, and between the organizational members and the participating organizational researchers. In most cases, the starting point of the effort is

Table 10.1 An eclectic generic "learning by design" change process

Phase 1: Project initiation
Initial definition of purpose and scope
Initial system scanning
Securing management commitment and role
Align intervention scope with business strategy
Establish criteria and measurement of success
Review of alternative mechanisms to lead effort
Phase 2: Formation of mechanism(s) to lead the learning by design effort
Phase 3: Developing a shared vision – envisioning
Phase 4: Systematic inquiry, analysis, and reflection on currently used learning mechanisms
Phase 5: Identification and exploration (of fit) of alternative/additional learning mechanisms
Phase 6: Developing the design of a "blueprint" for action
Phase 7: Implementation of changes – improvement processes for existing learning mechanisms and implementation of new learning mechanisms
Phase 8: Reflection on the "learning by design" planned change process

clear, but the processes tend to change over time based on new ideas, changing circumstances and activities.

The first phase involves the establishment of the change project's foundation. In this phase working on clarifying basic understanding about learning-by-design philosophy and orientation, expectations about the change process, the resources that it is likely to take to implement the effort, and the critical role that top management needs to assume are of the utmost importance. The intervention scope, goals, and expected outcomes must be compatible with the overall business mission and strategy. Top management must define the overall scope of the effort, articulate measurement criteria of success, explore alternative mechanisms, and make decisions about the mechanism to lead the effort.

Phases two and three center on the creation of the mechanism(s) that were chosen and establishing shared understanding of the effort's direction. Regardless of the mechanism(s) chosen, complete information about the change process, its intent, structure, process, and outcomes and how it fits the overall business vision and mission needs to be communicated to organizational members. The idea is to facilitate organizational dialogue that is embedded in the appreciative inquiry process. As such, one of the core tasks is to discover and disclose the organizational learning capacities – "dream of what can be" – the overall organizational envisioning process.

During *phase four* the effort moves into a systematic inquiry that centers on the identification and in-depth study of the learning mechanisms that evolved in the firm. The intent at this critical phase is to develop a deep level of understanding of what are the mechanisms and how they have evolved and to capture in detail how well they work – an inquiry into the true nature of the existing organizational learning mechanisms and organizational capacity. During *phase five*, the systematic reflective process that occurred in phase four is likely to explore the different design requirements that were triggered by the environmental business context, the different design dimensions and the choices that were made about the specific learning mechanisms. This new level of understanding of the existing learning mechanisms is likely to trigger the exploration of possible new learning mechanisms that are likely to respond to the emerging learning design requirements. The ongoing scientific inquiry, systematic analysis, and dialogue into the context and dynamic nature of learning mechanisms are likely to lead to choices about the development of the "next generation" learning mechanisms.

Phase six is all about making choices and the development of the blueprint for action. The choices are threefold: what learning mechanisms to implement, how to go about implementing them, and how to measure the performance and success of the learning mechanisms and the implementation process once implemented – the systematic reflection based on pre-established criteria and data. *Phase seven* centers on the implementation process of "new learning mechanisms" and the improvement process of the "old learning mechanisms." The entity that was chosen and created to lead the effort usually takes the lead in championing the activities in phases four, five, six, and seven.

The critical role of the leading entity is to communicate continuously with organizational members and top management, using a variety of communication tools. The need to have top management sanction the effort and fully participate in its activities cannot be underscored too much. It is vital to the effort and its success. *Phase eight* is a way to establish the ongoing learning processes and structures that will secure the organizational reflection-in-action that centers on learning mechanisms and their continuous improvement and development. As we have seen in the cases described in chapters 3 to 8, one of the "magic" consequences of a "learning-by-design" change program is that it provides the critical (and badly needed) balance between work intensity and business and human resources development.

▶ Inquiry Issues and Future Direction

As can be seen from the cases, the systematic reflections across the cases, and the integration of our studies with the existing body of knowledge, learning by design is an emerging area that requires much scientific inquiry and dialogue (see chapter 9). What follows is a discussion of six inquiry areas: the scientific merit of the proposed conceptual mapping of learning design requirements, learning design dimensions, and learning mechanisms; the scientific process of creating actionable knowledge about learning by design; the nature and role of leadership in learning by design; the nature of partnership in learning; the limits of learning by design; and learning by design and sustainable work systems.

The scientific merit of the proposed conceptual framework

In chapter 2 we advanced an alternative comprehensive framework that integrates learning, strategy, and sustainability. The theoretical foundation of the framework can be found in sociotechnical system theory, the resource-based view of the firm, and the emerging theories about business and human sustainability. The framework identified five clusters of factors that have an impact on the firm's profitability and sustainability. Thus, organizational competitiveness and sustainability are viewed as the outcomes of complex relationships between the design choices made around the organizational learning mechanisms, the firm's strategy and design, its resources and capabilities, and the business context.

At the center of the framework we find learning mechanisms. Looking closer at learning mechanisms, we have proposed an analytical model that sheds light on the key features of learning mechanisms. We have argued that organizational learning mechanisms are designed and managed in various ways.

The business context – called the mess (Ackoff, 1999) – creates learning design requirements. Those in turn lead to the managerial need to explore different learning design dimensions, and the choices made around specific design dimensions result in a specific profile of what we called organizational learning mechanisms (see figure 2.2). For example, in chapter 6, the context of the business environment dictated the need to create a work environment that fosters and facilitates learning. This in turn led to managerial choices: learning is viewed as an integral part of work; project team members are responsible for learning; and team members represent the variety of competence and disciplinary knowledge needed. The above resulted in the creation of a flexible architecture space design ("*ba*" as a learning mechanism) that facilitates human interaction for the purpose of learning, knowledge creation, and knowledge transfer within and between teams.

As we have seen in chapters 3 through 8, the proposed framework provides a comprehensive way to carefully examine current and future organizational learning processes, structures, and practices. Thus, the potential embedded in the use of our proposed framework for understanding and modifying current processes, structures, and practices seems attractive and fulfills an existing gap (Friedman, Lipshitz, and Overmeer, 2001; Garvin, 2000; Shani and Mitki, 2000). Bridging the theoretical gaps, however, requires further study at a much deeper level, devoted to the potential interconnectivity between specific theoretical tenets. For example, a key feature of our proposed framework is that it focuses attention on learning mechanisms and the linkages between learning mechanisms and business strategy, organization design, resources, capabilities, and business performance in terms of sustainability and competitiveness. From a managerial point of view, while one can probably assess the state of the firm's learning dynamics using the framework, figuring out causal relationships between the different clusters requires further development both at the theoretical and at practical levels.

Creating actionable knowledge about learning by design

Learning by design was viewed as an intentional effort by organizations to change the state of learning practices at work. Mapping out current practices, how they evolved, and how they work is a critical knowledge to uncover. Knowledge resides within the mind of individuals. In the context of work organization, we find micro-communities of knowledge whose members share what they know, values, and goals (Brown and Duguid, 1991). The ultimate success of a learning organization depends on how individuals and groups share with others what they know.

As was described earlier in this chapter, the foundation of the change process model can be found in action research, appreciative inquiry, and reflexive design methodologies. As such, the intentional effort to improve learning is viewed as an enabler of actionable knowledge creation since not only does it provide the platform, the mechanisms, and processes for the interaction between individuals and micro-communities, but it charges all involved to create a new understanding of current and explore future possible ways to organize around learning. Yet, sharing tacit knowledge, and creating shared understanding of individuals from different disciplines and experiences, requires significant commitment in terms of time and energy (Krogh, Ichijo, and Nonaka, 2000).

The intentional effort to transform an organization to become a better learning organization requires creating knowledge that is useful and relevant (Antal et al., 2001). Thus, actionable knowledge is viewed as knowledge that can simultaneously serve the needs of the living system (the organization and its members) and the scientific community (Adler and Shani, 2001). The interdisciplinary base of learning by design and the philosophy behind it provides an opportunity to create new actionable knowledge. For example, a recent study that focused on learning in teams concluded that successful teams engaged in real-time learning, analyzing and drawing lessons from the process while they were working and experimenting in improving the process (Edmonson, Bohmer, and Pisano, 2001). As we saw in chapters 3 through 8, a variety of structural learning mechanisms were developed by the companies. Yet, while these mechanisms seem to have created the context that allowed for sharing, learning, and the creation of new knowledge, more scientific research is needed in order to understand better the dynamics and possible cause and effect relationships between the different types of structural learning mechanisms and the process of creating actionable knowledge.

Leadership and learning by design

Learning is viewed as crucial for long-term organizational survival and growth (Garvin, 2000). Thus, management at all levels of the organization needs to be involved in enhancing learning. Recently the term "leading to learn" was advanced (Arvedson, 1996; Edmonson, Bohmer, and Pisano, 2001). At the essence of the argument one can find the notions that leaders play a critical role in fostering a learning environment, role modeling learning behavior, facilitating an ongoing dialogue about learning enhancements, exploring and experimenting with the implementation of different learning mechanisms, rewarding learning outcomes, and continuously improving learning processes. This has been underlined in several of the cases presented in this book.

Since this new emerging role of "managing and leading learning" seems to be of vital importance, more theoretical and practical knowledge needs to be developed about the role and about some of the management systems that must be developed and put in place. For example, Garvin (2000) argues that improving organizational learning needs to be added as a new goal for managers. This means that an organization needs to explore the creation of developmental processes that will enhance the managers' ability and skills to carry out the task.

At a basic level, the new emerging role is seen as a fundamental shift in management perspective and practice. By focusing on business and human sustainability the management orientation shifts towards a long-term perspect-ive. This shift requires the willingness to challenge current ways of thinking, joint discovery and envisioning of possible management practices that can facilitate system learning, design and experimental implementation of alter-native learning mechanisms, the creation of a learning culture, and the devel-opment of continuous improvement processes that will enhance sustainability. The emerging management role requires significant scientific research that will examine the nature of the role, its impact on key processes, and the pos-sible causal relationship between the role and organizational performance.

The nature of partnership in learning

As we have seen in chapter 9, learning by design is based on true partner-ship between organizational members, management, unions, and experts. At a basic level, partnership refers to the values, actions, processes, and conse-quences of sharing and/or creating something in common by two or more entities. As such, partnership requires a reason for existence, a common goal or a shared purpose. As we argued earlier, the purpose of learning by design is enhancing business sustainability both at the business competitiveness and the human development levels. Within organizations it is possible to identify many different stakeholders who may belong to different unions and profes-sional associations. Methods and strategies to acquire need further study, not least to illuminate the costs and benefits of such efforts. A general assumption in many quarters is that "it is not worth the effort"; there are star cases, such as the bank, that have succeeded in maintaining the balance for decades. From a scientific perspective, little is known about the nature of partnership, its key features, its dynamics, and its possible effect on learning and sustainability.

The limits of learning by design

Learning by design is an area that was developed and explored in this book. Learning has been an area of human concern for many decades, yet at the work-place the shift from training to learning seems to have occurred in the late 1980s. Even though organizational learning as a concept can be traced to the early 1970s, the scientific interest seems to have taken hold in the 1990s. This book attempts to add to our understanding of learning in organizational settings by crafting the book around a new conceptual framework that is centered around "learning mechanisms" and six companies that have made a systematic attempt at enhancing learning at the individual, group, and organizational levels.

Current working conditions demand that learning is integrated in work, that learning is experiential. The critical stage in experiential learning is reflection; why were our actions in a given situation followed by certain results/consequences? Research has shown that such reflection is difficult to structure without disturbing the process (Boud et al., 1993). Many (most) people cannot "reflect by numbers," especially in a group. Wilhelmson et al. (2001) made similar observations: people had difficulty in recounting their reflections and it was very difficult to separate "individual" from "collective" learning. Many of the ongoing discussions and dialogues at work between colleagues were reported as having generated personal lessons and new knowledge, without being associated with collective or team knowledge. The relations between individual and collective learning and means for supporting them in daily work in production need to be focused. How do communities of practice develop? How can the collective tacit knowledge be articulated (cf. Nonaka and Takeuchi, 1995; Nonaka et al., 2001)? What role do social networks play in the development of communities of practice and are there key individual roles?

In addition to "learning where they are," people will be "learning as they are," i.e., in order to increase the efficiency of learning in the workplace we need to know more about individuals' personal learning styles and how this is supported or obstructed in the workplace. Though we attempted to identify a number of star cases, there was only one division in one company that had this issue on its agenda and they have not managed to evaluate their experiences to date. Forslin (2001) has utilized an instrument based on Kolb's learning cycle to classify the learning patterns of mechanical engineering undergraduates and graduate engineers after several years of worklife experience. He found the "balanced" learning profile of undergraduate days had been changed to an "act–react" profile after the work pressures in design offices and production plants. How can different learning styles be described? How may they be supported, by cultural and structural learning mechanisms?

Learning by design and sustainable work systems

Developing sustainable work systems emerged at the beginning of this decade as a growing concern at the societal, organizational, and individual levels (Docherty, Forslin, and Shani, 2002). Learning is a key process for people's well-being and health in the workplace, helping to development their feelings of understanding, meaningfulness, and social community at work. Several research issues pertaining to sustainability in this context are:

■ How can all members of an organization gain insight into the need and benefit of regarding personnel as a key stakeholder in the company, whose development is a benefit for the organization as a whole and its various stakeholders in the short and long term? In this context, Hörte and Lindberg (1994), in an analysis of eighty cases, found that HRD and OD developments had more immediate impacts on productivity development than investments in new technology. Pfeffer (1998) and Collins and Porras (1995) have shown how companies that invest in learning for their employees are excellent performers. Kotter and Heskett (1992) have shown that firms that prioritize investors together with other stakeholders perform better than those focused solely on investors.

■ Yet there are still many companies that do not "follow the high road," as formulated in chapter 9, but hold their investments in personnel to a minimum. This has several dysfunctional consequences that need to be addressed in further research, namely the stress and possible burnout arising from the dissonance between employees' values in the workplace and management's values, not least regarding the nature of the workforce, its needs and aspirations. This dissonance is itself a main cause of burnout (Maslach and Leiter, 1997). How can this situation be identified and remedied?

■ There is clear evidence, however, that many people regard the opportunity to learn at work as a distinct threat, not an opportunity. A better understanding is required of the conditions that need to be created so that people can accept and commit themselves to learning (Schein, 2002). How can the sensitive balance between stability and development and change be attained and maintained? What are facilitating and hindering conditions and factors in dealing with this issue? Changing such value configurations is a very difficult learning issue.

■ A second issue in this context is the problem of "learned helplessness." Earlier or current unfavorable conditions of work have "taught" people that it is fruitless, meaningless, to get involved, to try to influence or change conditions, to aspire to learn new skills, etc. How can such vicious circles be broken? This requires a transformation in the organizational culture, at different levels in the organization.

■ The final sustainability issue is that of viability: How can interest and commitment to learning be maintained over time? Several of the most reported and admired examples of organizational learning have, since the initial reports, been "outsourced" by top management and are no longer used to the same extent within their "mother" organizations. Inter-organizational networks for learning have also a tendency to thrive for a few years, then die out (Thång and Wärvick, 2001). Is this functional? How can such tendencies be identified and met? How can a genuine interest in the issue of "learning" be differentiated from a passing interest in the fashion?

In summary, in the context of the increasing volatile business environment, sustainability in organizations means creating liberating, emancipatory mechanisms and building up internal learning capabilities to carry through reorganizations and continuous change successfully. As we have seen, the processes of learning and development in organizations, regarding experiential learning, tacit knowledge, communities of practice, creativity, and development in organizations are all of great importance but still require much further research.

▶ A Retrospective Conclusion

Most books end with a concluding chapter that summarizes the findings presented in the manuscript. At some level, achieving such an objective is not possible. The six company studies that were carried out in Europe, the USA, and Israel provide the essence of the book and, as we have seen, cover an enormous amount of information. Chapter 9 attempted to synthesize some of the information across cases, industries, and continents and integrate the knowledge around a few central themes such as the conditions, structures, and processes for sustainable learning organizations; the possible relationships between business strategy, learning, and performance; the possible relations between learning requirements, learning dimensions, and learning mechanisms; and the wide variations of learning mechanisms that emerged in the six companies studied.

In the first part of this chapter a possible roadmap or a generic intervention model for a planned change strategy that centers on the enhancement of learning was advanced. Some of the theoretical foundations for such a change model – action research, appreciative inquiry, sociotechnical system design, and reflexive design – were identified and briefly discussed. Based on our comparative inquiry, the second part of the chapter identified six possible clusters for future research: the scientific merit of the proposed conceptual mapping of learning design requirements, learning design dimensions, and learning mechanisms; the scientific process of creating actionable knowledge about learning by design; the nature and role of leadership in learning by design; the nature of partnership in learning; the limits of learning by design; and learning by design and sustainable work systems.

Recently, in an assessment of the development of organizational learning as a field of inquiry, Antal et al. (2001) identified the following seven emerging challenges: towards internationally comparative research; towards transdisciplinary theory building; towards knowledge creation through closer collaboration between scholars and practitioners; towards networks of organizations, communities, and environments of learning; towards learning and knowledge creation as embedded processes; towards actors at all levels and communities of practice crossing organizational boundaries; and towards learning as a strategic intent. A careful review of the first two chapters, which mapped out the field and presented a framework for investigation, the in-depth cases presented in chapters 3 through 8, and the last two integrative chapters reveals that as a whole our study faced most of the challenges articulated by Antal and her colleagues head-on and provided, to varied degrees, significant actionable knowledge and insight in all the areas.

Yet, as we have seen, due to the newness of the learning-by-design focus, while our study began to identify and shed some light on the emerging focus, the scientific knowledge is relatively limited. As such, specific directions for future research and learning were identified and briefly discussed. The transdisciplinary nature of learning by design and the process that was suggested for the implementation of learning by design in organizations (first section of this chapter) provide a platform for the continuous creation of actionable knowledge – towards the development of sustainable and competitive work systems.

References

Ackoff, R. L. (1999). *Re-Creating the Corporation: A Design of Organizations for the 21st Century*. New York: Oxford University Press.

Adler, N. and Docherty, P. (1998). Bringing business into sociotechnical theory and practice. *Human Relations*, 51(1), 319–45.

Adler, N. and Shani, A. B. (Rami) (2001). In search of an alternative framework for the creation of actionable knowledge: Table-tennis research at Ericsson. In W. Pasmore and R. W. Woodman (eds), *Research in Organizational Change and Development*, vol. 13. Greenwich, CT: JAI Publications, pp. 43–79.

Antal, A. B., Dierkes, M., Child, J., and Nonaka, I. (2001). Organizational learning and knowledge: Reflections on the dynamics of the field and challenges for the future. In A. B. Antal, M. Dierkes, J. Child, and I. Nonaka (eds), *Handbook of Organizational Learning and Knowledge*. New York: Oxford University Press, pp. 921–39.

Arvedson, L. (1996). *Leda att lära* (Leading to learn). Stockholm: Ekelids Förlag.

Boud, D., Cohen, R., and Walker, D. (1993). Understanding learning from experience. In D. Boud, R. Cohen, and D. Walker (eds), *Using Experience for Learning*. Buckingham: SRHE and the Open University Press, pp. 1–17.

Brown, J. S. and Duguid, P. (1991). Organizational learning and communitiues-of-practice: Toward a unified view of working, learning and innovation. *Organization Science*, 2, 40–57.

Bushe, G. R. and Shani, A. B. (Rami) (1991). *Parallel Learning Structures*. Reading MA: Addison-Wesley.

Cherns, A. (1987). Principles of sociotechnical design revisited. *Human Relations*, 40(3), 153–62.

Chisholm, R. F. and Elden, M. (1993). Features of emerging action research. *Human Relations*, 46 (2), 275–89.

Coghlan, D. and Brannick, T. (2001). *Doing Action Research in Your Own Organization*. London: Sage.

Collins, J. C. and Porras, J. I. (1995). *Built to Last: Successful Habits of Visionary Companies*. London: Century/Random House.

Cooperrider, D. L. and Srivastva, S. (1987). *Research in Organizational Change and Development*, vol. 1. Greenwich, CT: JAI Press, pp. 129–69.

Cooperrider, D. L. and Whitney, D. (2001). A positive revolution in change: Appreciative inquiry. In D. L. Cooperrider, P. F. Sorensen, Jr., T. F. Yaeger, and D. Whitney (eds), *Appreciative Inquiry: An Emerging Direction for Organization Development*. Champaign, IL: Stipes Publishing, pp. 5–29.

Docherty, P., Forslin, J., and Shani, A. B. (Rami) (eds) (2002). *Creating Sustainable Work Systems: Emerging Perspectives and Practice*. London: Routledge.

Döös, M., Wilhelmson, L. and Backlund, T. (2001). *Kollektivt lärande på individualistiskt vis – ett lärdilemma för praktik och teori* (Collective learning in an individual manner – A

LEARNING BY DESIGN: CHANGE AND FUTURE

learning dilemma for practice and theory). In T. Backlund, H. Hansson and C. Thunborg (eds) *Lärdilemman i arbetslivet*. Stockholm: Studentlitteratur, pp. 43–79.

Edmonson, A., Bohmer, R., and Pisano, G. (2001). Speeding up team learning. *Harvard Business Review*, 79(9), 125–33.

Eijnatten, F. M. van (1994). *The Paradigm that Changed the Workplace*. Stockholm, SE: Arbetslivscentrum and Assen, NL: Van Gorcum.

Emery, F. E. and Trist, E. (1969). Sociotechnical systems. In F. Emery (ed.), *System Thinking*. Harmondsworth: Penguin.

Forslin, J. (2001). *Personal communication: Seminar on learning styles in an Action Learning project on Intensive and Sustainable Work Systems*. Royal Institute of Technology, Stockholm, November, 2001.

Friedlander, F. and Brown, L. D. (1974). Organization development. *Annual Review of Psychology*, 25, 313–41.

Friedman, V. J., Lipshitz, R., and Overmeer, W. (2001). Creating conditions for organizational learning. In A. B. Antal, M. Dierkes, J. Child, and I. Nonaka (eds), *Handbook of Organizational Learning and Knowledge*. New York: Oxford University Press, pp. 757–74.

Garvin, D. A. (2000). *Learning in Action*. Boston, MA: Harvard Business School Press.

Herbst, P. (1974). *Sociotechnical Design: Strategies in Interdisciplinary Research*. London: Tavistock Institute Publication.

Hörte, S. Å. and Lindberg, P. (1994). Performance effects of human and organizational development and technical development. *International Journal of Human Factors in Manufacturing*, 4(3), 243–59.

Kotter, J. and Heskett, J. (1992). *Corporate Culture and Performance*. New York: The Free Press.

Kolodny, H. and Stjernberg, T. (1986). The change process of innovative work designs: New design and redesign in Sweden, Canada, and the US. *Journal of Applied Behavioral Science*, 22, 287–301.

Krogh, G. V., Ichijo, K., and Nonaka, I. (2000). *Enabling Knowledge Creation*. Oxford: OUP.

Lewin, K. (1951). *Field Theory in Social Science: Selected Theoretical Papers*. New York: Harper and Row.

Maslach, C. and Leiter, M. P. (1997). *The Truth about Burnout. How Organizations Cause Personal Stress and What to Do about It*. San Francisco: Jossey-Bass Publishers.

Mezirow, J. D. (1990). How critical reflection triggers transformative learning. In J. D. Mezirow (ed.), *Fostering Critical Reflection in Adulthood*. San Francisco: CA: Jossey-Bass.

Nonaka, I., Toyama, R., and Byosière, P. (2001). A theory of organizational knowledge creation: Understanding the dynamic process of creating knowledge. In M. Dierkes, A. Berthoin Antal, J. Child, and I. Nonaka (eds), *Handbook of Organizational Learning and Knowledge*. New York: Oxford University Press.

Nonaka, I. and Takeuchi, R. (1995). *Leading Knowledge Creation: A New Framework for Dynamic Knowledge Management*. New York: Oxford University Press.

Pasmore, W. A. (1988). *Designing Effective Organizations: The Sociotechnical Systems Perspective*. New York: Wiley.

Pasmore, W. A. (1994). *Creating Strategic Change: Designing the Flexible High Performing Organization*. New York: Wiley.

Pasmore, W. A. (2001). Action research in the workplace: The socio-technical perspective. In P. Reason and H. Bradbury (eds), *Handbook of Action Research: Participative Inquiry and Practice*. London: Sage, pp. 39–47.
200

Pasmore, W. A., Francis, C., and Shani, A. B. (Rami) (1982). Sociotechnical systems. *Human Relations*, 35, 1179–204.

Pfeffer, J. (1998). *The Human Equation: Building Profits by Putting People First*. Cambridge, MA: Harvard Business School Press.

Reason, P. and Bradbury, H. (2001). *Handbook of Action Research: Participative Inquiry and Practice*. London: Sage.

Rigano, D. and Edwards, J. (1998). Incorporating reflection into work practice. *Management Learning*, 29(4), 431–46.

Schein, E. (2002). The anxiety of learning. *Harvard Business Review*, 80 (3).

Schön, D. (1987). *Educating the Reflective Practitioner*. San Francisco, CA: Jossey-Bass.

Shani, A. B. (Rami), and Mitki, Y. (2000). Creating the learning organization: Beyond mechanisms. In R. Golembiewski (ed.), *Handbook of Organizational Consultation*. New York: Marcel Dekker, pp. 911–19.

Shani A. B. (Rami) and Pasmore, W. A. (1985). Organization inquiry: Towards a new model of the action research process. In D. Warrick (ed.), *Contemporary Organization Development*. Glenview, IL: Scott, Forsman and Company, pp. 438–48.

Susman, G. I. and Evered, R. D. (1978). An assessment of the scientific merit of action research. *Administrative Science Quarterly*, 23, 583–603.

Stebbins, M. W. and Shani, A. (Rami) (2002). Eclectic design for change. In P. Docherty, J. Forslin, and A. B. (Rami) Shani (eds), *Creating Sustainable Work Systems: Emerging Perspectives and Practice*. London: Routledge, pp. 213–25.

Taylor, J. C. and Felten, D. A. (1993). *Performance by Design: Sociotechnical Systems in North America*. Englewood Cliffs, NJ: Prentice Hall.

Thång, P. O. and Wärvick, G. B. (2001). *Kompetensutveckling för yrkesverksamma inom den västsvenska verkstadsindustrin: är det möjligt?* (Competence development for skilled workers in the manufacturing industry in the west of Sweden: is it possible?) Göteborg: Göteborgs University report 2001.

Index

Note: page numbers in *italics* refer to figures; page numbers in **bold** refer to tables; *n* after a page reference indicates a note on that page.